UNRESOLVED DILEMMAS

To Elina Haavio—Mannila

Unresolved Dilemmas

Women, work and the family in the United States,
Europe and the former Soviet Union

Edited by
KAISA KAUPPINEN
Finnish Institute of Occupational Health

and

TUULA GORDON
University of Helsinki

Ashgate

Aldershot • Brookfield USA • Singapore • Sydney

Published by
Ashgate Publishing Limited
Gower House
Croft Road
Aldershot
Hants GU11 3HR
England

Ashgate Publishing Company
Old Post Road
Brookfield
Vermont 05036
USA

British Library Cataloguing in Publication Data

Unresolved dilemmas : women, work and the family in the
    United States, Europe and the former Soviet Union
    1.Women - Employment 2.Working mothers
    I. Kauppinen, Kaisa II.Gordon, Tuula
    305.4'3

Library of Congress Catalog Card Number: 97-70908

ISBN 1 85628 461 1

Printed in Great Britain by the Ipswich Book Company, Suffolk

Contents

PART THREE: Unresolved dilemmas

Figures and table

1 Introduction: Dual roles and beyond

Tuula Gordon/Kaisa Kauppinen

During the past few decades the proportion of women in the labour force has increased dramatically in all industrialized societies, women form a considerable part of the working population. Most women also establish relationships and become mothers. Combining work and family has created considerable problems for women — problems that are not typically experienced by men. In the labour market sex segregation still persists, and it extends both horizontally and vertically. As long as labour markets remain segregated, and pay and prospects of those located in the predominantly female sectors are less favourable than in the predominantly male sectors, sex inequalities cannot be eradicated. This knowledge does not, however, lead very far towards an understanding of the processes involved. We also have to note that domestic circumstances and the main responsibility for housework and the care of the children still affect women; they enter the labour market *with one hand tied behind their backs*.

Families have been critically studied in feminist research, and they are considered one major source of women's subordination. The binary opposition between the public and private spheres needs to be examined. Women's entry into the public arena, even though partial, seems irreversible. Yet the public/private dichotomy is central in maintaining gender differences. Even when women enter the public sphere, they are seen as representing the private sphere, as is evident in the types of work women do (service work, health care, education, etc.). Similarly, when men enter the private sphere, they maintain the status conferred on them in the public sphere and, hence, have fewer responsibilities in the home.

The construction of the concept *dual role* has been ideologically significant in maintaining the public/private divide. Women's lives are not seen as an integrated whole — their work role is not supposed to alter their maternal and marital role in any fundamental sense. This conception of duality is challenged in this book. The term can be viewed as a rationalization covering the contradictions raised by the need to recruit women into the labour force, while still upholding their role at home. Until about the mid 1970s, women's participation in the labour force assumed a *U* shape: women worked outside the home before marriage, became home—makers when their children were born, and then returned to work outside the home in their middle years. In the mid—1990s women pursue a more continuous pattern of labour force activity.

A careful, systematic assessment whereby both continuities and changes are considered is important for women's position at work and at home,. The international perspective of this book enables an examination of the variety of processes in different countries, depending on the participation rates of women, the cultural understanding of femininity and masculinity, and the character of the welfare state.

Societies differ in the extent to which they provide special programs for employed women and men in terms of child care, maternity/paternity leave, flexible hours, and the degree to which gender ideologies call for a more active role of fathers in child care and household work. Depending on the benefits society provides, employed women and men engage in differing courses of action when managing the demands of combining work and family life.

One of the characteristic features of the *Nordic Model* has been the high participation of women in the labour market. From 20 years of age until retirement, 72 to 83 percent of the women and 81 to 92 percent of the men work in the five Nordic countries. Women and men are employed in different professions and have different employers. Women are underrepresented at the higher levels of organizational hierarchies, the percentage of female bosses being in no way proportionate to the percentage of female employees.

Increased international competition and an unstable labour market have forced companies to adjust through rationalization and restructuring. Flexibility is the main trend. The changing work conditions will lead to a harder work life for women.

In a competitive economy, companies are demanding more of their labour force, and men are also vulnerable to these pressures. Making the 60—hour job the norm for men will not further gender equality. This demand is in conflict with the equality programs that aim to further men's participation in their family roles. Today, more and more young men in the Nordic countries are trying to share parental leave — at least for one or two months. A new picture of fatherhood is emerging in which presence, closeness and care is combined with shared economic responsibility.

Even though women's participation in the labour market has greatly increased and men are challenging their old role patterns, the traditional gender division of tasks still holds. Most of the women have the primary responsibility for home and family. The women feel stressed by their jobs and they are often torn between the conflicting demands of everyday life. For women, the total work load increases with the number of children living at home, and the combined and conflicting demands of career and family life are accentuated.

In this book we explore both theoretical themes and empirical issues relating to the unresolved dilemmas of women on the tightrope between home and work, but we challenge the construction of this in terms of *dual roles*. Instead we view women's lives as more integrated, though also fragmented, but in more complex ways than what *duality* implies.

In general, labour market activity has enhanced women's economic independence. It also influences negotiations about the division of labour in the home. The degree of salary balance between the spouses affects their interaction and their child rearing practices. Nowadays, it is also easier for women to opt out of marriage; this is a strategy used by many professional women. Overall, changes in *the family* have been considerable, and the nuclear family, though still a strong ideological construction, is in practice one of several ways in which people organize their lives (e.g. dual career families, delayed marriage, single—parent households, cohabitation, serial monogamy etc.).

3

Women have relied on education a great deal in attempting to improve their position in the labour market in particular and in the public sphere in general. But the increased numbers of women participating in duration either as students or as teachers have not influenced the form and content of education a great deal. Those involved in decision making and in setting the framework for the educational establishment from primary to higher education have been primarily men. Thus a final unresolved dilemma to be explored is the relationship between women's participation and empowerment.

The exploration of the questions we have set in this Introduction continues in Part One. The framework is set by problematizing the welfare state. Analyses of welfare states, Anneli Anttonen argues, have concentrated primarily on citizen workers. These citizens have implicitly been men. When women are included in the analysis, the question has been about the status of their citizenship. The Nordic welfare states have attempted to ensure the social (as well as legal and political) citizenship of women — they have been termed women friendly.

In the context of the broader debate on citizenship and women Anttonen explores the Nordic model — is it really woman—friendly and does it really provide social citizenship for women? She concludes that a woman—friendly welfare state is a state for women worker citizens, but it should not be considered the end point of development (see Sarvasy, 1992, who argues that a *feminist welfare state* is needed).

Hobson continues the problematization of citizenship by considering the constructions of key words around the concept of independence/dependence. She explores the male/worker centered notion of independence — earning one's income in the market. Hobson argues that it is also important to consider social dependency in the family in order to be able to analyze the gender inequality hidden by general notions of citizenship. She explores the meanings and dimensions of *dependency,* and develops them by using a case study of *solo mothers* to gain a clearer understanding of the welfare state, and of unstated assumptions of dependency and independence in such states.

The authors of the articles in Part Two all reflect on the themes of this book by considering them in the context of specific issues or specific societies. Amy Wharton explores relations between service work and family life in order to understand how women experience their involvement in social reproduction in two different spheres — at home and at work. She analyzes the boundaries between the two spheres by looking at transitions from one to the other and developing their analysis into a discussion of continuity and discontinuity between work and family. Even though there are continuities between service work and family life, women nevertheless have to expend emotional energy when crossing the border between home and work. This energy expenditure is connected with the theme of the book, focusing on unresolved dilemmas. Nevertheless, the autonomy employment affords working women is important and positive, but the nature of that autonomy is complex and is affected by both work and family responsibilities.

Sharon Lobel explores psychological intimacy between women and men in the workplace. Most women and men work in jobs in which their co—workers are predominantly the same sex. But it is interesting to explore the implications changing division of labour between the sexes. In this context Lobel problematizes the dichotomies between work and non—work and work and family life by emphasizing the existence and importance of intimate relationships at work — such relationships do not solely exist in the terrain of the home and the family.

Svetlana Yampolskaya argues that recent changes in Russia have had both negative and positive consequences for the economy, the people, and the Russian family structures. Despite the increased freedom gained, women have suffered more from sexism and gender inequality. Because of the breakdown of norms and values in society, Yampolskaya believes it is important that the family be strengthened in current Russian circumstances, despite feminist criticisms of the family.

Since Estonia's independence from the former Soviet Union there has been a review of women's place in society. A strong theme has been an emphasis on home and family. Many Estonian women have also expressed a wish to reconsider their labour market orientation. The article by Anu Narusk questions the rationale behind this thinking.

Cynthia Fuchs-Epstein explores how *selves* are constructed and how *selves* change. Change is related to structural opportunities or constraints and possibilities in the terrain of culture to reconsider who one might become. She considers the implications of non—traditional jobs — how they are connected to changes in the self and the ways in which women and men understand these changes. Epstein problematizes the concept of single identities and dual roles. Changes in the structure highlight the construction of selves as multiple.

In Part Three the exploration of unresolved dilemmas continues. Janet Giele notes the world—wide modernization in women's life patterns and the continuing cross—national trend towards the extension and elaboration of family policy. She explores the interaction between changes in women's life courses and in the broader societal work and family institutions. Because of the multiple patterns of women's lives — simultaneous participation in work, family and continuing education — there is pressure to invent social arrangements to support such changes. Changes in women's typical life courses have positive effects in terms of flexibility and personal satisfaction. However, by working very hard, women pay a high price for their increased autonomy. Women's dilemmas may seem unresolved, but they are not constant or do they alter in the process of interaction between changes in women's lives and in work and family institutions.

Tuula Gordon's article explores how the *otherness* of women is constructed — historically women have been defined in relation to men. Romantic love, partnership, marriage and motherhood form the cultural context of women and resonate in representations of them.

Locating themselves outside the family provides opportunities for women, but it also places them in a contradictory and difficult position. She asks whether single women today have more independent possibilities in the context of the diversification of family forms and increased flexibility in the construction of gender. From empirical qualitative research on single women in London, the San Francisco Bay Area and Helsinki, Gordon concludes that constructing an independent life, reaching the status of the *individual* and obtaining full social citizenship are still areas of struggle.

Rosemarie Nave—Hertz's article on single mothers raises the question of possibilities for alternative constructions of women's lives. Not all women are located in the family and in the transitions between family and work in the same way. *Family* should not be taken for granted. Not all women are married, not all women have children, and not all women who have children are married. Issues concerning these women are often neglected in research that focuses on work and family, family being implicitly defined as nuclear. Single mothers in Germany have typically not made a positive choice to embark on such a life course, but have rather decided to proceed with an unplanned pregnancy. Subsequently their perception of their life course may certainly be positive. Nevertheless motherhood is still located in the context of the nuclear family, and women constructing alternative forms of motherhood do not find it straightforward.

Janet Giele noted the world—wide modernization of women's life patterns. In this context Hochschild and Tanaka's article provides an interesting snapshot of the cultural terrain inhabited by women in two countries with different sex—gender systems and different models of market economy. In some ways these women share the working mother's double day; in some ways they do not. Hochschild and Tanaka explore continuities and discontinuities by analyzing advice books for women. They concentrate on cultural collective bargaining — advice books describe cultural practices and beliefs that are bargained about. In both societies some cultural traditions are reviewed — the way forward for women is to reject many of these, but to foster some of them, as well as to create their own.

Safilios—Rothschild brings the discussion to the sphere of the private, the person, the emotional. She discusses the difficulties of combining a career and love; these difficulties, she argues, are greater than those of combining marriage with work. In order to clarify her argument she defines *career woman* specifically as one who invests a lot in her work. Thus not all professional women are career women, whereas skilled workers or office workers may be. Though women today are freer to be absorbed in their work than previously, the affective dilemmas discussed by Kollontai in the 1920s have not, however, disappeared. Love, by requiring absorbion, threatens a woman's way of life. Moreover, men who take it for granted that women are in paid employment may find it harder to come to terms with a lover's lesser willingness or availability to meet their affective and sexual needs. Thus though the high price that women pay for smooth transitions from family to work and back again, as discussed by Amy Wharton, might be resolved by positive changes occurring in women's lives, the affective dilemma between love and career, argues Constantina Safilios—Rothchild, remains. Thus she leaves us with a question: are unresolved dilemmas truly unsolvable?

We would like to thank Ms. Georgianna Oja for her language checking and Ms. Taija Veriö for word processing.

2 The welfare state and social citizenship

Anneli Anttonen

During the 1980s research on the welfare state relied increasingly on social citizenship approaches. The emergence of a modern welfare state in post—war Europe has been closely connected with the changing status of citizenship. Peter Baldwin (1990) speaks of a radical expansion of citizenship in post—war England. His main argument is that it was only with Beveridge and his most important interpreters, Marshall and Titmuss, that the notion of social citizenship became collectively anchored as a major turning—point in the evolution of Western society. Baldwin describes the Beveridgean welfare state as *the social citizenship welfare state*.

In *The Three Worlds of Welfare Capitalism* (1990), Gøsta Esping—Andersen divides the Western welfare states into social democratic, conservative and liberal regimes and demonstrates that the first type of regime has the most extensive social rights. According to Esping—Andersen (1990 p. 27):

> Social democracy was clearly the dominant force behind social reforms. Rather than tolerate a dualism between state and market, between working class and middle class, the social democrats pursued a welfare state that would promote an equality of the highest standards, not an equality of minimal needs as was pursued elsewhere.

Baldwin admits that Sweden has carried the principle of solidarity further than any other country, but even so he insists that Beveridge and Marshall are the fathers of the concept of social citizenship — and,

9

most important, that they coined the term in the spirit of liberalism not social democracy.

Theorists remain in disagreement as to whether the welfare state has followed a social—democratic or liberalist path in its development. A basic premise shared by both interpretations is that they explain the expansion of social rights as well as the welfare state itself from the vantage point of the status of the citizen worker.[1] Indeed, Carole Pateman (1989 p. 187) has observed that *the position of men as breadwinner—workers has been built into the welfare state.*[2]

Pateman (1988a p. 231) also observed that writings about the welfare state have very much been documents about the working class and its history. While we cannot deny the crucial role of the working class and its political struggles, it is equally clear that we need to have new stories about women and about the history of women's struggles. Pateman arrives at the critical conclusion that the welfare state is not only based on class compromise, on the regulation of class relations, but also on the regulation of gender relations.

There is an increasingly broad consensus of opinion among feminist scholars (see, e.g. Hobson 1991a; Langan and Ostner 1991; Leira 1992; Orloff 1992; Skocpol 1992) that mainstream scholarship is blind to gender on the welfare state. This blindness, the critics insist, applies both to cases in which the mainstream research tradition has primarily been concerned with income maintenance or income redistribution and to cases in which mainstream scholars have focused on the variation in the social rights of citizenship.

Social citizenship approaches open up an important theoretical perspective on the development of the welfare state. However, one problem with these approaches is that they have concentrated on the *masculine* domain of social policy, which has to do mainly with social insurance. The chief concern of these analyses has been with the social rights of the normal worker, namely the male citizen worker.

In a serious analysis of the connections between welfare state development and women's citizenship, we need to adopt an approach that differs from the mainstream view. The suggestion I have is that both citizenship and the welfare state be thematized as gendered constructs. One important methodological move as far as welfare state research is concerned is that the focus of attention should be shifted to the citizens as mothers and as women workers. This shift provides an important counterbalance to analyses based primarily on male citizen workers.

In the same vein of thinking the whole concept of the welfare state has to be reconstructed so that we can capture the gendered nature of social policy arrangements. For this purpose I have used the distinction I have proposed earlier between the *social insurance state* and the *social service state* (Anttonen 1990).[3] With the concept of the social insurance state I am referring to the part of the welfare state that guarantees the basic economic security of its citizens. The social insurance state has emerged to strengthen the status of citizens as economic providers through wage labour.

The social service state, on the other hand, is grounded in what has been described as maternalist social policy (see Skocpol 1992), which emerged around the turn of the century in Europe and the United States to strengthen the status of mothers, first as homemakers and as caretakers. The sphere of maternalist social policy did not evolve into a modern service state until after the Second World War. I assume that the social service state has had a particularly important role in the Nordic countries in expanding women's social citizenship.

In this article, it is my intention to explore the connections between the Nordic welfare state and women's social citizenship. Before moving on to look at the social insurance state, I go through the themes and debates of feminist research that structure my discussion. Then, I point out some of the characteristics which help to explain the scope and concept of the social service state. Finally, I consider the question of whether it is legitimate to speak of a radical expansion of women's social citizenship in the Nordic welfare states.

Bringing women in: Feminist scholars in search of subordinated women, undeserving mothers and dependent wives

Feminist research has produced many stories of the welfare state that differ from those of mainstream research. During the last 15 years, as women have received increasing attention first as the targets of social policy interventions in the 1970s and later as key actors and professionals in welfare state projects, we have become more and more convinced that the category of gender provides an important startingpoint for the conceptualization of the development, current status and future of national welfare states. *Initially feminist scholars discovered women as subordinated, not yet full citizens.*

The first to discover subordinated women was the Anglo— American debate that was much inspired by socialist feminism. State social policy was interpreted as patriarchal and as repressive against women. Elizabeth Wilson's (1977 p. 7) definition the *state organization of domestic life* neatly crystallizes the tradition of socialist feminism in the 1970s: patriarchy works alongside capitalism to control and regulate the life of women with the support and backing of state social policy.

In its early years social policy hardly guaranteed any rights to women. Daughters and wives were economically dependent upon fathers and husbands. The male breadwinner rule provided the foundations for social policy. Joan Acker (1989 p. 5) describes the contents of early social policy as follows: social policy was created by the labour—capital compromise, which initially involved, on one hand, efforts to replace male wages lost through injury, death, or unemployment and, thus, efforts to ensure the survival of the man and his dependents. But the compromise also involved efforts to *protect* women and children from the harmful effects of industrial work.

In her history of American social policy, called *Regulating the Lives of Women* (1988), Mimi Abramovitz draws attention to a very clear and deep gender division within this system. On one hand, there is the privileged group of wage earners who are in normal paid employment and who enjoy extensive earnings—related social security, endorsed by legislation. On the other, there are the members of the low—income group, who are not in regular paid employment and who have no such rights. Most of these people consist of single mothers, who throughout the history of social policy have had to submit themselves to various controls of family and marital relations to qualify for public support. Abramovitz demonstrates that means— tested programs deriving from the tradition of poor relief have tended to be repressive and to maintain poverty rather than to open up new opportunities for women.[4]

Another line of debate inspired by Anglo—American feminism revolves around the dichotomy *breadwinner/housewife*. Carole Pateman (1989 p. 187) points out that the dichotomy breadwinner/housewife, and the masculine meaning of independence, were established in Great Britain by the middle class of the last century; in the earlier period of capitalist development, women (and children) were wage labourers. A *worker* became a man who had an economically dependent wife to take care of his daily needs and look after his home and children.

In light of the theory of Carole Pateman (1988b, 1989; see also Anttonen 1990), the emergence of the welfare state can be seen as a manifestation of modern patriarchy based on fraternal contracts and rights. Democratic civil society was constituted not by ruling fathers but by *free brothers*. Democratic citizenship was originally based on ownership; many struggles were required before it expanded to wage labourers. Women, in turn, were incorporated at the first stage into the emerging democratic society mainly through family and marriage.

Individualization in terms of civic, political and social rights was originally a deeply masculine project in which the personal autonomy and economic independence of men required the subordination of women: unlimited personal autonomy cannot be a universal right. By naturalizing the female sex, denying women's rights and demands, and strengthening the division between the private and the public, men as a powerful gender succeeded in keeping women as natural exiles in a society for free brothers.[5]

Civic and political rights were expanded to apply to women as well, but the process was slow. Structural changes in capitalism have made it possible for large numbers of married women to enter paid employment, and equal—pay legislation in the 1970s, which in principle recognizes the wage as a payment for the individual, may give the impression that the male breadwinner/female housewife model has seen its day *And it was always a myth for many, perhaps most, working—class families* says Carole Pateman (1989 p. 189).

Anglo—American feminist research has shown not only how strong and profound the mechanisms of women's subordination and patriarchal control are, but also have also learned that women do not form a distinct, homogeneous group. Social policy reveals its nature as an instrument of control most clearly in cases in which no male breadwinner exists and the woman has to turn to society for help. Abramovitz (1988 p. 3) uses the distinction between deserving and undeserving women, which is familiar from poverty research The underserving group includes, among others, poor single mothers.

Feminist research has brought women's subordination into daylight and demonstrated that social policy has been instrumental in maintaining a profound inequality between women and men. This has been a major concern for feminist research: to draw attention to the patriarchal characteristics of the welfare state. Most particularly, the model of economic subsistence that is based on wage labour and the social security system, which compensates for wage labour, continues to favour men at the expense of women.

However, social policy has another history as well. Theda Skocpol (1992 p. 31) observes that although *so many of today's fledgling feminist theories of the welfare state argue that modern social policies express dominant male interests and reproduce 'patriarchal' relations between genders in ever changing way*, it is also important to look at the activities of women's groups in shaping early modern social policies.

Citizen mothers and women worker citizens

Feminist research in the Nordic countries has been less committed to theories of women's subordination and patriarchy than Anglo—American research — although the tradition does have some following in the Nordic countries as well (e.g. Hernes 1987; Holter et al. 1984). It would clearly be a simplification to argue that women have had no role in social policy except that of an *object* of deprived citizen who need protection. Indeed, there seems to be a growing wave of opinion now that the welfare state has grown out of women's interests and that the project has opened up important new opportunities for women.

The social citizenship approach requires that we also look at the *founding mothers* of the welfare state.

In Finland research on the founding mothers of the welfare state has drawn attention to the key role of women's political and social activity from sewing circles and philanthrophy to women's professional association (e.g. Kuusipalo 1990; Simonen 1990; Saarinen 1992). By the turn of the century, women were already taking an active role in the field of social and health work. Anne Ollila (1993) speaks of *social mothering* as a legitimate pathway for women from the private to the public sphere. It is important to uncover the dichotomization of early citizenship along gender lines.

The Finnish historian Irma Sulkunen (1991 p. 121) argues that the very concept of the democratic citizen is and has always been genderbiased. It did not offer promises of shared equality; all the rights and all the duties, it implied, tied the citizenship of women primarily to the family and to the private sphere, while the citizenship of men was accordingly linked with the public and with worklife.

It is necessary to add that women were incorporated into the emerging democratic society not only as wives and daughters but also as citizen mothers. *Citizen mothers were expected to show high moral standards and to be enlightened members of society.* They were also expected to bring up a new generation of healthy and respectable citizen workers (c.f. Sulkunen 1987; Hirdman 1990b).

In this sense the male breadwinner norm was influential during the early 20th century in Finland, as well as in the other Nordic countries. Bourgeois women were deeply concerned about the increasing employment of women in factories, which was not only thought to be a serious threat to the morality of women themselves but also to the morality of homes, future generations and society at large (Vattula 1989; Julkunen 1993). And although women's paid employment was already at a comparatively high level in Finland, particularly among the industrial and agrarian population, it is difficult to describe the work these women were doing as an emancipatory path from the private sphere to the public one. They had to work out of necessity.

At the beginning of this century the right to motherhood was at least as equally important as the right to paid employment, especially for working—class women. Up until the 1950s, the hero of womankind was an enlightened citizen mother who devoted her life and skills to childbearing, housework and philanthropy. The ideal of the citizen mother was highlighted immediately after the Finnish Civil War (1917—1918), and again during and after the Second World War.

Some scholars (e.g. Julkunen 1990; Sulkunen 1991) have adopted the concept of the domain of feminine social policy, but it does not refer to the poor—relief type of regulating policy that Abramovitz and Fraser spoke about earlier. Rather, the domain of feminine social policy is characterized by such determinants as motherhood, caring, nursing, helping, upbringing, education — the whole sphere of social reproduction. This sphere of social mothering has paved women's way from the private to the public and from philanthropy to professionalism in the modern welfare state.

In the Nordic countries the male breadwinner/dependent wife rule has largely broken down (Lewis and Ostner 1992). Furthermore, it has always existed as a regulative ideology and ideal that was pursued (even by women themselves, as Irma Sulkunen [1991] has shown) rather than as a dominant ideology. In practice, the housewife institution had only a marginal significance. With reference to the classical study by Elina Haavio—Mannila (1968), it can be argued that both poor agrarian Finland and the more affluent industrial Finland needed the labour input of its women. Therefore the model of breadwinner/housewife does not adequately describe the essence of the Finnish gender system even before the 1960s.

The issue of women having the right to make an independent choice between going to work and staying at home was isolated from the family and made a public issue as early as the beginning of the 20th century. According to Haavio—Mannila (1968), however, the gender issue resurfaced in the mid—1960s. Riitta Jallinoja (1983) says that the turning point came in 1966 with the founding of Association 9, whose goal was defined as the convergence of gender roles. Anne Holli (1991), in her studies of Finnish equality policies, confirms that the 1960s marked the beginning of a policy stressing the similarity of men and women. Gender differences became a negatively loaded objective.

Overall, the decade of the 1960s was a golden age of policies of *gender equality*; there should have been very good prospects for making real progress. Haavio—Mannila (1968 pp. 43—44) showed that, in terms of wage labour and education, Finnish women have long been ahead of women in the other Nordic countries. Finnish women appeared to be looking ahead to a very bright future indeed. The gender issue had been transformed into one of equality and the women's movement was strongly campaigning for gender equality.

During the 1960s, wage labour became the norm of gender equality. The task set for state power was to facilitate the fitting together of wage labour and the home: there were increasing calls for better day—care services, longer maternity and paternity leaves, and the right for parents to stay at home to look after a sick child. In addition, starting from the 1960s, there were increasing calls that men should share equally in looking after the children and doing household chores. The citizen mother was no longer the vantage point for the campaigns of the women's movement.

Today, with the high level of women's paid employment in the Nordic countries, the most appropriate notion is without doubt the *woman worker citizen*, a concept introduced by Barbara Hobson (1991b).

This review of Anglo—American and Scandinavian feminist research has pointed at some important differences. However, these differences do not necessarily derive from the research traditions concerned but rather come from the differences in the societies in which the researchers work. There exists no universal way to conceptualize the relationship between women and the welfare state. National projects may have been motivated by the same endeavour to strengthen the family institution that is based upon the male breadwinner rule or by the solution of the working class question, but over time they have evolved differently and thus assumed different forms.

The very idea of the welfare state: Social insurance for citizen workers

The modern welfare state is a complex structure whose key principles can be captured in the concepts of the social insurance state and social service state. The social insurance state grew up to safeguard the position of wage earners, whereas the social service state acts to guarantee the continuity of caring in societies in which the responsibility for caring no longer lies primarily with women. The main difference between the social insurance state and social service state lies in the status of the benefits they provide. The former is preoccupied with income maintenance and economic independence, the latter with care—taking and coping with daily life.

In most countries the welfare state has been built upon the basic idea of compensating the wage earner for lost income. Heide Gerstenberger (1985 p. 69) has said that the *introduction of social insurance represents one of the most important milestones in the development*

17

of the bourgeois state. The very fact that the system is possible means that it was preceded by a broad social contract which renegotiated the relationships between the working class and the capitalist class. Peter Baldwin (1992) has a similar interpretation of the emergence of social insurance, but he makes a clear distinction between the classical pension for wage earners and the British—Scandinavian people's pension.

Baldwin (1990, 1992) asserts that the British Beveridge plan, leaning on Marshall's doctrines, introduced a new concept of citizenship. In post—war England, Beveridge was charged with the task of creating a comprehensive, complete system of social insurance in which all citizens found their place.

> All citizens were to become recipients, but at the same time all were to become contributors to the social insurance system. By universalizing social insurance all citizens, even those who had formerly been self—reliant, were now made dependent on the state. (Baldwin 1992 p. 5.)

This *radical expansion of citizenship* became possible in the post—war climate because, during the war, citizens had become accustomed to sharing many risks. The classical social insurance programs (the best—known example being the Bismarckian social insurance program) that had been created around the turn of the century did not have the same solidary motivation but were instead restricted to certain professional groups.

The *social citizenship welfare state* aimed at national unification by combining:

> - ... two extremes of possible human social experience: on the one hand, the medieval view of society as something like family writ large: hierarchical, paternalist, communal; on the other hand, the extreme liberalist view of society as a mere conglomeration of autonomous, individualistic monads, brought together only incidentally by the pursuit of self interest (Baldwin 1992 p. 5).

There can be no doubt that the institutionalization of social insurance is an important turning—point in the history of bourgeois nation states and the redefinition of citizenship. However, following the arguments that Carole Pateman has presented in her book *The Sexual Contract* (1988b), I would like to argue that this kind of new social contract was not only a compromise between capital and labour, or between socialism and liberalism, but also a compromise based on a sexual contract.[6]

The introduction of social insurance can be seen as an integral part of the process of modernization in which men attempted to break loose from the medieval view of society as something like family writ large: hierarchical, paternalist and communal. The signing of a new social contract only became possible when the paternalist rule broke down and paved the way to a stronger civil society. However, the breakdown of paternalism did not immediately give women the same opportunities as men.

In the Anglo—Saxon countries, where liberalism started, men were expected to be breadwinners. In cases of sickness, injury or old age, a legal right to personal income was guaranteed by social insurance. Women were expected to be wives and mothers, unpaid housekeepers and caretakers. Individualization in terms of civic, political and social rights had been originally a deeply masculine project.

These deliberations on the duality of citizenship and the sexual contract provide a different kind of basis for evaluating the introduction and success of the social insurance principle, as well as women's citizenship. The social citizenship welfare state that developed in Great Britain after World War II was not based on the idea of universal citizenship, for it was designed for *perfectly normal persons* (an expression used by Beveridge, see Baldwin 1992 p. 13). *Perfectly normal persons* meant the same thing as male wage earners; housewives were excluded from insurance coverage.

It is only the Nordic version of the social citizenship welfare state, based on people's pensions and on earnings—related social security, which guarantees that *all benefit, all are dependent; and all will presumably feel obliged to pay* (Esping—Andersen 1990 p. 28). All citizens are covered by social insurance not only as workers, but also as non—workers.

Hernes (1987 p. 140) has observed, however, that even in the Nordic countries women have *until recently been mainly citizen mothers, protected and supported in this role by a paternalistic state.* In addition, she stresses that

> social democratic hegemony has concentrated its attention almost totally on the citizen as worker. The social democratic citizen is the citizen worker, a male family provider, a working class hero. HIS rights, identities and participation patterns were determined by HIS ties with the labour market and by the web of association as well as corporate structures that had grown up around these ties.

In Finland, both the Social Democratic Party and the trade unions had an instrumental role in the introduction of statutory earnings—related pension programmes; these were not achieved until the 1960s.[7] In addition to these earnings—related pension programs, there is also a national flat—rate people's pension program, which was originally introduced with the 1937 National Pensions Act. The chief advocates of this system have been the Communists and the Centre Party, the latter representing mainly the agrarian population.

The Nordic model for the social insurance state is not designed only for perfectly normal persons, that is, for male citizen workers and farmers. It is important to stress that mothers have been eligible for earnings—related maternity allowances since the introduction of sickness insurance legislation in 1963. And in spite of the critical comment cited in the preceding paragraph, it is fair to conclude that the Nordic social insurance state, which is based on the principle of universality, also has benefits for women who have not received payment for employment and who are not covered by earnings—related insurance.

My conclusion then is that the Nordic social insurance state forms an integral part of women's social citizenship. It has expanded the social rights of all women, not only those engaged in wage employment. However, the duality of citizenship has remained in place even in the Nordic social insurance state, where the distinction between earnings—related insurance systems and flat—rate people's pension schemes (which guarantees minimum subsistence in pensions, maternity benefits and unemployment benefits) upholds a profound asymmetry in terms of citizen statuses. The citizen mother is still not regarded as a perfectly normal person.

Barbara Hobson (1991a p. 15) has made the observation that, within the feminist welfare state regime, the norm of citizenship should be a single mother:

> All women are potential single mothers and main providers in families. This would lead to policies that are universalistic and compensatory: for example universalistic policies would include daycare, care of the elderly and handicapped as citizen rights.

This comment is related to the fact that the right to work and the right to one's own money do not necessarily guarantee the right to decide on one's own life. Autonomy defined in economic terms is a profoundly masculine ideal because there are always people — children, the elderly and the handicapped — who need care. But these dependent people cannot necessarily buy the care they need, even with money, nor does money alone release women from their care—giving obligations.

The social service state for women: The case of Finland

Feminist research has shown that, throughout recorded history, women have carried the main burden and responsibility for looking after the family and relatives, as well as for taking care of the household and livestock. This is still the case, even today and even in countries where women have moved out of the family in large numbers to take on paid jobs. But there have been other important changes, most notably the process that Hernes (1987) has described by her slogan *reproduction going public*. There has been a radical change in the division of caring work between the family and the rest of society.

Against this background it comes as no surprise that the concept of caring has attracted much attention among feminist researchers both in the Nordic countries and elsewhere throughout the 1980s.[8] The ongoing debate on caring has made visible the unpaid work that women do in and around the home and with the family and relatives, as well as the reproductive labour they do on a wage—labour basis. At the same time, increasing attention has been given to welfare services that have received only marginal attention in mainstream research and, accordingly, in welfare models.

Today, the welfare state is also a *social service state* or an evolving *caring state* (see Leira 1992). The public sector has assumed increasing responsibility for caring functions, especially in the Nordic countries, which boast the most impressive statistics for organized day care. Indeed, comprehensive welfare services are among the most distinctive characteristics of the Nordic model. In addition, these services are chiefly funded by public money and organized on a professional basis.

The Nordic welfare policy is characterized primarily by the *universality* of income security and social services. The central government and local municipalities play a key role in the implementation of social policy. Social rights are based on citizenship, and therefore the clientele of the welfare state is very large and unsegmented. Welfare policies have been explicitly geared towards promoting equality among citizens. This goal has not only been pursued by a policy of income distribution, but inequalities have also, and importantly, been smoothed out by providing services.

Birte Siim (1988 pp. 175—176) has made an important observation about a key difference between the Scandinavian and Anglo—American model:

> In Denmark and in Sweden women have to a greater extent come to rely on the state as consumers of public services, and only to a smaller degree as social welfare clients. The opposite is true in Great Britain and the USA, where women have come to rely on the state primarily as clients.

There are also commentators (e.g., Wolfe 1989) who feel that the Nordic countries have gone too far and that excessive caring and protection on the part of the public sector serves to undermine and weaken community ties and family morals. However, many feminist researchers have a different interpretation of the institutionalization of the social service state. According to Birte Siim (1987), universal access to welfare services has helped to make women less dependent on men as well as on the market, even though it has also implied various new dependencies. Leila Simonen (1990) talks about alliances between women and the state, and Hernes (1987) speaks of a woman—friendly state.

In *Welfare State and Women Power* Helga Maria Hernes (1987 p. 14) has the following argument: *Nordic democracies embody a state form that makes it possible to transform them into woman—friendly societies.* In Sweden, Yvonne Hirdman (1990a), and, in Finland, Raija Julkunen (1992) have, among many others (e.g., Jones 1990; Lucas 1990; Simonen 1990; Acker 1992), argued that the Nordic model has paved the way for a woman—friendly social policy.

The concept of a *woman—friendly state* provides an interesting starting point for discussion on the meaning of the Nordic social service state to women. However, since the notion of the social service state is not established in the same way as the notion of the social insurance state, my analysis of the social service state is necessarily an empirical study and grounded in the case of Finland. In fact, the analysis should be read as an attempt to find a new and meaningful way of dealing with social services and women's social citizenhip. Inevitably, it is a preliminary effort.

In Finland the modern welfare state project got underway in the 1960s. The foundations for the social insurance state were established towards the end of the decade with the consolidation of the corporatist bargaining model. It was later that the social service state became institutionalized.

The peak years in the growth and expansion of social welfare and health care services[9] came in the 1970s and 1980s. In terms of money spent on social expenditure the social insurance state is far more extensive than the social service state (Palm 1988 p. 24). During 1960—1985 Finland's social expenditure increased about sixfold. The two items with the fastest growth rates were pensions and health care services. The growth of social services began to gather momentum towards the end of this period.

Measured in terms of staff numbers, the public sectors which grew the most rapidly during the period between 1970 and 1985 were teaching and education, nursing and health care services, and social welfare. According to the results of Alestalo (1991 p. 16) the

23

proportion of teaching and research staff out of all public—sector wage earners increased between 1970 and 1985 from 15.9 to 21.9 percent. and in social welfare from 4.5 to 10.7 percent.

In 1985 a proportion as great as 44 percent (Alestalo 1991) of all wage—earning women in Finland were working in the public sector. Over half of these women were engaged in teaching, nursing, health care and social welfare. In 1990 the total staff number in social services was 104,809,[10] of whom about 50 percent were engaged in children's day care. The combined share of home—help services and old—age welfare, as well as children's day care out of all social service posts and offices was 79 percent.

Children's day care and the care of elderly and disabled persons constitute the backbone of the social service state.

As far as feminist research is concerned, it is important to look at social services because first, the vast majority (over 90 percent) of employees in social services comprises of women. Second, women use social services to a greater extent than men. In many cases they are vitally important to women. The availability of day—care services means that women can make the important choice between paid employment and staying home, whereas social and health services for the elderly and the handicapped, make it possible for them to remain in the labour market. However, they are also important for the independence and autonomy of persons in need of care — although this topic remains beyond the scope of my paper.

Women's citizenship in light of the social service state

It can also be assumed that the social service state has led to a change in what is considered the content of citizenship and social rights. I shall now make a brief excursion into two social services: home—help services and children's day care. Both of these examples help shed light on the development of the social service state, on the feminization of the welfare state, and on the content of citizenship.

Home help has a long history in Finland. The Mannerheim League of Child Welfare launched a professional home—help service in Finland as early as the 1930s. The purpose was to compensate for a mother's absence from home because of illness or childbirth (Simonen 1990).

The first law on home help came into force in 1950; it made home help the first social service for which local authorities received state subsidies. But it was only with the National Municipal Home Help Act of 1966 that the service was expanded so that every family and individual was entitled, in principle, to receive home—help.

Since the 1960s, this service has grown very rapidly. In 1960 the total number of home helpers was around 200; by 1980 the figure climbed to 8,200 and by 1990 to over 12,000 (*Sosiaalipalvelujen henkilökunta* 1990).

The expansion of municipal home—help services is one indication of the shifting boundary line between the private and the public. Home help was originally introduced as a service to compensate for the absence of mothers in the family and on small farms. Later, municipal home helpers were also needed to look after sick children when the mother went to work. Today, the need is greatest in old age welfare, and it provides a much appreciated opportunity for the elderly to stay at home instead of having to move into an institution.

From the view of working—age women, a new type of caring profession has also developed with the growth of municipal home—help services. Starting from the 1960s, the increasing number of vacancies in home—help services has provided tempting training and career opportunities especially for women moving out of the countryside into towns. From the very outset, municipal home help has been a typically female occupation. Futhermore, it has been an integral part of the domain of feminine or maternal social policy that has been built by women and women's organizations. (see Simonen 1990.)

Home—help services were developed in response to the needs of agrarian society. The service was started at a time when it was still taken for granted that it was women's responsibility to look after the children, the home and the livestock. In the 1930s, the compensating service of home help was developed to strengthen the position of women as citizen mothers. Home help was not developed to secure the position of the mother as a woman citizen worker. It was not until the 1960s that it was transformed into such a service.

Children's day care is arguably the most important social service in Finnish society today. Half of the country's social service expenditure goes into children's day care, and half of the social services staff is

25

engaged in this field. Children's day care has, in fact, become a matter of national pride for Finland, where it is regarded as an important indicator of the country's high level of welfare. Even so, the first national day care act requiring local governments to provide day—care services to families living within their jurisdiction, was not passed until 1973.

However, the history of children's day care is much longer. The first Finnish kindergartens, dating to the 19th century, were privately owned or run by foundations and associations. They were strongly motivated by pedagogic and poor—relief considerations, but the number of these early nursery schools never met the real need. In fact, they were also developed to secure the position of women as citizen mothers (Kurikka 1992).

The first calls for public day care were made around the turn of the century. However, it was only with the debate on gender roles that started in the late 1950s, with the reformistic movements of the 1960s and the reorganization of the women's movement that the public debate began to gather momentum — perhaps too much for the government's good.

Elina Haavio—Mannila (1968 p. 187) wrote about the day—care issue in 1968. She pointed out that in Finland, society has been able to follow the example of Eastern Europe and the other Nordic countries in providing organized day—care services for working mothers only in exceptional cases. In the 1960s it was estimated that every other working mother who had children under seven years of age did not have access to adequate day—care services.

The first calls for public day care were made around the turn of the century. However, it was only with the debate on gender roles that started in the late 1950s, with the reformistic movements of the 1960s and the reorganization of the women's movement that the public debate began to gather too much momentum for the government's good.

Furthermore, increasing numbers of mothers of small children were moving out of the home to take on paid jobs as early as in the 1950s, although it was only during the 1960s that the *mother's right to choose* won broader recognition (Kuronen 1989). At the same time, as the demand for female labour increased (employers were now also in favour of women's wage labour), labour relations were normalized.

Part—time work started to recede and full—time employment became the norm for all wage earners. All of these factors combined to set into motion the day—care reform in the early 1970s.

The main force behind the campaigns for day—care reforms at the beginning of the century and later were women. Indeed day care as a whole remained a strictly female issue for a long time. This trend is understandable in view of the fact that day care and women's wage employment are closely intertwined. In all the Nordic countries, women take a very active part in the labour market. Finland, however, differs from the rest of the Nordic countries in the sense that full—time employment is more common.

After a series of inevitable political disputes and compromises, the first National Day Care Act came to include two different systems. Local governments were charged with the responsibility to support, first, the building of kindergartens and, second, supervised day care in private families. This latter option was recorded in the law partly because the advocates what is called the mother's wage[11] remained in the minority (Alanen 1981).

Since the introduction of the day—care act, the municipal day care system has expanded very rapidly in Finland. During the past 20 years, the number of staff engaged in children's day care has more than tripled. In 1990 personnel in kindergartens numbered 26,521, and personnel in supervised family day care totalled 23,359 (*Sosiaalipalvelujen henkilökunta* 1990).

In the 1980s the Finnish day care act was revised radically because there was still a chronic shortage of day—care slots. Towards the end of the decade, development efforts in the field of day care were also frustrated by a shortage of nursery staff. The new act, which was endorsed in 1984, not only required local governments to organize day—care services, but day care became a subjective right. At first every guardian of a child under three years of age had the right to get his or her child into municipal day care. Then the right to the day care was given to one or the other of the parents in the form of a home care allowance, if the parents decided not to take advantage of municipal day—care services.

Home—care allowances[12] are paid during a period of approximately 24 months after the expiration of maternity and parents' leave up until the time that the youngest child is three years of age. The original intention was that, by 1995, the law would apply to all children under school—age, but this decision has now been reverted due economic austerity measures.

The day care reform is thought widely to mark a turning—point in terms of the expansion of social rights. The main difference between social insurance benefits and social services has been precisely in their legal status. Citizens have not enjoyed the same subjective right to social services as in the case of earning—related benefits — in other words, citizens have not had the right of appeal. In this regard it would seem that the new day—care act is altering the tradition upon which the social citizenship welfare state was originally built.

Municipal home—help services and children's day care provide two different examples of how the social service state has become institutionalized. At the time they were created and launched, both of them were services for citizen mothers, but they have developed in response to the needs of woman worker citizens as well. They have also led to a process which I have called the feminization of the Nordic welfare state (Anttonen 1990). The social service state is distinctly a domain of female social policy.

The Nordic welfare state: A woman—friendly state?

The 1960s was, in many ways, an important turning point. The social service state started to assume a more concrete form as a new gender policy began to evolve. In conjunction with this development the male breadwinner rule began to lose its ideological potential. Its practical meaning had already dissipated earlier. The norms of social policy were now developed more and more often with a view to the needs of woman citizen workers; the traditional juxtaposition of the citizen worker and the citizen mother was no longer a self—evident starting point.

It is generally assumed that the main force behind social reforms in the Nordic countries has been represented by Social Democracy.[13] However, the debate that was waged in the 1960s on gender equality and gender policy, as well as the research carried out in these areas, indicate that the institutionalization of the social service state and gender policy are closely intertwined. The comment by Hernes (1987

p. 17) that the welfare state and the struggle of gender equality are interlinked also applies to the situation in Finland.

During the 1960s, wage labour became the norm of gender equality. The institutionalization of the social service state since the 1970s made the continuing expansion of women's wage employment possible and vice versa. The continuing expansion of the public sector created new jobs for women. The labour force and the welfare state were feminized in pace with the continuing growth of the Finnish national economy and the GNP shares of social expenditure (see Palm 1988 p. 97).

The Nordic welfare state has opened up new opportunities for women, first as citizen mothers and later as woman worker citizens. On one hand, this development can be explained by historical factors such as women's early suffrage and participation in politics and wage labour. On the other, explanations can be found in the welfare state itself, such as in the universality of social security benefits and services, the policy of full employment, and the positive equality effects of education.

What we have to realize is that, in societies which remained agrarian well into the mid—20th century, gender divisions did not become so deeply entrenched during the early stages of modernization as was the case in continental Europe or Britain. Moreover, it was difficult to define the tasks of women in the same way as in countries which had a large and wealthy bourgeoisie; and even though working—class women and women on small farms might have been attracted to the ideal of the citizen mother, very few families could afford to live according to the ideological doctrines of the housewife society. Women were used to working out of necessity.

I agree, however, with Raija Julkunen (1992), who suggests that the weakness of the male breadwinner model explains the emergence of a woman—friendly social policy. Especially the development of the social service state during the 1970s and 1980s was determined by women's right to work — this is most clearly seen in day—care legislation. Women's right to wage employment has not been called into question during the past two decades. A woman—friendly welfare state is a state for women worker citizens. It has failed to achieve essential convergence in the position of mother citizens and woman wage workers, even though there has been some movement in this direction. Motherhood does not in itself guarantee an adequate livelihood or sufficient social benefits

At the time I wrote this paper, it seemed that the Nordic welfare state model had come to the end of its road. The collapse of socialist regimes in the East and the breakdown of social democratic hegemony in the West have seriously undermined people's faith in social policy based on solidarity. In addition, the deep economic recession of the early 1990s has strengthened the appeal and attraction of market—liberalist economic and social policy doctrines.

Social welfare and health—care services are being slashed and government officials are still trying to find new items on which they can save money. Various welfare—state commitments, such as those contained in the day—care act, have been dropped. At the same time, the public sector has come under unprecedented attack. Public services are said to be expensive and bureaucratic; they are also thought to violate the individual's autonomy and the principle of consumerism. Instead of the social service state, a project has started to build up a welfare mix society in which less weight is given to the public sector and professional caring. These changes have various effects on women's lives, but in the fluid situation that now prevails it is extremely difficult to anticipate the future course of things.

Indeed, what once was the most radical day—care reform in the world may well be dismantled in Finland in the future; at least it seems that social service rights will not be expanded. On the contrary, the record—high level of unemployment (in January 1995 19 percent) has led to a situation in which the demand for day—care services has been declining, and, as a consequence, municipal day—care services have been cut back. Women's unemployment is making increasing numbers of welfare state professionals redundant. However, the problems we have are not only due to an economic crisis, there is also a political and ideological crisis and possibly the politics of gender equality is also suffering a major setback.

The institutionalization of the woman—friendly welfare state has been grounded in a policy of full employment. In the current situation of massive unemployment, we might well see a sharper distinction develop between male and female wage earners and women increasingly defined through motherhood and caring. This would

30

effectively bring back the traditional juxtaposition of the citizen worker and the citizen mother.

For the first time in its short history, the Nordic welfare state is being put to the test. We are no doubt going to see soon how woman—friendly it really is. As yet it is too early to say where the present crisis will lead. It is possible that the woman—friendly Nordic welfare state will turn out to be a historical experiment. However, we have to keep in mind that women's political weight is greater than ever before.

Notes

1   I have borrowed the concepts of citizen worker and citizen mother from Helga Maria Hernes (see Hernes 1987 pp. 135—163).

2   Mainstream research on the welfare state has been chiefly concerned with analyzing the position of citizen workers and their rights and struggles. There is no doubt whatsoever that the hero of welfare state development is the *citizen worker*, the male family provider (Hernes 1987 p. 140).

3   Arnlaug Leira (1992) has recently made a similar distinction between an economic provider state and a caring state.

4   Following much the same line of argumentation, Nancy Fraser (1989 p. 149) says that the American welfare state is divided into masculine and feminine practices whereby *one set of programs is oriented to individuals and tied to participation in the paid work force — for example, unemployment insurance and Social Security. A second set of programs is oriented to households and tied to combined household income — for example, AFDC, food stamps, and Medicaid. This set of programs is designed to compensate for what are considered to be family failures, in particular the absence of a male breadwinner.*

5   The founding fathers of modern western philosophy have also repeated this story: for example, Hegel thought that women naturally lack the attributes and capacities of persons who can enter civil society, sell their labour and become citizens. Women were held by Hegel to be natural social exiles who belong to the private world. (Pateman 1988b pp. 235—238.)

6   Without going into the details of the theoretical debates (see, e.g., Pateman 1988a, 1989; Hirdman 1990a; Julkunen 1992), my argument is that the sexual contract includes both implicitly and explicitly approved principles (some of which are recorded in legislation) as to how society defines gender relations, divisions of responsibility, and labour and citizenship statuses.

7   They not only cover ordinary wage earners, but also farmers and people with their own businesses.

8   For example Waerness 1978, Finch and Groves 1983; Ungerson 1987, 1990, Tronto 1989.

9   The expansion of the health care system falls beyond the scope of this paper.

10 In 1990, the total number of posts and offices was 108,264, of which 93 percent belonged to the public—sector under the state, local municipalities or federations of municipalities and the remaining 5 percent were non—governmental. The vast majority, or 93 percent of the staff, comprised women. The proportion of women has remained more or less unchanged since 1979 (*Sosiaalipalvelujen henkilökunta* 1990 p. 24). In 1990, the proportion of those working in social services out of the total labour force was about 4 percent.

11 This is not the same thing as the universal system of child allowances which was first introduced in 1948.

12 The allowance consists of a statutory basic amount plus a supplement that varies between different municipalities and which is means tested.

13 In 1966 the Social Democrats were back in the government after a long period of absence.

3 Remaking the boundaries of women's citizenship and the dilemma of dependency[1]

Barbara Hobson

We have seen the emergence of a feminist literature that both challenges the dominant theories and concepts of citizenship and suggests alternative theoretical frameworks.[2] Beginning with Carole Pateman's pathbreaking analysis of the patriarchal grounding of social contract theory, there has been an intense interest in the implicit norms and assumptions around citizenship. This research has revealed the gendered construction of the key words that form the basis of dominant theories of citizenship: dependency/independency, private/public, needs/rights.

Despite a growing interest among feminist scholars in gender and policy regime analysis, it has mainly been a one—way dialogue. Not only the theoretical frameworks, but also the empirical measures of dominant policy regime research on welfare statism assess the institutional features in welfare states in relation to the protection, social provisions, and entitlements of either an average non—gendered industrial worker or a male head of household (Hobson 1990; Orloff 1993). Esping—Andersen in *The Three Worlds of Welfare Capitalism* (1990), broadened the terrain of welfare state theorizing to encompass the relations between *family*, state, and market. However, he did not problematize gender in any of the three realms. - Basically, his theoretical and empirical analysis still assume a male worker/citizen model (Anttonen in this volume). This assumption is primarily evident in the concept of decommodification, which takes for granted the fact that people have been commodified, and it presumes that distributional conflicts exist only between workers and employers. Distibutional conflicts between husbands and wives and the ways in which gendered power relations in the family shape labour market decisions are not conspicuously absent. When conflicts among male and female workers appear in the analysis, they are seen in terms of competing sectors (men in private sector work and women in public sector work), rather than as gendered wage differentials and opportunity structures within occupations and sectors. Whereas distributional conflicts in the market are seen as the core of power resource analysis, the gendered distribution of power in the family is dislocated from the market state nexus. Esping—Andersen (1987 p. 20) asserts that the activities of the welfare state are interlocked with the market and the *family's* role. The family is treated as a category and not as a set of relations that are shaped by the state or market (Ostner 1993). Implicit in his analysis of the three types of welfare regimes is an assumption that the family functions as a unit, a sphere of welfare activity that provides services or is serviced by the state. In *The Three Worlds of Welfare Capitalism*, the family is the main provider in corporatist/conservative and liberal welfare policy regimes; the state only interferes when the family fails in its role to service its members. However, in the social democratic policy regime, the state takes responsibility to service family needs and thus frees the individual to develop his/her capacities — it allows women *to choose work rather than household* (italics added) (Andersen 1990).

This inference reveals the pervasiveness of a view of citizenship based on independence and dependence from the market. Nowhere is the gender analytic vacuum more obvious in models of welfare state research than in its failure to recognize care work: individuals are dependent on others for care and much of this care work is unpaid. Even in Scandinavia where the state has taken over some of the responsibility for the care of children, the elderly and the handicapped, empirical studies of the division of labor in Scandinavian households reveal that women rarely have a choice between household or market work. Scandinavian women work a double shift of domestic unpaid labor and paid market work, as do most working women with families.[3]

To incorporate gender analytically into the policy regime typology implies first a recognition of the family as the site of distributional conflict. Second, one needs to insert a missing hyphen in the links between the state, the economy, and the family: state/family—

economy, or state/economy—family. In addition we can say that labor market policies stratify the distribution of resources in the family: not only the allocation of time and money, but also the ability to make claims (Sorensen and MacLanahan 1987; Pahl 1988; Haavio—Mannila 1989). Who has the stronger position in the labour market among couples is expressed in daily life patterns (who is responsible for household tasks and childcare), but it also can be seen in the career trajectories of spouses in households: who invests in education and employee training programs; who is involved in work organizations and professional bodies (Hobson 1990; Haavio—Mannila and Kauppinen 1992): all facets of social citizenship. In addition a range of policies (tax systems, parental leave and child sick days, and public provision for day—care), provides incentives for increasing women's activity in the labour force. Greater participation in market work, in turn, tends to alter the distribution of paid and unpaid work in the family.

Among feminist scholars, there has been a growing recognition that economic and social dependency in the family is a critical site for theorizing about gender inequality. Empirical analysis of economic dependency among couples and time budget studies of the division of paid and unpaid work have revealed the inequalities that result from the dynamics of power and dependency in the family over the life course. They have shown that women who take the main responsibilities for caring in the family tend to have a marginal position in the labour market because they are likely to have an intermittent work history (Sorensen and McLanahan 1987; Haavio—Mannila 1989). Furthermore studies have demonstrated the economic and social costs of dependency in cases of divorce (Eckelaar and MacLean 1986; Millar 1992). This rich empirical research has laid the basis for new approaches in the feminist analysis of dependency. Such analyses consider the discursive landscape around dependency and its social policy dimensions in different societies.

Little agreement exists among feminist scholars in the search for alternative models. The question of how to develop new theories and paradigms of policy regimes that acknowledge both the unequal distribution of resources in the family and the role of care in the formation of citizenship is an unresolved dilemma. This problem goes to the heart of Pateman's analysis of what is called Wollstencraft's dilemma: how to recognize women's caring and domestic contribution (her unpaid work) and how to provide opportunities for and access to women's influence and contribution in the economic and political spheres of life. Within the feminist research on social politics and welfare states, this dilemma is posed in terms of the compensation for care work. Should one aim for gender differentiated citizenship that assumes women's roles as mothers and constructs a policy matrix to compensate for women's caring wage? (Ostner 1993). Or should one posit a gender neutral notion of citizenship that encompasses the participation of all parents in care, employment, and the making of policy (Hobson 1993; Siim 1993)?

I do not presume to solve this dilemma, but rather to highlight the weaknesses in both positions and suggest some criteria for constructing a paradigm for a social policy regime that would permit a comparative analysis of gendered social rights. Such an analysis would require a category of social rights that is inclusive enough to reach the distributional conflicts in the family and a framework for policy regime analysis that addresses the ways in which policy shape the power relations between men and women in families. Thus I begin with a discussion of dependency as a core concept for building a framework for women's social rights. Then I focus on the solo mother as a category for analyzing variations among welfare states, what I refer to as gender policy regimes. I analyze the poverty rates of solo mothers in five countries and how different policy regimes tend to frame women's universe of choices of paid and unpaid work. In the conclusion I delineate the dilemmas for the construction of a social policy regime attuned to women's social citizenship in light of the current policies of retrenchment in welfare states.

Dimensions of dependency

If we begin with the question of why dependency is a core concept for theorizing about gender and welfare states, we need to use several levels of analysis. The meaning of dependency reflects of a range of values and norms in a society. It appears as a social text about who is worthy and who is unworthy, what we define as active and passive citizenship. It is a keyword that interprets what is work and what is *productive work*.

Dependency is a social construction in welfare states. For example, when wives and children are referred to as dependent in the policy discourse, it is assumed that economic transfers confer dependency on someone or some institution. However, it is rare to find an allusion to husbands' dependency on wives for care in policy debates (see Knijn 1994; Saraceno 1994). Because citizen status is coupled with worker status in modern welfare states, those dependent upon income from their families or the state have tended to be labeled as *dependents* — implicit in this term is the lack of independence and its corollary, the lack of autonomy and self—reliance (Fraser and Gordon 1994). In some contexts there are both gender and racial/ethnic components in the persona of the dependent. For example, the black welfare mother epitomizes dependency in the United States, whereas the American elderly, who receive publicly financed medical benefits and social services, are not seen as dependent but as entitled to public provisions (Gordon 1994). Finally, when power relations in families are adressed, it is important to note that the family has also been a site of resistance against oppressive regimes. This statement applies to the Afro—American family both before and after slavery and the strategies of families when confronted by the tyranny of the state in former Soviet bloc countries (Marx Feree 1995).

To recognize that dependency is a social construction in welfare states, however, does not necessarily rule out its relevance for capturing variations in the situations of women in different welfare states. With this statement I want to suggest that dependency is still a useful analytic tool for understanding specific power relations in families and identifying the economic and social location of women and men in the home and labor market. Thus, in this individual context, we can talk about women's economic dependency in the family as a reflector of a broad spectrum of women's social rights.

In the article *No Exit, No Voice* (1990), I suggested a framework for understanding the power dynamics in households. This framework laid the basis for discussions of women's social right to form autonomous households (Orloff 1993). Employing Hirschman's (1970) classic formulation of exit and voice as strategies that work in tandem, I presented two sides of this dynamic, first, that economic dependency limits a woman's ability to opt out of bad marriages and, second, that, not having any exit possibilities, she has a limited voice in household decision making (Hobson 1990). When applied to the bargaining position of men and women in families, Hirschman's framework of exit and voice implies the following conditions: first, the more dependent, the weaker the voice, second, the lower the earnings potential, the fewer exit possibilities, third, the fewer the exit possibilities, the weaker the voice.

Dependency can also be seen as a gauge of social rights if we employ Esping—Andersen's dimension of stratification in social policy regime analysis — whether the distribution of resources is more or less equal. If we take Esping—Andersen's premise (1990) that the welfare state is a system of stratification in its own right, that it is an *active force in the ordering of social relations* (p. 23), then women's economic dependency in the family should be brought into an analysis of the ordering of relations. A self—evident reason for including women's economic dependency in families in analyses of inequality in welfare states is the fact that women who have been economically dependent on husbands face a risk of poverty after divorce. Heightened awareness of the costs of dependency after divorce is apparent in the discourse around the femination of poverty. Furthermore, in countries such as Sweden, where a small proportion of women is not in the labor market (less than 7 percent of married women were totally dependent on their husband's income in 1991[4]), mothers who are solo tend to be poorer and have a much lower standard of living than solo fathers (Hobson and Takahashi, in press)

Much of the empirical work on variations in welfare states has concerned the level of benefits and the distribution of resources. Comparative studies of welfare states have tended to use the distribution of family income as a barometer of inequality in societies. The underlying assumption is that resources are distributed equally in families and families are stable units. In fact, research has shown that resources are both consumed and distributed unequally and that cases of concealed poverty in families can be found at any income level (Pahl 1988). In comparative studies, the categories of weak and strong welfare states often fail to take into account whether entitlements are given to breadwinners and not spouses (Sainsbury 1989). Nor do they address the ways in which social policy shape the division of paid work in the market and unpaid work in the household; few take into account social services, for example. (Borchost 1994.)

If we compare the actual levels of dependency in different welfare states, it becomes evident that clusters and categories that reflect standard comparative measures of inequality in welfare states do not capture a critical dimension in gender inequalities.

Using the Luxembourg Income Study (LIS), I have been able to look at women's economic dependency in several Western European countries. By economic dependency, I mean the gap between women's and men's share of the family's earned income. (Sorensen and McLanahan 1987; Hobson 1990.)[5] When I introduced economic dependency into comparative research models of overall inequality based upon the distributions of total household income, I found that the relationship is rather weak (Hobson 1990, 1994).[6] Certain countries, such as Germany and the Netherlands, that have a fairly low overall income inequality have extremely high dependency rates for married women. The United States with the most unequal distribution of household incomes has relatively low economic dependency.[7]

In this analysis the source of the cross—national variations of economic dependency is based upon how much women work. In those countries with the highest dependency levels the proportion of married women who do paid work is relatively low. The Netherlands, in the comparative studies of the distribution of income across families in the 1980s, was seen as one of the least stratified societies; yet, in terms of gender differences in economic resources within families, it appears to be one of the most unequal. It has one of the highest levels of women's economic dependency. In the 1990s, a surprising number of married Dutch women were still totally dependent on their husbands' income (49 percent).

Policy regime theorizing has gone beyond conventional welfare state research that has compared levels of social expenditures. The models focus on the content of welfare policies and how they extend social rights. However, if we take the content of social policy and introduce a gendered analysis, then it seems logical to incorporate the dimension of women's economic dependency. Suppose we again consider inequality in the family in the three welfare regime clusters suggested by Esping—Andersen: the liberal, corporatist/conservative, and the social democratic.

The liberal welfare regime is characterized by means—tested benefits associated with stigma. By guaranteeing only minimum benefits, the state encourages the work ethic and private insurance schemes. Canada, Australia, and the United States exemplify the liberal regime type. The corporatist/conservative regimes, such as Germany, France, Italy, and Austria, are committed to preserving status differentials. The state has replaced the market as the provider of welfare but social insurance and services assume a non—working wife. Family benefits are geared toward maintaining the traditional family and motherhood. The cluster of the social democratic policy regime represents those countries that express the principles of universalism, broad social rights, and have developed programs that decommodify workers to the greatest extent. Included in this group are the Scandinavian countries and the Netherlands.

When we look at inequality in the family during the 1980s and early 1990s in different welfare states, it is difficult to find consistent patterns in the three welfare regime clusters (Hobson 1994). For example, in the liberal welfare regime, we find, that in the late 1980s, only 19 percent of Canadian women were totally dependent on their husband's earnings, whereas in Australia over 28 percent of married women were without earnings. In the United Kingdom, 39 percent had no earnings of their own. Comparisons of Sweden and Norway in 1991 showed that married women had different locations on the dependency scale. Swedish women had a dependency level of 0.26, while Norwegian women tended to be more dependent on their husband's income with a rating of 0.34 for average dependency.

Neither the empirical measures nor the conceptual frameworks employed in policy regime analysis are sensitive to gendered dimensions. When gender is brought into the analysis, the basic assumptions of the social rights tradition are called into question

Social citizenship in terms of gender

Pederson (1994) in her comparative and historical studies of gender and welfare statism, has made the point that Marshall's framework of social citizenship, which has been the theoretical mainstay of scholarship on welfare states, actually narrowed the scope and role of welfare states by arguing that class divisions generated in the labor market were the only real source of inequality between citizens. This stand is evident in the work of social—democratic theorists such as Korpi and Esping—Andersen, who considered the central axis of power brokering as revolving around working class mobilization and social democratic party politics (Esping—Andersen and Korpi 1987). In this analysis of power structure and power resources in welfare states, women as social actors lack an agency with which to shape citizenship rights.

The most problematic concept for constructing a theory of women's social citizenship is that of decommodification because it obfuscates the ways in which gender differences have been built in welfare states. The states that appear to have institutionalized welfare states, principally the Nordic countries, have developed policies that cover a range of rights to job security, educational retraining supports, health care, and parenting. But the construction of dependence and independence in this context often assumes a citizen worker (who is employed full time and whose attachment to the labor force entitles him or her to the most generous entitlements).

Taken at face value, we could say that housewives are decommodified in societies where policies have helped to make the male breadwinner wage secure and protected from the risks of the market. Their wives, with policy incentives that encourage them to do unpaid caring work in the home, are thus freed from market dependence. Absurd as this may seem, the decommodification of wives is on the agenda in many countries. It is in fact official policy discourse around the remaking of state/economy relations in post—communist societies. Maternalist and nationalist ideologies have emerged to *decommodify* women workers and dismantle the services provided by the state for social reproduction (Dimova 1995; Kotowski 1995; see also Heinen 1995). However, the economic realities in these countries do not permit a single breadwinner model.

Rather than take decommodification as a point of departure, we might begin by asking how social policies have encouraged women to be commodified and thus less dependent on husband's incomes. Second, we can consider the gendered outcomes of policies that supposedly decommodify individuals. We must keep in mind that social policies can promote a gendered allocation of time between paid and unpaid work through channeling benefits to male breadwinners, for example, through pensions and unemployment benefits — but they can also perpetuate a male breadwinner model indirectly through tax penalties for dual—earner couples. Studies of women's labor force participation reveal the importance of the individual tax system for encouraging women to enter the labor market (Gustafsson and Bruyn—Hundt 1992). In practice, the tax incentives for women to join the labor force in Sweden made it difficult for women to remain at home. (Every kronor women earned became extra income taxed at a low level.) At the same time, the expanded service sector provided jobs for Scandinavian women (Rein 1982). Indeed policy and markets seem to work in tandem, not decommodifying workers but commodifying them.[8]

In addition, not to be forgotten, is the fact that policies allowing women to have a continuous attachment to worklife, such as day—care and parental leave, are often built around worker status and time in the labor force. Take, for instance, the Swedish case: parental leave benefits are based on an individual's income during the previous year.[9] Moreover, day—care places are reserved for women who are in the labor force.[10]

Considering the gendered outcomes of policies, it is useful to think in terms of gender when the effects are evaluated of activities permitting employees to be paid while pursuing activities other than working, whether they are child bearing, family responsibilities, re—education, organizational activities, or even leisure—time activities (Such policies are highly developed in the Scandinavian welfare states). If we look at the decommodifying programs that are generally used by Swedish mothers, for example, parental leave or the right to work part—time up till a child is six years of age, we can see contradictory consequences of the discrimination against women in the work force and a highly segregated labor market — ghettoization of women workers in the public sector (Acker 1991; Persson 1991). Conversely, decommodifying programs that men tend to utilize, such as job retraining and education and union organizational work, tend to enhance their labor market position. Because women and men have had and continue to have different connections with the labor market, activities that weaken a woman worker's dependence on the market may also have the unintended effects of weakening her position in the market.

How couples use benefits that are universalistic in scope and gender neutral is shaped by the dynamics of power and dependency in the family. Again we can take the example of Swedish parental leave policy. Up until 1994,[11] this policy gave the right to all parents, either mothers or fathers, to leave the labor market for 12 months to care for young children and receive 90 percent of their salary. A study of parental leave among Swedish couples (Haas 1992) found that a wife's relative and absolute contribution to the family economy were the two best predictors of whether a man took leave and how long he remained at home. Therefore the question of who takes leave is often a reflection of a person's location within the family — who has the higher earnings or earnings potential; who is considered the breadwinner.

Beyond decommodification

Recognizing the need to extend the boundaries of policy regime theorizing, some feminist scholars have suggested a gendered dimension beyond decommodification. O'Connor (1990) has argued for supplementing decommodification with a concept of non—dependency in personal life, insulation from personal and public dependence and insulation from market pressures. In a similar vein, Orloff (1993) has suggested that we develop a more generic concept of independence that would encompass *individuals* freedom from compulsion to enter potentially oppressive relationships in a number of spheres. This concept would include the role of the state in mediating a range of relations from the market to family to race relations in communities. Lewis and Ostner (1994) have proposed an alternative paradigm for a gender policy regime that proposes a different set of criteria for constructing social policy based upon variations in attachment to the male breadwinner ideology, a weak, moderate, and strong male breadwinner typology.

These formulations revolve around the policy implications of dependencies in welfare states. They raise some probing questions about the stated and unstated norms surrounding a male breadwinner wage. Moreover, they implicitly argue for the exit option in marriage and for the autonomy and freedom of solo mothers to be able to choose not to marry.

In the following section, I introduce the idea of a family wage, and, through its policy dimensions, I consider how it is encoded into divergent policy regimes based on the situations of solo mothers. I have selected solo mothers for this analysis because they allow a discussion of different dimensions in welfare states, for example, claim structures, the organization of care, and more generally the unstated assumptions about dependency and independency in welfare states.

Although solo motherhood is not necessarily a permanent status, solo mothers can move in and out of marriage and couple relations, I would argue that they are a central category for developing a theory of women's social citizenship. First, there are increasing numbers of women in western societies who spend part of their lives as solo mothers. Second, solo mothers are addressed as a category of mothers with special needs and problems in much of policy discourse. Finally, from the stand point of justice, solo mothers can be viewed as a highly disadvantaged group in terms of their resources, which include money, time, and social networks (Hobson 1994). If one assumes that all married mothers are potential solo mothers (given the increased risks for divorce in all Western industrial societies over the last decades), then the kinds of state support solo mothers receive indirectly shape the equality in families. Thus how solo mothers are incorporated into the larger policy frameworks can be seen as an indicator of the strength or weakness of women's social citizenship, whether women are treated as persons, with the social rights to form households.

Solo mothers and policy regimes

In order to capture how social policies shape the economic and social lives of solo mothers in different welfare states, I examine the variations in poverty rates in five countries. Then I turn to the different income packages of solo mothers in these countries and consider whether they are fitted to the clusters or models of welfare regimes.

The data for this analysis of solo mothers were taken from the LIS, and all mothers between the ages of 20 and 50 years with children under 18 years of age were included in the sample. For purposes of comparability, I have selected the following five countries, which represent different types of welfare policy regimes within the dominant paradigm: the United States and Great Britain as liberal policy regime countries; Germany as the conservative corporatist; Sweden as the social democratic country (Hobson 1994); and the Netherlands, which is aligned with the social democratic countries in some studies and as conservative/Christian, alongside Germany, in other analyses.

In comparing the poverty levels of solo mothers in these five countries, it is not surprising to find Sweden and the US at opposite ends, Sweden with the lowest rates (4.3 percent) and the US with the highest (58 percent).[12] Less obvious are the variations in poverty among the other three countries, and they seem to confound expectations of welfare policy regime models. Alhough Britain and the United States are paired as liberal welfare states, the British solo mothers are relatively less poor than their American or German counterparts. In Britain women's relative poverty is about 14 percent, whereas in Germany it is a surprising 22 percent.

Income packages of solo mothers do not mirror Esping—Andersen's clusters of regimes either. For example, solo mothers are the most dependent on wages in Germany, the corporatist/conservative regime, and in the US, exemplifying the liberal regime. In fact, the income packages of solo mothers in Germany and the US are similar; in both countries earnings comprise the main source of income and social transfers comprise between 20 and 24 percent. In all five countries, private transfers comprise a very small proportion of solo mother's income sources. The family is persuaded to be the main source of welfare in the corporatist/conservative and liberal welfare state regimes. But even among these countries, not more than 7 percent of solo mothers get the main part of their income from private transfers.

When the main source of income among solo mothers, either earnings or wages is identified, reveals a range of policy options

45

around paid and unpaid work. Moreover, when the two main categories of solo mothers, as either most dependent on wages or transfers for their income package, are analyzed, the extent to which the breadwinner ideology provides a relevant framework for understanding women's social citizenship can be determined.

In Sweden, the case in which the male breadwinner wage is said to be weakest (Lewis and Ostner 1994), a mixed income package is found for solo mothers. It is composed of social services, transfers, and wages. Considered to be the archetypal worker citizen model in policy regime analyses, Swedish solo mothers receive benefits on the basis of their status as solo mothers, as workers and as citizens. As citizens, they receive a child allowance, and, as low income persons, they are eligible for a housing subsidy. Solo mothers are guaranteed income maintenance payments if fathers are not able to provide support. As workers, solo mothers not only have the possibility of a day—care place, but are given priority in the day—care queue and have reduced fees since most of them have lower incomes than two earner couples (Gustafsson 1990). They are also accorded rights as workers in the form of job protection after parental leave, the right to work part—time until the child reaches the age of eight years. Solo mothers in Sweden are labour—force participants, as are the vast majority of mothers in Sweden. However, solo mothers are dependent on social transfers for a significant portion of their income package. If we compare groups of solo mothers whose main source of income is wage earning with those whose main source of income is social transfers, we find that there is actually less of a poverty gap between them than in either Germany or the US.

Great Britain and the Netherlands have very low proportions of solo mothers in the labor force, and we would expect this situation in these strong male breadwinner countries. Yet Germany does not follow this pattern. In Germany 59 percent of solo mothers have earnings as their main source of income. Among solo mothers who rely on social transfers for most of their income, German women are among the poorest; 49.5 percent of them have incomes below half the median income, whereas only 10 percent belong to the earning category. Once again the German and American solo mothers have features in common. Both have almost identical proportions of mainly earners (58 percent in the United States and 59 percent in Germany). Similarly solo mothers dependent in the United States upon transfers for their main income source are highly disadvantaged; 89 percent have incomes below the median. (See Figure 3.1.)

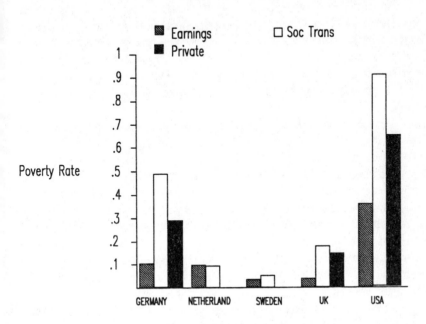

Figure 3.1 Poverty rates of groups of solo mothers

Germany and the United States, though different in their policies towards families and welfare, the United States having fewer policies to support families, exhibit a disjointed social policy around motherhood and care. Both reveal a gendered policy toward mothers that privileges married mothers and bifurcates the mother/worker and the mother/housewife. In both cases, the structure of benefits and services distinguishes the options and activities of the working mother from the non—working mother and the solo mother from the married mother. The highest levels of poverty are found among solo mothers who are dependent on social transfers (see Figure 3.1); yet there are few policies that support mothers who seek to combine work and family responsibilities (Kammerman and Kahn 1986 1991; Gustafsson

1990). In Germany and the United States a wide economic gap exists between families with mother—headed households and households maintained by couples or fathers. In effect the organization of benefits not only favors those with worker status, but also delegitimates and stigmatizes those who are mother carers unattached to a breadwinner. In comparing solo mothers in welfare states, we can see that solo mothers are worse off when there are contradictory policies that divorce the experiences of the married and unmarried mother and produce separate systems or tracks of welfare and work, as in Germany and the United States.

Instead of decommodification as a barometer of social rights, a more useful strategy is to consider compensations for care in different gender policy regimes. Nancy Fraser (1995) has divided these gender regimes into two ideal types that reflect the main currents in feminist theorizing on women's social citizenship: the *care giving parity model* and the *universal breadwinner employment model*. The caregiving parity model would promote equity through supports for women's informal care giving. The employment model would provide day care and services that permit women to become participants equal to men in the labor market. At first glance, these ideal types appear to represent the Dutch and Swedish policy regimes, since both reveal coherent strategies toward the organization of paid and unpaid work, and thus solo mothers are fitted into a policy logic around compensation for women's caring responsibilities. However, before the variations in compensatory care policies can be analyzed, it is important (1) to consider the basis of entitlement, whether mothers at home are compensated for care work as service, (2) to analyze the degree of institutionalization of public provisioning, and (3) to determine whether the level of benefits maintain a solo parent household or assume a couple with a male breadwinner.

In the Netherlands, for example, solo mothers are compensated for their caring activities by what amounts to a social wage. A small proportion of benefits is targeted for solo mothers as carers of small children; however, their main income source comes from social transfers that are given to all persons with low incomes or those outside the labor force. But unlike other unemployed persons, solo mothers have not been expected to search for paid work. The benefit levels have been high and approximate a social wage. More than 95 percent of Dutch solo mothers mainly dependent on social transfers for their income would have been poor if they did not receive them.[14] Furthermore, the poverty rates are the same (9 percent) among solo mothers who depend on earnings and those who depend on transfers as the main income sources. Until very recently solo mothers were given their benefits regardless of whether they were cohabiting with someone other than the father and solo mothers saw their benefit as a social right to care (Knijn 1994). Thus Dutch solo mothers have been able to form households in their own right and obtain benefits for their care giving. I have referred to the Dutch system as a mother carer—citizen model (Hobson 1994). Nevertheless, the formal basis of entitlement for Dutch solo mothers has been social assistance, and the recent initiatives to cut public sector spending in Holland have placed solo mothers in a vulnerable position.

Sweden has the highest proportion of women in the labour force and the most extended public day—care services. In addition, solo mothers in Sweden have the highest proportion of earners among those of the five countries, but it would be misleading to suggest that Swedish solo mothers have achieved equity in wage earning and approach a universal breadwinner family model. As persons who are doing both breadwinning and caring, they are disadvantaged in the labor market when competing for jobs with men who do not have the main responsibility for care work in families. As persons who must manage a household, solo mothers are time pressured since they tend to work more hours than mothers in couples, who often opt for a 20— to 30—hour week to ease the double burden of paid and unpaid women's work — an alternative that few solo mothers can afford

Recent Swedish legislation has mandated that all municipalities guarantee a child between one and ten years of age a place in day care or in an after—school care program. But reductions in money allocated from the central government and ceilings placed on tax increases have meant that, in many communities, day—care centers do not have extended hours or they charge extra fees for children who stay after five o'clock in the afternoon. What has been an apparent citizen model (Hobson 1994) is now moving toward a two—parent worker model.

Motherhood has been a basis of entitlement in Great Britain, and solo mothers have been given benefits as non—earning mothers who lack a breadwinner. This arrangement, I suggest, expresses a mother—needs model (Hobson 1994). Social assistance, tax structures, and a lack of day—care facilities are barriers against solo mothers increasing their economic activity (Land 1994). Changes in the law during the 1980s have discouraged solo mothers from combining even part—time work with the means—tested income supports for social mothers and British solo mothers have the lowest labour force activity among EU countries (Millar 1994). Few British solo mothers have viable alternatives to income sources other than welfare transfers; Joshi (1990) concludes that there is no gain and in some cases, economic losses are incurred by solo mothers who take employment. The same situation is also true for solo mothers in the Netherlands, but in Great Britain benefit levels are much lower in that solo mothers have not had a social wage for care. (However, in relation to benefits awarded to other disadvantaged groups in England, supports for solo mothers and their children have been relatively generous.) Less poor than either German or American solo mothers, those in Great Britain still do not fit the universal care—giving model.

In some respects the United States has a care—giver model based on mother needs. Of course, the extremely low level of benefits makes it impossible for solo mothers not to work and many perform shadow work. The current US policy of the mid—1990s represents a rejection of motherhood as a basis of entitlement (Mink 1995; Hartmann and Spalter—Roth 1994). Mounting political pressure to create a national policy to force all welfare mothers to become self—supporting and to undermine the *welfare dependency* of solo mothers resulted in legislation that limited the number of years a solo mother can receive benefits to care for dependent children. However, this shift towards a universal breadwinner employment model has no broader policy framework, since the Unoted States continues to have the weakest mandated job protections system or maternal leave benefits among Western industrialized countries, minimal public care services for children or the elderly and a labour market that sustains discriminatory wage patterns for women and blacks.

In Germany, social policy has a gendered structure in which mothers' claims are often linked to their status as wives (Esping—Andersen 1990; Lewis and Ostner 1994). In this context care work is not compensated per se. The majority of married women have access to generous social provisioning through their relation to a male breadwinner, directly in pension schemes and indirectly through a tax system that highly privileges couples. Mothers are given a care subsidy, but it is assumed that this is a supplement to husbands' income, not a caring wage. Thus solo mothers appear as a deviant group outside the framework of a policy regime based upon a breadwinner wage, and they encounter poverty and marginalization (Kulawik and Reidmuller 1991).

Unresolved dilemmas in women's social citizenship

No pure model of social policy regimes organized around work or motherhood exists in post—industrial societies, and this situation is a reflection of the growing numbers of mothers who now participate in the labour market and are members of solo parent families.

In the search for new strategies, feminists are confronted with the historical record that documents the failure of feminist movements to secure mothers a decent standard of living on the basis of their service as carers or achieve equity through paid employment. Lewis and Ostner (1994) maintain that no government has attached a substantial value to caring work, an irony that pervades an analysis that appraises welfare regimes on their ability to recognize women's unpaid work. Nor have those who advocate a universal breadwinner model addressed adequately the conditions under which most women work (the dual burden of paid and unpaid work) or the fact that few women work enough hours or earn wages high enough to maintain their families. Finally the recent discussions about the long oppressive work schedules of the paid and unpaid work of Eastern European women have raised questions about women's rights as workers.

Several feminist scholars now maintain that it is no longer feasible to construct a theory of women's social citizenship without valuing women's unpaid care work (Ungersen 1990; Knijn 1991). Clare Ungerson affirms women's right to choose to care and be compensated for their caring work (Ungerson 1990). On the other hand, there are strong arguments for women's right to choose not to care (Land 1983; Hobson 1990). Yet can we envision a social policy regime that equally supports a mother's wage for caring and a system of services and provisions that would allow mothers to be integrated into worklife? The question of choice is even more elusive in this period of welfare state retrenchment and restructuring. Policies toward solo mothers are highly contested in many welfare states, and they have been set in a discursive landscape of a culture of dependency in many countries.

The competition for scarce resources has produced a policy discourse and a set of initiatives that scapegoat solo mothers. For example in the Netherlands, an intense debate about the supports for solo mothers has led to policies that will require solo mothers to seek labor market work. So far this requirement has applied only to solo mothers if there are day—care slots available for their children or a family member is available to take over caring responsibilities. Since few day—care slots exist, the immediate impact on solo mothers' right to care is hard to gauge. However, benefits have been reduced and a new stipulation in the law would deny solo mothers the right to be the head of a household and receive benefits if she is cohabiting with someone who is a breadwinner, a variant of the man in the house rule test for benefits (Knijn 1994). Such policies imply a change in the principle of a social wage for care. If fully implemented, they would constitute a break or divorce in the treatment of married mothers and solo mothers. A gender policy regime that approximated the care— giving parity model is now being reconsidered as too expensive. The greater risk of poverty for solo mothers presages the increased economic dependency of women in marriage as their exit options are closed off.

An intense debate on the cost of solo mothers to the state has been waged in Great Britain over the last few years this debate has culminated in new legislation, the Child Support Act. The new law places the burden of support for solo mothers and their families on the fathers, who must pay the state directly for the support of their children and the benefits for the caring parent (most often their divorced wife), even if they have other families to support. The Child Support Act is not aimed at increasing the benefits for solo mothers, but rather at shifting the responsibility to the absent father and reducing the welfare budget (Lister 1994). There is also a stipulation in the law that can deny benefits to solo mothers who refuse to supply the name of the putative father. The law places divorced women back into dependent relationships with former husbands, who could demand renewed contact as a result of their contribution. For women who left husbands because of violence against their children and themselves, this is denial of fundamental civil rights. It implies a rejection of the basis of social citizenship in Marshallian terms: what citizens can claim from public authorities in terms of economic supports and services during periods of distress.

Solo mothers have not been targeted in the Swedish policy debate. But many of the debates, as well as the intense pressures to reduce public services affect single—parent families more adversely than two—parent households. In the 1990s a conservative coalition government enacted legislation for a care voucher system that permitted parents to choose care subsidies instead of public day care. With the return of the Social Democrats in 1994, the care voucher system was repealed. The choice to be full—time carers was never an option for solo mothers, given the meager care subsidy. In fact, the choice to care and not to care appears more and more linked to a women's wage earning capacities in the current Swedish economic crises with high unemployment and slashing of public services.

As these cases in transition suggest, trying to contruct policy modules that fit around supports for mothers to be at home or in the labor market presents a dilemma. If systems that support a social wage for caring are advocated, the option of public services for care that allow women to combine work and family life may have to be relinguished. Alternatively, if we maintain that all mothers have a social right to affordable day care, then women who want to be full—time carers may have to be denied adequate compensation to protect them from the hazards of economic dependency — the inability to leave a marriage.

Feminists continue to seek to find a solution to Wollstencraft's dilemma that goes beyond the dichotomy of equality and difference (Jones 1990; Phillips 1991; Lister 1993). Fraser (1995) highlights the pitfalls in posing the dilemma in the framework of equality and difference and suggests a more complex set of criteria for feminist theorizing around women's citizenship. The care—giving parity model, even its ideal form in terms of benefits and entitlements, would not address core features for gender equity, those of anti—marginalization, income equality and equality of respect. Though these models of equity feminists have proposed may appear utopian, she asserts that they are not radical enough. According to Fraser the alternative, universal breadwinner model does poorly in leisure time, androcentrism and does not only fair in overcoming income inequality and marginalization. Her solution to achieving gender equity in post industrial welfare states is to induce men to be more like women by having them take on more caring responsibilities and caring roles.

How to accomplish this goal requires more than a series of thought experiments; it needs real policy instruments. For example, one might think about a punitive system of carefare, a policy equivalent to workfare now being proposed for welfare mothers to force them into the labour market. In the carefare system those who do not contribute their share of care work have lower pension benefits. Another strategy is to offer economic incentives for men who care, which is the current strategy in Sweden, where parental leave has been amended so that eligibility for a full benefit year requires that each spouse takes at least one month of parental leave, which is compensated at 90 percent of their salary. The most optimistic scenario is that all fathers will demand that their employers let them take advantage of the daddy month rather than lose the full year. And more importantly, during their month of full—time care taking, they become sensitized to the demands of care work, and ultimately couples begin to renegotiate and divide unpaid work more equitably.

Besides the fact that it is hard to imagine which concrete policies produce this transformation of men toward care—giving roles, this strategy does not address to the growing numbers of women living in households without partners. Rather than an expansion in social citizenship rights for solo mothers, one finds a narrowing of possibilities and a convergence in policies that approach solo mothers as a problem group in many welfare states. There are several parallels in this policy terrain, but all have the common goal of removing the state's responsibility for supporting solo parent households. One route is towards greater economic dependence on former husbands, who are then coerced by the state to pay for the support of children and former wives. Another is towards forcing solo mothers to become the household breadwinner with fewer income maintenance benefits and social provisions for mothering. Finally there are general social and economic pressures to form two parent households.

social provisions for mothering. Finally there are general social and economic pressures to form two parent households.

On the one hand, these trends can be seen as the result of the recession and economic crises facing many welfare states, accompanied by concurrent conservative ideological assaults on the public sector as overgrown and unproductive. But, on the other, the lack of support for compensating solo mothers for their burden of care work is also due to the current feminist dilemma in Western industrial societies — as more and more women become active in economic and political spheres of society, it becomes harder and harder to mobilize political energies that argue in favour of social benefits for unpaid care work when large groups of organized women are demanding expanded day—care facilities, more services for the elderly, and legislation for pay equity.

Notes:

1   This research has been supported by a grant from the Swedish Social Science Research Council and the Swedish Work Environment Fund. I would like to thank Jaokim Palme for all his help with the LIS data and for his invaluable suggestions for this paper. I would also like to thank Tuula Gordon, Kaisa Kauppinen, and Peter Hedström for their comments.

2   There is rich and varied literature on women's citizenship. Some of the most well known are books by Nancy Fraser (1990), Susan Okin (1989), Carole Pateman (1989), Anne Phillips (1991), and Iris Young 1990.

3   Surveys done in 1984 showed that Swedish women work an average of 48 hours a week (18 hours in a paid job, and, 20 hours in unpaid household work). Men average about 37 hours a week in paid and unpaid work, with only 7 hours of household work (Flood and Klevmarken 1990).

4   These estimates are based on an analysis of the most recent Swedish survey data of the LNU. We included all married women between the ages of 24 and 55 years in our sample.

5   LIS is an ideal data set for analyzing economic dependency because it has some of the most highly comparable cross—national data on income sources for Western industrialized societies. For a complete description of the statistical analysis and data source, see Hobson (1990).

6   I used a standard measure of inequality in comparative research, the distribution of total household incomes adjusted for family size (the Gini coefficient).

7   The dependency rates for the mid—1980s are 0.62 for Germany, 0.64 for Netherlands, and 0.51 for the United States.

8   The argument has been made that, in Sweden employers, unions and policymakers, developed various strategies to entice women into the labor force during the 1960s and 1970s because of a labor shortage and apprehension about bringing in foreign workers. See Nyberg (1989).

9   For those who have not been in the labour force there has been a flat rate benefit of a minimal amount — about 10 dollars (U.S.) a day.

10   Those who are not employed have had the lowest priority in the day—care queue; recent policy has offered all families a day—care place.

11   The most recent changes in the parental leave law reduce the benefit level to 80 percent for 10 months and a mandatory mother and father month for the other two at 90 percent.

12   I have used a standard convention for calculating the relative powerty rates: all solo mothers with incomes below half the median income, adjusted for family size, are defined as poor.

4 Women, work and emotion, managing jobs and family life

Amy Wharton

The connections between work and family have been examined by numerous scholars (Crosby 1987; Voydanoff 1987; Haavio—Mannila 1989). Women have been an important focus of these studies, given researchers' findings that employed women bear more responsibility for housework and child care than their male counterparts. Hence employed women have a *second shift* at home (Hochschild 1989). Despite researchers' interest in work—family relations, most studies of this issue pay relatively little attention to the specific types of work women perform for pay and for their families for free and the ways these characteristics shape the kinds of *unresolved dilemmas* women experience.

By focusing on a particular type of work — namely, *emotion work* — that is performed primarily by women employed in service jobs for pay and by women as care givers in the home, this chapter aims to initiate research on this unexplored set of topics. In particular, I examine the relations between service work and family life, seeking to understand the ways women experience their simultaneous involvement in these two spheres of social reproduction and the consequences of these experiences for the kinds of *unresolved dilemmas* women perceive. Analyzing data collected from interviews with women service workers, I examine how employment in a service job shapes the experience and meaning of family life, and how responsibilities for family care giving affect women's orientation to service work.

Conceptions of the relations between service work and family life

Services have come to play an increasingly important role in virtually all industrialized economies. In the United States, the service sector in 1988 accounted for 72 percent of gross national product (GNP) and 76 percent of employment (Bowen and Cummings 1990). Moreover, most observers view these estimates as conservative because they exclude the *service elements* of the manufacturing industries (Groonos 1990). Women have been central to the service revolution in all industrialized countries (Saraceno 1984; Ward and Pampel 1985; Lyson 1986). As Smith (1984) argues, the increase in U.S. women's participation in the labour force after World War II was fueled in part by the expansion of the service sector. Accordingly, Urquhart (1984) shows that the employment shift to services in the United States did not result from workers' migration from one sector to another, but rather from the *expansion of the labor force and especially the increasing participation of women.*

Most discussions of service work and its impact on women examine the economic consequences of employment in a service—related occupation or industry (e.g., Smith 1984, Glass et al. 1988). For example, Smith (1984) argues that the low wage rates paid by service—sector industries have contributed to the feminization of poverty. Using occupations as the units of analysis, England (1992) found that jobs requiring *nurturance* pay lower average wages than comparable jobs not requiring this activity. Although her focus was not service per se, these results highlight the connections between the *people processing* aspects of service delivery and the devaluation of work associated with women. More generally, several researchers have examined the implications of a service economy for racial and gender stratification (Glenn 1992; Lorence 1992).

The consequences of the service revolution do not stem solely from its economic impacts, however. Services diverge in important ways from manufacturing, imposing different demands on workers and new concerns for employers. Bowen and Cummings (1990) locate the distinctiveness of services in three defining attributes: they are *intangible*, consisting of experiences that are rendered, as compared with objects that are possessed; they are produced and consumed simultaneously; and services depend upon customer involvement in both their production and delivery. As a result of these characteristics, many service jobs require *emotional labour*, or the *management of feeling to create a publicly observable facial and bodily display* (Hochschild 1983). Because women are overrepresented in service jobs, especially those involving direct contact with the public, women are more likely than men to hold jobs requiring emotional labour (Hochschild 1983).

The distinctiveness of services also stems from their connections with social reproduction. This concept refers to the array of activities and relationships involved in maintaining people both on a daily basis and intergenerationally (Glenn 1992). Many service jobs involve reproductive labor that has moved out of the household and into the market economy. These jobs, such as those involved in food preparation, child care, and care for the elderly, thus bear some resemblance to the care—giving tasks historically performed by women in the home (Saraceno 1984; Abel and Nelson 1990). In particular, the activities associated with family care—giving, like those involved in paid service work, also require emotion management (Wharton and Erickson 1993). Viewing service from the perspective of social reproduction thus calls attention to its connections with gendered care—giving work performed in the family.

Like the economic consequences of the service revolution, the social consequences of this development are hotly contested. On one hand, some view the expansion of services as part of a broader cultural shift towards postmodernity, where appearance and superficiality are celebrated and the ability to distinguish image and reality disappears (Jameson 1984; Erickson 1991). In this view, service workers confront a distinctly new form of alienation characterized by a loss of touch with their feelings and, hence, themselves (Hochschild 1983, Paules 1991). These feelings of self—estrangement also threaten workers' well—being in non—work arenas, spilling over from the workplace into other interpersonal relations. To the extent that service jobs are disproportionately filled by women, women (and perhaps their families) should bear the most emotional and psycological costs of the service revolution. Other discussions of the service economy offer a more benign picture. For instance, Kanter (1977) suggests that the expansion of services may function to reintroduce or reinforce familial kinds of relationships and familial norms in the occupational world. In this view, the spread of service orientation is associated with the diffusion of family—based interpersonal norms throughout the workplace. As service workers who often have family involvements themselves, women are important bearers of these norms and relations, and they are paving the way for a different, more humane occupational world, characterized by a convergence between work and family norms.

These contrasting views rest on differing conceptions of service and the changes its expansion has entailed in work organization. More important, they make different assumptions about women's experience of the relations between service work and family life. In the process, they also draw different conclusions regarding the *unresolved dilemmas* women experience, for instance, those claiming that service work creates a potential for new emotions—based forms of alienation stress, the discontinuities between service work and family life. For Hochschild (1983), these discontinuities stem from the nature of emotion management in each sphere. In particular, women control their own emotion management efforts at home, while, in the workplace, these efforts are controlled by employers. The transformation of unpaid *emotion work* into paid *emotional labor* qualitatively alters the conditions of its performance. Though both may contribute to social reproduction, service—related emotional labor bears little resemblance to the unpaid emotion work women perform in the private sphere. The fact that the emotion—management skills required of service workers on the job are at odds with those demanded at home creates the potential for work—family conflict and individual psychological stress. Hence, this view implies that women service workers with families face specific work—family dilemmas that stem from the emotional demands of their work and family roles.

By contrast, Kanter's perspective at least implicitly views the boundaries between service work and family life as more permeable, continuous, and less conflicted for women. In particular, she implies that the demands of family—based social reproduction are not qualitatively distinct from those found in paid service work. Hence nothing prevents women's family—based identities and strategies from positively spilling over into the workplace. From this perspective, service workers with families may have few work—family dilemmas. In fact, this view implies that these workers may be better off than other women workers with families, given the assumed continuities between their work and family roles.

As these divergent scenarios suggest, the consequences of service work for women and their families are not well understood. Studies of women's paid service work are increasing (e.g., Leidner 1993), as is research on social reproduction in the family (e.g., DeVault 1992), but few have attended directly to the connections between these realms. Similarly, while studies of work—family relations are growing more generally (e.g., Haavio—Mannila 1989), attempts to understand the links between service work and family life are largely missing from this body of literature. As Saraceno (1984) notes:

> But very little is known about the split many women experience in themselves, between being family members performing services for their families, and being professional workers performing analogous services for pay and for others ... As the main persons responsible for the care of family members, women increasingly have to cross continuously shifting boundaries, making links while defending separations.

The continuing role of service work as a major employer of women, many of whom also have family responsibilities, makes the relations between service work and family life sociologically important. More important, by exploring women's experiences of the relations between service work and family life, we may gain a better understanding of the *unresolved dilemmas* faced by this group of women workers and their families. Does the performance of service—related emotional labour pose psychological dangers for women workers with families, and increase work—family conflict? Or, is this group of women workers less affected by the *unresolved dilemmas* confronted by other women with families?

In the analysis and discussion that follow, I address these questions. My central argument is that portrayals of service work and family as inherently discontinuous and conflicted *or* continuous and integrated are both overly simplistic. Instead, I show that research must be sensitive to the sources of service work—family continuity and discontinuity, and I illustrate some of the factors that structure these

61

linkages. Approaches that assume either conflict or integration between service work and family life are also limited by their inability to consider the actual strategies used to manage relations between work and family. These one—sided approaches neglect possible conflicts and contradictions engendered by people's efforts to negotiate multiple institutional demands and memberships. Most important, failure to examine taken—for—granted assumptions about the relations between service work and family life may lead to inaccurate conclusions about the nature of the *unresolved dilemmas* faced by this group of women workers and their families.

Research methods

The primary data for this study were collected from interviews with 20 women during the spring and summer of 1989. Each interview lasted between one and two hours. Supplementary data were gathered from a mailed survey completed by each respondent. Both the interview and the questionnaire focused on the respondents' work and family lives, and on their efforts to manage participation in both spheres.

These data were collected as part of a larger study of male and female service workers employed by three companies: a seventeen—branch bank, a large hospital, and a hotel. Samples of workers from these companies first completed the mailed questionnaire. Attached to the questionnaire was a request for people willing to be interviewed about the issues in a more open—ended and in—depth manner than the survey format allowed. I especially wanted to interview employed women with family responsibilities and was particularly interested in interviewing women whose jobs involved a direct service component (e.g, requiring extensive contact with the public as customers or clients). The 20 women whose interviews comprise the data for this study met these criteria. Accordingly, all respondents were employed at least part—time and had family responsibilities. Eighteen were currently married or cohabiting with male partners, while two were single parents. All had at least one child; half of the women had two. Their average age was 35 years and all were white.

All the women worked in service—related occupations, although there were important differences between the types of jobs held. Approximately half of the women were employed by a large hospital as nurses, health therapists, and technicians or as secretaries/receptionists.[1] Because all 11 of these women described their jobs as involving direct contact with patients and their families, these jobs were classified as *human service* positions. The public contact required in such jobs is more intense and typically of longer duration than the contact required in other *frontline* service jobs, such as those of the remainder of the sample. These other nine women worked in hospitality and banking, holding jobs such as bank teller and waitress/bartender. Although these jobs also involved extensive public contact, the contacts tended to be more fleeting and, hence, less personal than those typical of the hospital workers. Only two women reported having supervisory responsibilities and both supervised bank tellers.

No claim is made that these respondents were representative of women service workers with families. In particular, the sample did not incorporate the experiences of minorities. In addition, the women volunteering to be interviewed for this study may have been those for whom work—family issues are particularly salient.[2] For instance, many of the women interviewed expressed sentiments similar to this bank worker:

> My mother was a working mom. She worked full—time, and that was really at a time when there was a greater percentage of moms that stayed home. She struggled with that the whole time we were growing up. But at least it was more cut—and—dried for her. She knew what she was up against and she just had to deal with it. For me, it's really different. It's a touchy emotional subject, whenever it comes up and wherever it comes up. Whether you're talking to your best friend, your sister, or somebody you just met — anytime the subject comes up, you have to be very careful, because it's very emotional, very charged.

The results can be used to extend or challenge existing conceptual frameworks regarding the relations between paid service work and family care giving. In particular, the results can help illuminate the sources of service work and family continuity *and* discontinuity as experienced by women with families. Those for whom these issues are personal and *emotional* may be the best sources for this exploratory work.

Transitions: The boundaries between work and home

According to Friedland and Alford (1991), the major contemporary institutions of home and work both possess a central *logic* or set of *organizing principles,* consisting of both *material practices and symbolic constructions.* In Friedland and Alford's view (1991), institutional logics represent the parameters within which experience and behavior must be understood:

> Institutions constrain not only the ends to which their behavior should be directed, but the means by which those ends are achieved. They provide individuals with vocabularies of motives and with a sense of self. They generate not only that which is valued, but the rules by which it is calibrated and distributed.

This statement implies that people are, to some degree, accountable to institutional requirements and expectations. At the same time, however, because people *live across institutions,* they must learn to reconcile and negotiate between mutiple institutional symbols and practices (Friedland and Alford 1991).

An important process associated with *living across institutions* concerns the transition from one sphere to another. The women in this study confronted multiple types of boundaries between work and home that had to be crossed on a daily basis. As will be seen, some perceived the boundaries between work and family as more permeable than others. In addition, regardless of the permeability of the work—family boundary, women experienced both positive and negative spillover between job and home. In contrast to the findings of both Hochschild and Kanter, women did not perceive the relations between service work and family life in unilateral terms as either continuous and integrated *or* as discontinuous and conflictual. Instead, their experiences were multifaceted and shaped by particular features of their situation.

Negotiating physical boundaries

Some boundaries are undoubtedly confronted by all workers with families, regardless of the type of job, while others reflect the particular demands of service work. For example, since only a minority today performs work for pay at their place of residence, most workers confront a physical separation between home and workplace. As Kanter (1977) shows, this separation is associated with changes occurring during the process of industrialization, changes that were especially pronounced for the white middle class. Zoning restrictions regulating the intermingling of residential and commercial buildings, and the growth of suburbs are two mechanisms through which work and family have been historically kept physically and geographically separate.

Because all of the women in this study had to travel to work, all confronted a physical boundary between family and job. Most regarded the physical distance between work and home as one important influence on their ability to move between institutional spheres. Several women commented on the physical separation between work and home and the ways that separation facilitated or interfered with their ability to make the psychological and emotional transition between these realms. Many knew exactly how long it took them to travel between work and home and described the ways they used this time:

> I have quite a drive to get home, between a half—hour and forty minutes. And that I've found to be real important. When I was married before, I had two stepchildren who weren't exactly angels. I would get off work and come home in five minutes. I had work stress to unwind from and stress at home at the same time. During that time, I had a very difficult time. Then I got transferred to a place where it took me an hour and a half to get home. I was able to use that time to unwind from work, to kind of get myself out of work mode and put myself into home mode — get myself in tune with what's going to be

> waiting for me at the other end. That's something I like now.
> I'm able to think for maybe fifteen minutes, unwind and recap
> my day, and then put myself into home, and see what's
> expected of me there.

> It's nice to walk home. That really helps a lot, just having that
> kind of transition from one place to another. I find that as I
> walk home, I think about the day. That does help. It's a whole
> lot better than racing out and driving up the hill and getting
> here.

Even the women who did not comment on the process of traveling to
or from work described the way they negotiated the transition
between spheres. For example, this nurse worked the afternoon shift
at the hospital:

> On days that I work, I typically don't do anything away from
> home. I don't do doctor's appointments, I don't do dentist
> appointments, I don't go shopping, I don't do groceries. I just
> stay home, read the newspaper, have my coffee. Sometimes I'll
> be in my gown until one o'clock . . . So in a way it's almost like
> being lazy, because when I go to work, then it's all systems go.
> So don't ask me to do anything that requires thinking on the
> days that I work. Don't ask me to coordinate picking kids up
> from school and getting them to the dentist and having
> haircuts. Keep my errands for my days off.

Along similar lines, a bank worker described her need to spend a
transitionary fifteen minutes at her desk before going home. When asked
how she spent that time, she explained:

> I straighten my desk. If I have any personal phone calls to
> make, I'll make those. I sit and think and I have a couple verses
> that I read. Basically, I change my breathing pattern and I
> physically force myself to start relaxing. I get so worked up
> throughout the course of my day. I use so much energy that it's
> bam—bam—bam. Then to calm down and be a calming figure
> on the kids at night, that's hard. That's real hard.

In summary, all of these women used the physical separateness of work and home as a resource for managing the transition between realms. The fact that home and work were geographically distinct facilitated movement from one sphere to another by providing time to move between institutional logics. This time is important, because the movement between institutional spheres involves not only a shift in locale, but also a more fundamental shift in orientation to self and others.

Coming back to being Mom

As women moved between work and home, many described a process of altering themselves and their expectations to accomodate the institutional demands of the sphere they were entering. As illustrated in the earlier quotes, it was not uncommon for women to describe their return from work as an opportunity for self—transformation. Phrases such as *I need to put myself into home and see what's expected of me there* or *when I get home I can just be me again* are two examples. Another woman expressed it this way:

> I'm away from my children a lot of hours as it is, but I also want to give them the best side of me when I'm with them. They don't get that if I just am rushing around and I have no transition time to come back to being their mom. What they get is a very cranky, tired person that says *Give me my distance,* instead of a mom that says *I've missed you all day, come close.*

This process of self—transformation reflects the shift in expecations and demands that occurs as women move from one institutional logic to another. As Friedland and Alford (1991) note, identities are not fixed, but instead are adjusted as people move between settings and social contexts. People's experience of crossing institutional boundaries, and the associated shifts in self—understanding that occur, have not received much attention in the work—family literature, however. Though far from definitive, the data reported here suggest that these issues deserve closer scrutiny from researchers. In particular, crossing institutional boundaries requires greater or lesser amounts of work on the self. The physical separation between job and family is one factor facilitating these efforts. As is shown in the following discussion, the perceived degree of continuity between spheres appears also to influence the emotional effort associated with crossing institutional boundaries.

Because the women in the study were all employed in public—contact service jobs, it is impossible to assess whether their descriptions of the work—family transition differ from those of other types of women workers. What is clear, however, is that this transition did not occur in the same way under all conditions, nor was the experience similar for all women interviewed. In particular, some women experienced transitions between work and home as less abrupt than others and therefore reflected a view of these spheres as relatively continuous. Others, however, experienced work and home as less integrated and more discontinuous. For these women, transitions between spheres were marked, and the process of self—transformation was more dramatic and recognized. To understand the sources of these differences, we must look closer at women's experiences of continuity and discontinuity between work and home, and the way these experiences are shaped by women's particular work situations.

Continuity and discontinuity between work and family

As noted earlier, some authors emphasize the continuity between service work and family, while others assume that these institutional logics are fundamentally discontinuous. Service work and family life are experienced as continuous to the extent that their respective institutional logics are perceived as compatible. In other words, the expectations, demands, and norms associated with one setting are relatively consistent with those associated with another. By contrast, conflicting or incompatible institutional logics are likely to generate feelings of discontinuity between service work and family. The women in this study described service work and family life as integrated and continuous in certain respects and as discontinuous and conflicted in others. In these circumstances, it thus becomes important to examine the sources of work—family continuity and discontinuity, the factors that explain differences in women's experiences, and the psychological consequences these experiences engender.

Continuities between work and family

Experiencing work and family as continuous means that the organizing principles and interpersonal demands of each are seen as consistent and reinforcing of one another. Because many paid service jobs occupied by women involve tasks historically performed by women in the home, some assume that women service workers should experience a high degree of continuity between their work and family lives. Indeed, many women commented on the similarity between job requirements and family expectations:

> What's going on at home is the same kind of thing as if you're at work: A lot of people coming and going and kids in and out.

> One of the good things about my work is that I really don't have to be much different than at home. When I come home, I don't perceive that I have much of a change. I'm still a care giver with my children.

> At work I have to be assertive, sometimes forceful. I have to be able to think on my feet and make quick decisions. But I pretty much do that at home as well.

All of these women worked in human service positions. In fact, none of the women who observed these kinds of similarities between job and family were employed by the bank or hotel. This pattern of response may reflect real differences in the demands of these jobs. The skills and interpersonal demands associated with human service jobs may be objectively more similar to those associated with women's family roles than are the demands of other jobs held by women in the sample, such as bank teller. In particular, the type of emotional labor required by human service positions may be similar to the emotion work women perform at home. Women in these circumstances thus perceive these realms as more continuous than women whose work and family roles differ in the type of emotional labour they require.

Positive and negative spillover: Psychological consequences for women

Kanter's (1977) suggestion that service jobs reflect *a familial orientation* implies that the expectations associated with these positions are relatively compatible with those found among family members. As noted, consistent with Kanter, some women service workers did perceive similarities between their job and family life. These similarities in expectations might be assumed to result in positive spillover between work and home. *Positive spillover* implies that people's work and family lives enhance one another and that the management of work—family relations is not psychologically damaging. There was some evidence for this argument. In particular, perceived similarity in work and family expectations led some women to feel that their interactions with people on the job made them more effective interpersonally at home:

> I think it [influence of work on family and family on work] flows both ways. I think because I deal with people so much there [work] that it just helps me relate to them [family members].

> [Working with people] just helps me relate better. Because I deal with so many different kinds of personalities and different problems, it helps me better understand the needs of people that I live with.

At the same time, others experienced the *continuity* between work and family life as a source of stress and therefore revealed an important flaw in the view that similarity in institutional logics eases the experience of crossing institutional boundaries. Indeed, as argued elsewhere, precisely *because* women are expected to be care givers at home *and* work, they may experience strain (Wharton and Erickson 1993). For these women, having to attend to others both on the job and at home may result in feelings of role overload and, eventually, emotional burnout. In this view, role overload involves a greater

70

number of prescribed activities than an individual can handle adequately or comfortably (Kelly and Voydanoff 1985), while emotional burnout represents one consequence of this state. In these respondents' words:

> Well, you know, it's awful, but I feel at work like I'm paid to always be there for someone reaching out for me and needing me, and when I come home and I have an eight—year—old and a two—year—old and a thirty—four—year—old always after me for something, too, I just want to say: Wait a minute! Who's going to give it back to me?

> There are times when you come home and you're just really drained and your family asks something of you and you just have to tell them: Hey, I gave it all at work and I don't have anything left. My pockets are empty. There's just nothing left and you'll have to be patient and wait until I regenerate myself.

> There are days when you just give everything emotionally that you have to give at work and then you come home and there's nothing left. All you want to do is just either sit down and cry like a baby, or just go to bed and thank god that the day is over.

In summary, some types of women service workers perceive continuity, rather than conflict, between the interpersonal demands of their work and family roles. Continuity, in turn, can facilitate positive work—family spillover whereby skills gained in one setting are applied to another. Though these findings are, at one level, consistent with Kanter's perspective, there is an important difference. Instead of using skills learned in family life to solve job—related problems, the women in this study viewed their work—related interpersonal skills as enhancing their skills in family care giving. At the same time, perceived similarity in work—family demands does not imply the absence of work—family stress. Though its particular causes are not well—understood, the data suggest that women who perform the same kinds of interpersonal activities at home and on the job are vulnerable to role strain.

71

Discontinuities between work and family

Discontinuities between work and family life also emerged in the women's comments. These discontinuities were reflected in comments describing dissimilarities or inconsistencies between job and family. They referred to several aspects of work—family experience. First, and most important, women observed discontinuities between the expectations for emotional expression associated with each sphere. Consistent with Hochschild's (1983) observation that performance of paid *emotional labor* often requires workers to display emotions they may not necessarily feel, many women felt they were more *themselves* at home and could more freely express their feelings in the family than in the workplace:

> In your family you just don't hide your feelings as much, whereas in a job, you do, because you want any stranger that you're involved with to have a good impression. You want them to think you're a good person. Your family sees all aspects of your personality.

> When you're at work, you're out in front and you're holding your stomach in [laughs]. When you get home, you let your stomach grow. I'm more relaxed at home.

> I'm who I am when I'm at home. I don't fake my feelings around my kids. I've cried in front of my kids, I've been depressed and I've let them know that. I've tried not to control any of my emotions around my kids because I don't want them to control theirs.

These sentiments were expressed primarily by women not employed in human services, but rather in jobs such as bank teller and hotel reservation clerk. These data are consistent with the earlier discussion regarding perceived continuities between work and family. Recall that women employed in human services were more likely than others to see similarities between job and home responsibilities and demands. By contrast, women employed in less contact—intense service jobs reported a greater disparity between their at—work self and the person they are at home. Though both types of service jobs require emotional labor, women employed in human services may find it more difficult to not be themselves on the job and to fake their emotions than women whose jobs involve less intense contact with the public. For instance, when asked if she ever displayed emotions with her patients that she did not really feel, one nurse explained:

> I don't have a good feel for that. It would be hard for me to do that. Nursing is such personal work and you're dealing with people that are in crisis. It's just hard to be distant and put on an automatic smile. Maybe some nurses do. I don't know.

A related theme that emerged in women's observations about the discontinuities between work and family life concerned the degree of control they exercised in each sphere. Ross and Mirowsky (1992) found that the employed report a greater sense of mastery over their life than the unemployed. Along the same lines, Paules (1991) suggests that women, especially working—class women, value autonomy on the job because they are denied this at home. Though different in many respects, these studies suggest that women should feel more efficacious in the workplace than in the family.

Consistent with this prediction, all of the women who spoke about this issue believed their ability to control their surroundings was greater in the workplace than at home. Control on the job provided a sense of satisfaction, which often stood in contrast to women's lesser sense of efficacy in the family:

> Work actually is a welcome break for me. Work is for myself. These little bodies aren't climbing on me all the time and wanting my attention. At work, I have more control. I have a set schedule and I can do things and I know what to expect.

Women's greater sense of control on the job was also reflected in their belief that work was less frantic and more orderly than at home:

> There were days that I'd go through the whole day and realize that, oh, I hadn't eaten anything that day. I fed everybody else

73

> a couple times, but I hadn't eaten. The nice thing about work is
> you get a coffee break or you can have an adult conversation.

Hence, in contrast to those who would encourage women workers
to carry familial orientations into the workplace, women in this study
derived satisfaction from work precisely because it differed from the
chaotic nature of family life. A bank worker captured the irony of this
view. When asked about the kind of person she wanted to be for her
children, she responded:

> It's interesting ... I want to be the same person I've been all
> day to my customers. I want to be the person who's really got
> the time and interest in them. I want to hear about their day, I
> want to talk with them, I want to walk with them ...

In other words, at least some women viewed their opportunities for
autonomy on the job as providing a desirable model for family life.

Positive and negative spillover: Consequences for women

Hochschild's (1983) argument implies that women who perform
emotional labor on the job may suffer negative psychological
consequences. These consequences stem primarily from the self—
alienation that occurs when employers dictate workers' emotional
demeanor. Hochschild (1983) devotes less attention to the potentially
positive consequences of emotional labor and the ways these may
enhance women's non—work lives, however. Quantitative analyses of
the larger dataset from which these interviews were drawn (e.g.,
Wharton 1993), as well as Paules' (1991) qualitative study of
waitresses, indicate that the performance of emotional labor does not
have uniformly negative consequences for workers. The women
interviewed for this study also reported some positive consequences
associated with having to manage their emotions at work. Most
important, performance of emotional labor provided an opportunity
to exercise control on the job and display competence:

> On my job, I feel like I'm totally in control. I have to smile,
> maybe when I don't want to smile and be totally on top of

everything. And not let your guard down. If you're having a bad time at home or something's going on, you can't let that show through at work.

There were other ways that discontinuities between work and family life resulted in positive consequences for women. Most important was the belief that, because work and family demands are different, these realms can be kept distinct. Workers can be buffered from family stress while on the job and from work stress while at home. As these bank workers noted:

> Unless it's something really major at work, when I leave that building I'm no longer a bank teller and I'm no longer worried about that company. That's what I try to do anyway. I think it saves your sanity.

> They don't mesh a lot, my work and my home life. I think it's good that way. For me it works, anyway.

> I think there's room for both work and family as long as you can leave your job at your job. And I try to leave my family at home when I go to work . . . I try to keep them separate but I need them both.

Experiencing a sense of discontinuity between work and home was a source of stress for at least some women, however. Consistent with Hochschild's (1983) argument, these women were supposed to act on the job in ways that were antithetical to family members' expectations for behavior. When work and family cannot be kept separate as has already been described, women's interpersonal relations in the family may become conflicted. As these women explained:

> My job requires me to not show my emotions. I can't give an attitude. My husband shows his emotions much more than I do and he perceives me as cold sometimes, which is very true. I have to be very factual and sweep emotion under the rug. It's what the job is like and that's just the way I've learned to be.

75

I consider myself a perfectionist and I consider it a curse . . . Medicine draws perfectionistic types of people, because it is life and death. You don't just do something sorta right, you do it one—hundred percent. I think that spills over into what you expect in a relationship. You expect perfection in your relationship with your husband and with your children and it can be a curse.

Sometimes when I come home, I don't want to be nice. I want to be left alone, or I want to say: Okay, time out for fifteen minutes. Let Mom readjust. My husband's noticed it, too. He'll come in and see me at work, and then when I get home, I might be in a totally different mood. He'll say: Well, I just saw you a few hours ago and you were just fine. I say: That's because I have to be that way at work! He'll say: Can't you carry it over more?

I have to walk around a lot at work and say *Good job, that was a real, real good job with that customer, good job here,* and all that kind of stuff. I think maybe the reason I don't do it with my husband is because I assume that he could reason well enough to know that he's doing a good job. I don't feel I have to verbalize what I feel . . . I think that having to verbalize it all the time at work and then coming home and trying to sound sincere about it . . . I don't think it works.

In summary, women service workers perceived important areas of discontinuity between job and home in my study, and these areas were mainly consistent with those discussed by Hochschild (1983). Women employed outside human services were more likely than human service workers to portray work and family in these terms, however. In addition, as discussed earlier, discontinuity between work and family life was psychologically disruptive for some women, and a source of satisfaction for others. Identifying the conditions under which these negative or positive consequences occur should be an important goal of future research.

Women have played an important role in the development of a service economy in the United States. Like employed women more generally, many of these women have partners and children, and most of them have the primary responsibility for the physical and emotional work necessary for maintaining family life. The historical continuity between paid service work and the domestic tasks associated with the family has been the source of increased speculation about the connections between the emotional labor women service workers engage in on the job and the emotion work of care taking at home. Do women service workers *humanize* work by bringing a familial orientation to the job? Or has the commodification of service work so altered its character that women service workers are the first victims of a new kind of emotions—based alienation? The answers to these questions, in turn, imply different conclusions about the nature and severity of the *dilemmas* faced by working women with families. In its emphasis on the emotional continuities between service work and family life, one perspective implies that women service workers with families should face fewer work—family *dilemmas* than women whose work and family demands are more discrepant. By contrast, a second view highlights the emotional discontinuities between service work and family life, and argues that women service workers with families face greater, and perhaps more psychologically severe, work—family *dilemmas* than other women.

Though the qualitative findings discussed cannot provide definitive answers to these questions, they do raise important concerns about both perspectives. First, this study suggests that portrayals of service work and family life as inherently continuous and integrated *or* as discontinuous and conflicted are both overdrawn. In fact, the women in this study reported both continuity and discontinuity in their work and family lives. The type of emotional labor performed at work may be one factor that accounts for differences between the women who commented mainly about continuities between work and family and those who observed more discontinuities. The type of emotional labor required of human service workers, such as nurses, may encourage workers towards more sincere expressions of empathy and emotion than the type of emotional labor required of workers who encounter the public in banks and hotels. Because women almost universally described the family as a place where they could express their true feelings and selves, it is not surprising that the human service workers were more likely than others to view work and family as continuous in important ways. Hence accounts that stress the continuities between service work and family life may be valid for certain types of occupations (and family configurations), while perspectives emphasizing discontinuities may more accurately describe others. These results thus imply that similarities and dissimilarities between work and family, even for service workers, are multifaceted.

A second implication of this study concerns the consequences of work—family continuity and discontinuity. Women who experience work and family as essentially continuous are not necessarily freer of work—family stress than those who experience these realms as discontinuous. Each type of experience may have either positive or negative consequences for women. For instance, women who perform emotional labor on the job may find that the interpersonal demands of their job are inconsistent with those associated with their family role. Under some conditions, these inconsistencies are experienced as stressful and problematic, such as when the need to *sweep emotion under the rug* at work conflicts with a partner's desire for emotional expressiveness in the relationship. In other circumstances, the discontinuities between work and family are precisely what enables women to manage their work and family lives. Identifying the conditions under which women experience discontinuity as a source of distress or satisfaction should be a high priority for future research. Similarly, women who feel that at work they *really don't have to be much different than at home* are not necessarily better off than others. Though these women may be able to use skills learned in one setting to solve the problems of another, they may also be vulnerable to a form of emotional burnout. This possibility underscores the earlier point that the connections between service work, family life, and women's well—being are more complicated than assumed by accounts that stress the similarity or dissimilarity between service jobs and the home.

In exploring the continuities and discontinuities between service work and family life, this study also calls attention to the complex role of autonomy in working women's lives. Like the women Paules (1991) interviewed, the women in this study derived satisfaction from the feelings of control they obtained from the job. What Paules suggests but does not demonstrate, however, is that women value control at work more highly to the extent that such control is lacking at home. The data described are consistent with this argument. For these women, work provided an environment that was often less chaotic than family life and hence was seen as more susceptible to intervention and control. The respondent who wished to be able to relate to her children as she did her customers is the best expression of the complex way control figured into these women's lives. When service jobs require emotional labor, control over emotional expression is undoubtedly diminished, as Hochschild (1983) suggests. Women with families, however, may not necessarily become alienated, but may respond more like the waitresses in Paules' (1991) study. The opportunity to manage emotion on the job thus may become an opportunity for self—expression lacking in non—work arenas. Not all women may respond this way, of course. Nevertheless, studies of women's work, including jobs involving emotional labor, should be sensitive to the ways that women's views of job autonomy may be affected by their family responsibilities.

This study began by describing the work—family transition. Though studies on work—family relations have proliferated, the process of *crossing borders* remains relatively uninvestigated. My data suggest that women carefully manage their movement between institutions and devote considerable emotional effort to the work—family transition. Because work and family are organized according to different *institutional logics*, movement between spheres requires that people alter themselves. As we have seen, not all transitions require the same degree of personal transformation. It may also be the case that the emotional effort varies depending upon whether women are moving from work to home or vice versa or depending upon the relative salience of each role. The broader point, however, is that understanding work—family relations and the *dilemmas* they pose, requires attention not only to work and family, but also to the process of moving between these realms.

To conclude, I return to a suggestion offered at the beginning of this chapter. Research on work—family relations would benefit from continuing efforts to examine specific types of work and family characteristics. In her review of the work—family literature, Lambert (1990) concludes that multiple processes link these two spheres. Her perspective is skeptical of approaches to work—family relations that privilege apriori a model of conflict or integration. This study concurs with her assessment. Instead of assuming either conflict or integration, continuity or discontinuity, researchers should seek to identify the conditions under which one or the other may be true and should explore the positive and negative implications of each for women's service work and family lives. Further research is needed before we can determine whether a service society helps resolve or exacerbates the *dilemmas* faced by working women and their families.

Notes

1   Secretaries and receptionists are not typically classified as *human service* workers. The job descriptions of the three hospital workers we interviewed who were employed in these positions justified this categorization, however. In particular, these women's jobs required significant, and sometimes emotionally intense, contact with patients and their families.

2   To examine the possibility that the women interviewed were different in meaningful ways from the married or cohabiting women in the larger sample, we compared these two groups' responses to a variety of questionnaire items. These comparisons revealed few differences between the groups. For instance, although the interviewed respondents were slightly younger, less educated, and less satisfied with their jobs than the married or cohabiting women in the larger sample, both groups reported similar levels of work—family conflict. Though more fundamental differences between the groups cannot be ruled out, these comparisons suggest that the women interviewed for this study were not significantly different from their married or cohabiting co—workers in the larger sample.

5 Psychological intimacy between women and men at work

Sharon A. Lobel

Why should we study psychological intimacy between women and men? Women and men can love and care for one another, trust and respect each other, communicate openly and be available to help and support each other. Such relationships, however, are usually assumed to occur either in marriage or in non—marital relationships that involve sexual intimacy.

Psychological intimacy between women and men in the workplace is a topic that has received scant attention, and, when it has, it has mostly been in the context of relationships involving attraction and romance. Indeed, in anthropology, there are few references to socially approved close friendships between women and men without significant sexual implications (Bell 1984). Nonetheless, as described more fully later, women and men can have psychologically intimate relationships without sexual intimacy. In such relationships, sexual attraction may or may not be present for either or both members of the couple.

There are several reasons for adressing the gap in research on psychologically, intimate relationships between women and men in organizations. First, as more women enter the work force in the United States and other countries, there is a greater likelihood that such relationships will become more prevalent. In the workplace, as elsewhere, increased interaction with others provides opportunities for interpersonal affection to develop (Haavio—Mannila et al. 1988).

Second, as noted by Gutek, Cohen and Konrad (1990), the increase in the number of working women, coupled with job desegregation has contributed to greater sexualization of the environment, with a corresponding increase in harassing and non—harassing forms of sexuality. For example, Kauppinen, Haavio—Mannila, and Kandolin (1989) found that among Finnish policewomen, there was a high frequency of complaints about sexual harassment and also a high frequency of marriage with colleagues. Relationships involving sexual harassment are obviously deleterious, but non—harassing sexual relationships can also engender negative consequences, such as legal suits and feelings of jealousy, anger and abandonment (Mainiero 1986). Therefore, it would be helpful to identify forms of interaction between male and female co—workers with potentially positive individual and organizational consequences.

Third, a body of research suggests that personal relationships cannot be relegated to a domain that is separate from work (Haavio—Mannila 1994; Lobel 1993). Whether sexuality is viewed as an inherent attribute of the person or as a response to situational cues, it is surely difficult to confine its expression only within non—work relationships. Thus, relationships which are psychologically, but not sexually intimate may in some cases have an element of sexual attraction which is not acted upon. Therefore, in the debate over what constitutes appropriate sexuality at work, perhaps the psychologically, but not sexually intimate relationship deserves more attention.

Fourth, as in the human relations tradition (Likert 1961, 1967), some scholars and practitioners have argued that informal relationships yield benefits by helping organizations achieve business goals. In other words, rather than simply accept personal relationships as a fact of organizational life, some people have argued that personal relationships ought to be encouraged among employees (Macher 1986). Given the potential negative consequences of some forms of relationship between women and men, as well as questions about conflicts of interest between personal and organizational aims, we need a better understanding of the nature and effects of close relationships that cross gender lines. Such research needs to address both the impacts on the organization and well—being of the participants in the relationship.

In this chapter, I describe relationships between male and female co—workers who are psychologically, but not physically, intimate. Psychologically intimate relationships are characterized by feelings of love and caring, high trust and respect, open communication, and mutual accessibility. Gender differences in the frequency and nature of psychological intimacy with a co—worker, and the effects of psychological intimacy with a co—worker on the work group, on the relationship with the spouse, and on mutually supportive behaviors related to job and career performance are reviewed. I also examine the impact of psychological intimacy with a co—worker on performance outcomes.

Gathering information about psychological intimacy

The research reported in this chapter used data from two sources, an exploratory study and a quantitative survey.

In the absence of previous empirical studies on non—sexual, psychologically intimate relationships between male and female co—workers, Lobel, Quinn and Warfield (1990) decided to gather exploratory, qualitative data that could be used to generate items for a quantitative survey. In a letter to 900 randomly selected members of a national professional training and development association, we asked individuals who had experienced non—sexual love relationships at work to answer six open—ended questions. The questions requested the individual to describe the following in his or her own words:

1   the participants in the relationship;
2   how the relationship began and subsequent key events;
3   indicators of closeness and deterrents to sexual involvement;
4   personal and organizational payoffs and costs of the relationship;
5   unique characteristics of the relationship; and
6   perceived frequency of similar relationships in the workplace.

Fifty people responded. We examined the responses for common themes and selected sentences to include in the questionnaire items for the quantitative survey. Given the exploratory nature of our study, we relied on our judgment to select representative statements about indicators of closeness and about personal and organizational payoffs and costs. These statements were included in the sections of the quantitative survey measuring feelings and attitudes towards the co—worker and spouse, and the personal and organizational impacts of the relationship. After we completed our statistical analyses of the quantitative survey, we returned to the qualitative data for representative statements to enrich our interpretation of the quantitative findings.

The survey population was comprised of persons who resided in the United States and who had participated in the executive education program at the business school of a large midwestern university during the previous three years. All of the 709 female participants were included in the survey sample. Because of a larger number of participants from Illinois, Indiana, Michigan, and Ohio relative to the numbers from other states, every third male from these states and every male from other states was selected until 1,000 males were identified to receive surveys.

The survey was mailed to the 1,709 sample members along with a cover letter inviting participation in a nationwide study of friendships between male and female co—workers. The letter emphasized, that even if the person had only superficial relationships at work, his or her responses were important to the study. Anonymity was guaranteed; in fact the questionnaires were not numbered in any way.

We received 1,044 completed surveys, yielding a 61 percent response rate. The complete anonymity which we provided to respondents made it impossible to identify which members of our survey sample comprised the respondent group.

Quantitative data analyses were conducted on a subgroup of persons who indicated that they were not sexually intimate with the co—worker in the relationship in question. Among the 968 respondents in this subgroup, there were 527 men and 441 women. The median age was 38 years. On the average, women were younger than the men (38 versus 41 years) and had been employed by their current employers fewer years (9 versus 12 years). Of the respondents 80 percent indicated that they were married, 9 percent said they were *unmarried but committed to a relationship,* and 11 percent said they were *uncommitted.* Altogether 87 percent of the respondents held managerial positions. The median salary was USD 50,000 with a minimum of USD 18,000 and a maximum of USD 680,000.

In the interest of space, I have not described the development of the measures and the quantitative analyses in detail. Instead, I have provided a brief description of the various questionnaire items.

The section of the questionnaire measuring general attitudes towards relationships between women and men included potential obstacles to developing a friendship with a person of the opposite sex, such as shyness or a belief that people of the opposite sex have different interests. For questionnaire items dealing with feelings for a co—worker of the opposite sex, the respondents indicated the extent of agreement with statements such as *We feel love for each other*.

The respondents also described the frequency of particular behaviors in interactions with the co—worker, such as working overtime together or visiting each other's homes. The effects of the relationship on performance outcomes, such as job involvement, commitment to the organization, and size of most recent merit increase were assessed. The respondents also provided a self—rating of performance on two items adapted from Tsui (1984), namely, *I am performing my job the way my superiors would like it to be performed* and *I have fully met my superior's expectations in my roles and responsibilities*.

The nature of psychological intimacy between female and male co—workers

In 194 cases, the relationship described in the percentage, selected *other* to describe the position of the other person in relation to the self. The men were more likely than the women to be describing a subordinate and women were more likely to be describing a peer. The median number of years the subjects had been acquainted was three.

The data analyses revealed three types of psychological intimacy with a co—worker. For all three types, the women were more likely than the men to report that their relationship with a co—worker of the opposite sex was psychologically intimate.

In the first type of psychological intimacy, the respondents described their feelings with statements such as *There is an exhilarating 'chemistry' between us* and *We have a desire to be together*. This type of relationship was depicted by a male respondent as follows:

> I have few people in my life that I trust and confide in like her. The only reason it isn't sexual is our respect for each other, as well as our marriages.

A female respondent said:

> I tend to fall in love with people I meet at work and [with whom I] share a close working relationship.

The second type of psychologically intimate relationship was characterized by a respondent's willingness to devote time and energy to another person in the absence of obligation to do so. Said a male respondent:

> I did not view her as sexually attractive. She was like a good friend I trusted in for input and help.

Said a female respondent:

> He is part of my moral support but not part of my sexual satisfaction.

The third type of psychologically intimate relationship involved friendly, mutual interest and respect, without the *charged* emotions of the first type. Said a male respondent:

> I have a number of solid relationships based on respect, acceptance, and what I would even call Christian love (Agape), but the extent of involvement is kept to a work — or a friendship—relationship and has not developed into a dyadic one which might or would threaten my marital commitment.

The respondents indicated a variety of behavioral indicators of psychological intimacy. For example a female respondent said:

> He made a special trip to my office every morning to see how I was, discuss some of the things we both did the evening before at home with our families. We used to go to the park together at noon and walk, feed the ducks; sometimes he'd personally pack a picnic lunch for both of us; sometimes we didn't eat at all.

There were no significant differences between the women and men in the frequency of shared social activities outside of work, for example, going to parties or dinner together. There were also no significant gender differences in the frequency of shared work—related activities with a co—worker of the opposite sex, such as working overtime or working on important projects together. Nonetheless, the women were more likely than the men to agree that they communicated with the co—worker about non—work related subjects, for example, talking about spiritual things or having long, private discussions.

The men were more likely than the women to believe that developing a male—female friendship is difficult. For example, the men were more likely to agree that people of the opposite sex have different needs and interests and that they did not know how to develop friendships with the opposite sex, despite a greater desire to do so, relative to women. The men were also more likely than the women to agree that *Men—women relationships are sexual for me not just friendships* and that *friendships with the opposite sex should be reserved for marriage*. As might be expected, those who in general believed that developing an opposite sex friendship is difficult were less likely to report psychological intimacy with a particular co—worker.

How does psychological intimacy with a co—worker of the opposite sex affect work performance? According to the human relations tradition, supportive, personal relationships between co—workers inspire positive work—related attitudes (Mayo 1933; Kahn and Katz 1960, Likert 1961, 1967). Emotional support from a supervisor or co—worker directly minimizes interpersonal tensions and satisfies a worker's needs for affiliation and approval. Consequently, recipients of co—worker and supervisor emotional support feel more satisfied with themselves and their jobs. These effects can be achieved with a single, significant source of support.

Consistent with the human relations tradition, psychological intimacy with a co—worker was positively associated with other forms of work—related support. In particular, participants in psychologically intimate relationships said they helped each other reach work goals, shared career information, and provided useful feedback.

The first kind of psychological intimacy, namely, the one characterized by feelings of *chemistry* and love, was associated with greater commitment to the organization and job involvement, more positive self—evaluations of performance, and higher merit increases. Said a female respondent:

> He helped my career enough that I'm now a VP and became one at 33. I worked like a dog and made him look good. We had lots of success.

Said a male respondent:

> This is an opportunity for me to talk to someone who is experiencing the same pressures and issues at work. [There is] better understanding without threats of vulnerability that another man might present.

There were no significant gender differences on the scales measuring performance outcomes, including job involvement, self—evaluation of performance, organizational commitment and size of most recent merit increase.

How does psychological intimacy with a co—worker of the opposite sex affect the work group? Office romances, especially those between a superior and a subordinate, have been shown to engender negative consequences, such as gossip, jealousy and resentment. Co—workers perceive that personal/sexual resources are being exchanged for those of the career domain (Mainiero 1986). In psychologically intimate relationships, although the participants are not sexually involved, co—workers may think that they are or may still resent the special privileges that seem to be inherent in the personal relationship. The data showed that the women who reported feelings of love for a male co—worker reported evidence of complaints and tensions in the work group as a result of the relationship:

> A couple must be very mature to have a serious relationship with a co—worker. You must be able to separate your work and personal lives. Even if the couple demonstrates their ability, there will be others at the workplace who will be non—believers.

For men, work group impacts were perceived to be mostly positive.

Said a male respondent:

> We had a wonderful responsive staff — creative and productive. The organization benefited from this dynamic.

What is the relationship between psychological intimacy with a co—worker of the opposite sex and psychological intimacy with the spouse? For women, greater psychological intimacy with a co—worker was associated with less psychological intimacy with the spouse when the relationship was primarily characterized by feelings of *chemistry* rather than feelings of friendship, trust and respect alone. According to one female respondent:

> The only cost I can think of has been some resentment and/or conflict with our spouses who may not trust us as much as we deserve.

When the relationship was primarily characterized by friendly, mutual interest and respect, without the presence of *charged* emotions, greater psychological intimacy with a co—worker was associated with greater psychological intimacy with the spouse. For example, a male respondent said:

> Male/female relationships can truly be non—sexual and have a different kind of love which binds them. This can be a spiritual or brotherly/sisterly bond and I believe this is what this individual and I share. Our friendship has been meaningful enough that it has strengthened the relationships with our spouses and we each know this and appreciate and respect one another for such a bond.

Conclusions

This research aligns with existing literature on the meaning of work that argues against artificial dichotomies between work and non—work domains, instrumental and expressive activities, work and family life (e.g., Brief and Nord 1990; Lobel 1993; Haavio—Mannila 1994, Wharton and Erickson 1993).

The findings suggest that there are gender differences in general attitudes towards opposite sex friendships. Women tend to be more interested in developing and cultivating such friendships, and they perceive fewer personal or social obstacles to doing so. Consequently women are more likely than men to develop a psychologically intimate relationship with a co—worker of the opposite sex. Thus one consequence of increasing numbers of working women in the workplace may be an increased probability, for both women and men, of participation in a psychologically intimate relationship with a co—worker of the opposite sex.

These data suggest that psychological intimacy with a co—worker of the opposite sex provides several benefits for the participants and the organization. In particular, these relationships serve as an important source of job and career support; participants offer useful feedback, information, and help in reaching work goals. When the relationship involves feelings of love, both women and men report that they feel more motivated and satisfied with their jobs. Participants also report greater organizational commitment, more positive self—evaluations of performance, and higher merit increases. In other words, as human relations theorists have argued, personal relationships can benefit the organization, as well as the persons involved.

Research has shown that personal relationships with women are more beneficial to both men's and women's well—being than are relationships with men (House et al. 1988). If women provide higher quality emotional support than men (Wharton and Erickson 1993) and if relationships with women are more beneficial to men's well—being than are relationships with men for women's well—being, then we would expect that the positive effects of psychological intimacy would accrue especially for the male participants in these relationships.

Although this research did not reveal differences between men and women on measures of work performance, more female than male participants in psychologically intimate workplace relationships reported negative impacts of the relationship, such as complaints and tensions in the work group and less psychological intimacy with the spouse. In some cases, the impacts were serious. For example, one participant said:

> A colleague [also a personal friend] and her boss were fired for having an alleged affair. I have no way of knowing the truth, but she has told me that they were not having an affair; it's not worth it if appearances can influence one's position at work.

Thus, although the psychologically, but not sexually intimate relationship represents an option for male and female co—worker relationships, reactions of co—workers indicate that there are challenges for participants and others in attempting to integrate personal and public life.

The degree of reciprocity of emotional support and the long—term impacts on men's and women's well—being clearly require further attention. Several other questions about the nature and impact of psychologically intimate relationships also merit future research. How crucial is the support of a partner to women's and men's career development? Precisely how do close psychological bonds between women and men affect family relationships? Is organizational culture related to frequency and type of psychologically intimate relationships? Should we foster cultures which nourish these bonds?

6 Russian families past and present

Svetlana Yampolskaya

A great number of changes happened in the late 1980s in Russia. The transition from dictatorship to political freedom, from total control over the individual to personal independence, and finally from strict social order to chaos in all spheres of life took place. All aspects of people's activities were affected; a person's self—awareness was shocked.

Of course the family could not escape and had to undergo certain changes as a result of current events. The changes became a good reflection of all the processes happening in society and a vivid indicator of the country's condition after perestroyka. All contradictions and problems the family had before were strained to a breaking—point. The same trend took place in other aspects of people's lives. Problems of work and leisure, problems of everyday life, and personal problems all intensified to a great extent. Along with the positive changes, tension and stress escalated.

The economic situation which was not very good before perestroyka had a major effect on families over the years. Increased unemployment, a decreased number of professional jobs, rapidly declining wages, and hyperinflation had a strong negative impact on the population in general and on the family in particular. According to the statistical data of 1989, 86.5 percent of Russian families were *poor*, and only 11 percent fell into the middle income category (Tidmarsh 1993).

However, political freedom and personal freedom did not affect the family in a positive way either. Misunderstanding the idea of freedom and the absence of experience of freedom have led to chaos in almost all aspects of Russian life. Thinking that they could do anything, people lost their feeling of responsibility, their feeling of duty, not only in their social activity but also in their families.

With the loss of all beliefs, a general depression took place within and outside the family. The family could no longer provide moral support for an individual as it had earlier, and it could no longer protect its members. Uncertainty and insecurity became the family's experience.

Too much freedom and independence, which suddenly burst into the family, resulted in its helplessness and hesitation. At the same time the government did not provide or develop any new social policy. Being engaged with fighting over power, the authorities did not think about the family unit any longer. In the face of all the economic problems, family issues did not seem important. However, since it is the family that is responsible for the quality of the labor force, for social control over its members and for socialization, it is the family that society must begin with when trying to solve social and economic problems. Even taking into account all feminist arguments about the future of the family (Bernard 1972; Christensen and Heavey 1990; Narusk 1994), Russia has to accept that, under given circumstances (when deep economic crises take place), strengthening the family is very important for societal reconstruction. This idea has been expressed in Osheverova's article *If the state doesn't take care of the family, there will be no one to take care of the state* (Osheverova 1992).

The Russian family and its problems under socialism

After the Russian Revolution of 1917 the government declared support and protection for the family. All social policy concerning the family was explained as measures to help and strengthen it. All resolutions of the Communist Party began with the words: *For the purpose of strengthening the Soviet family* . . . and then the decrees came one after the other: prohibition of abortion, prohibition of bearing a child at home, establishment of difficulties for the divorce procedure, for example. Even when actions taken towards the family were softened, and divorce and abortions became easily available, they still had a negative effect and in reality turned out to be against women and children.

Gender equality in the workplace

Like everyone else women were declared to be free. They were *free* to work outside the family; they were *free* to take care of the family; they were *free* to work as much as men did. According to Soviet legislation everybody had *the right to work*; in other words everybody *had to work*. People who did not work outside the family were subjected to imprisonment. Women were not an exception. They were forced to work.

Everything was arranged in such a way that no one could escape working. People who did not work did not have a pension when they retired. Non—working persons were deprived of food and goods distribution. And again women, even women with many children, were not an exception.

Women had to work for one more reason. Their husbands could not support the family. One income was not enough. Even with two incomes people could hardly make both ends meet. The Soviet government *took care* of that too.

Of course there were some men willing to take a second job. But even this initiative was suppressed. According to Soviet legislation, people were *not* allowed to have two jobs. Some exceptions were made for certain professions, mostly unskilled and extremely low—paid jobs.

Women had to work outside the family, but at the same time they wanted to work. They also wanted to have a family and to raise children. The data testify to the fact that, despite all difficulties of life, women are mainly oriented to combining two roles — that of mother and that of worker (Rimachevskaya 1993). To be able to combine family life and career making, women needed more time. Women were asked many times: *What would be the best for you?* About 80 percent of the women answered: *To work part time.*

However for a long time part—time work was not possible for anyone. Even when officially women who had small children were allowed to work part—time, it was up to the manager to give or not to give this permission, and obtaining this permission was very difficult. Managers (even female managers) did not like these arrangements. They did not want to have additional problems. They also clearly indicated that, if a woman would like to work part—time, it was better for her to look for another job. One more time women failed to obtain a chance to improve their living standards.

Even obtaining a permission for a flexible schedule was a problem. Managers allowed women to come to their workplace one or two hours later only if a woman could prove the necessity of such a schedule. In some cases they had to start work at 7 a.m. or at 8 a.m. even though the kindergartens did not open until the same time.

Even men with small children could not ask for a flexible work schedule. They were not allowed to take sick leave to look after their children either. Only women could obtain such a leave. An exception was made when the mother was in prison or dead.

Thus the Soviet government reinforced patriarchal views of the family and therefore also gender inequality. It should be noted that antiquated notions of the family and the woman's role were always strong in Russia. Working hard on the image of a woman in public life, Soviet propaganda did not pay any attention to private matters. According to the ideology of socialism, individual problems, and personal life, including family life, were not important issues.

Women as workers and housewives

On obtaining an equal position with men at the workplace, women's role at home did not change much. They were still responsible for all the housework, the upbringing of the children, and serving their husbands.

The Russian Revolution of 1917, the subsequent policies of Stalin and, finally, a developed socialist system had changed almost all norms of society. Rejection of religion, unacceptance of ownership, different work ethics, different leisure—time patterns and people's interaction were introduced. The traditional division of labour in the family and women's duties in the family were the only norms that remained the same. Men had to be served. Children should be raised primarily by the mother. It was a shame if a man had to do

95

housework. It was a female activity and should be done only by women. This is what the unwritten regulations said. Women did not discuss or argue about it. They shared the same norms, the same traditional views.

It should be pointed out that the prestige of a housewife is very high in Russia. A study of women in Leningrad, Penza and Moscow showed that all the women placed great importance on the prestige they received from being good housekeepers (Slesarev and Yankova 1969). Some of them said: *A good housewife always finds time, strength and the means to put the house in order*, or *A good housewife is not too lazy to do the washing and clean up the apartment once more*.

Most women continue to think that they have to meet all the traditional expectations their husbands and relatives have. But some of them did change their way of thinking. As a result they had to choose between family and a solo life—style. Men's way of thinking did not change. *Women are adapting more quickly to changes in economic opportunity and need, than men to changes in women* (Hochschild 1986).

At the same time the Soviet government succeeded in persuading women to work. It became everybody's belief that a woman had to work outside the home. And if she did, not she was disregarded.

> The communist ideology was reflected even in the attitudes to work: it was not only an instrument of earning money but also a means to personal development. This ideology of work meant that, to be a *good woman*, the woman was to participate in work outside the home and, so doing, be a good citizen and a role model for the children (Haavio—Mannila and Kauppinen—Toropainen 1994).

Women did not have a choice. Social pressure to meet all requirements was too hard. There was no way for women to avoid working outside the family. And, it turned out, there was no way to escape domestic chores either. The problem of *second shift* appeared (Hochschild 1989). The gender relations in the family and sexual division of housework remained unchanged. In the USSR the total work load on women (production and homework together) made up 76.3 hours per week, whereas for men it was 59.4 hours (Posadskaya 1993).

Women were responsible for their work in the workplaces, and also for doing the domestic chores. It was their responsibility to take care of children and to take care of men. A wrinkled shirt on a man openly said that he had a bad wife. His co—workers felt sorry for him. Women also knew that they would be treated like bad wives, or *bad* women if they did not provide good service for their husbands. These regulations were strict; according to sociological data *all* married women spent twice as much time on housework than their single counterparts, including single mothers.

The bigger family a woman had, the more she had to work. Providing food for the family and standing in line, getting goods were female activities too. It was not easy to get them done. Everyday life in Russia was extremely difficult.

Shortages of food and goods meant that women (but not men) had to spend extra hours standing in lines. The lack of prepared food meant that women had to spend extra hours in the kitchen. Shortages of restaurants and lack of money meant that women had to cook every meal. Service was hardly available and women had to develop different abilities to obtain certain things. Making and fixing clothing were necessary skills women had to develop. They also had to be cautious using a private service — private business was illegal and prohibited.

Even the workhours of shops were a problem: all shops were closed by 6 or 7 p.m. when people finished work. Women used their lunch hours for shopping. Men used their lunch hours for lunch.

Housing was another distinct problem for all Soviet families. Endless arguments between generations sharing one flat and conflicts between neighbors sharing one kitchen and one bathroom took place because of the housing shortage. One more child in a family was sometimes a disaster because of the lack of space. One more abortion could be a disaster too because it threatened a woman's health. Medical care was very poor and unreliable. Contraception was completely unavailable.

Women and children

Women were encouraged to have many children. Soviet propaganda worked very hard at it. But shortages of kindergartens and housing and the unavailability of clothing and food for children sent Russian women the opposite message. Despite the strong persuasion of the authorities the Russian family remained small, but the number of abortions was increasing annually.

Child upbringing was one more burden Russian women had to bear. Men normally did not assist much in taking care of children. According to sociological studies only 28 percent of fathers took actual part in child raising (Auley 1981). Women could not expect any assistance from the State either. In spite of the fact that women loved and wanted children, they appeared to add another hardship to women's everyday life. Keeping in touch with children's institutions, helping them study and looking after them were also women's duties.

We have, first of all, to take care of women, the general secretary of the Communist Party Brezhnev kept repeating at each Congress of the communists. But nothing was done. And women had to continue to carry their burdens. Because of the special social policy, developed by the Soviet government women had inherited the double shift, extra strain and overloading. Almost all the problems they tried to solve were actually created by the State.

Being forced to work full time, women did not perform very well at their workplaces. Many of them did not improve their qualifications. Fifty—seven percent of the women declared that they even had no intentions of improving their qualifications (Porokhnik and Shepeleva 1975). The family suffered too. The tension women brought to their families, with children out of control, made marriages very fragile. As many women said, in the workplace they thought about the family, at home they thought about the work. In spite of the nice declaration about helping the family communist authorities made family life extremely hard in every way.

Leisure in the Russian family

The Soviet government even interfered with family leisure time and destroyed this aspect of family life. Six—day work weeks and three—shift work schedules were introduced, and the family weekend was broken. Besides, husbands and wives usually had different shifts, and thus they were forced to spend their free time separately. They could not even plan to spend their vacations together because it was almost impossible to have them at the same time. Moreover, if they had children they could have vacations only in summer when all children had holidays. But summer vacations were always considered a luxury. Ordinary people could take summer vacations only a few times in their entire life.

When planning a vacation soviet people always tried to get a reservation in a resort — to get a *putevka*. Of course it was in short supply also. If a person was lucky he or she could get one. To get two for a husband and wife was only possible for people who held high positions. Thus, as a result, most spouses spent their vacations separately.

Staying for a month without their spouses, men and women were naturally attracted to others and became involved in liaisons. Some of the relationships led to broken families. A study of divorce hearing shows that the most frequent reason for the collapse of a family is not the replacement of an old love by a new one but an old love being sacrificed for a casual liaison (Kharchev and Matskovsky 1978).

Spending free time apart automatically resulted in spouses developing a different set of friends. They needed somebody to spend leisure time with. Finally spouses had different friends, different patterns of free—time spending, different vacations at different times. The only thing they shared was everyday life and everyday problems. The sociological study carried out by Yankova showed that about 30 percent of Muscovites explained their divorce after more than five years of marriage by their strong orientation to romantic love and their neglect of *the prose of life* (Yankova 1975).

Communist control of the Russian family

The dictatorship of the Communist party was absolute. Communists kept all aspects of individual life under control. The family was their main preoccupation.

Controlling the family was important, first, because it is the place where all socialization processes took place and, second, because it was a convenient tool with which to influence people's minds. As soon as babies were born they were supposed to be taken to children's institutions and be brought up by the State. Lenin's idea was partially realized, and there were some kindergartens where children were brought on Monday morning and picked up on Friday night.

Since the State failed to take care of children completely, it was the family who was responsible for the rest. The leaders of the Communist Party had to make sure that children got a *proper* upbringing.

Spreading fear among the population (those who did not agree with Soviet ideology could get in trouble) the Soviet government had a guarantee that parents would control their children's *proper* way of thinking because they wanted them to be safe. There were almost no families in which parents talked about missing relatives, discussed the political system, or expressed their disagreement with current policy. On the other hand, spouses were also afraid to misbehave and to be punished. Any wife could complain about her husband to the local Communist Party Organization. Any husband could do the same about his wife. People were encouraged to do so.

People's relationships (not only between spouses) were openly discussed at the Communist Party meetings and at working group meetings. *Guilty* people had to follow the instructions Communist leaders made for them. Otherwise punishment would take place. It could affect all phases of a person's life. The Communist Party not only controlled adultery, matters but also divorce problems. Communists immediately lost their career opportunity if they got divorced. People who wanted to hold high positions and who had an unhappy marriage had to choose between personal life and work. Many husbands kept their families only because they were career—oriented.

An interesting fact was that women were not punished for a divorce to the extent that, probably because of the general idea that men were responsible for initiating and keeping the marriage. Women could threaten men. The Communist Party control was strong. People who would denounce a person were many. Men had to be careful.

There was also control over sexual life. Literature on sexual matters, any kinds of information about sex and sexual relationships was censored, and asceticism was advocated. For a long time sexuality was a prohibited topic. Many tragedies took place because of the lack of knowledge or unavailability of sexologists.

As a result the Soviet family was under control from all sides. Child upbringing, any kind of misbehaviour, and spouses' relationships were subjects of Communist Party concern. Party control over the family was one of the most amazing and special characteristic of the Russian family.

Russian family's response to communist development

However, all kinds of prohibitions and controls led to unexpected and opposite results. The family, like the economy, adapted itself to the socialist system and developed new and tricky forms of life—style. The purpose of this adjustment was to survive. But survival included cheating the State. Cheating became one more interesting characteristic of the Russian family and Russian life. It took place at work and at home at the market and at State shops, and in businesses and in love. Distrust became the norm of life. It was brought into personal relationships, and it relentlessly kept ruining them. It was wrecking family and personality too. People led two—faced lives.

The family, as the most sensitive institution, absorbed all special traits of the newly created socialist society and reflected all negative standards of the communist regime. Like the entire country, the family had a legal and an illegal life. Alcohol addiction and extramarital affairs became a hidden side of family existence. First it was primarily men's preoccupation; then women drifted into it. Hard working conditions, husbands' alcoholism, and the double strain set the stage.

Measures taken by the Russian government to strengthen and stabilize the family had an opposite effect. Russian authorities failed in everything they wanted to achieve by leading certain policies on family and marriage. Moreover, all the direct and indirect actions taken by the Russian government towards the family had the most negative impact.

Because of the problems of the country, the Communist Party was dissatisfied with the declining birth rate. Their major concern was to obtain enough people for the future labour force. Therefore it increased the length of maternity leave and the size of the monthly payment during the first year after birth. Propaganda was also used to convince people to have more children. However, the Russian family remained relatively small, with only one or two children. In addition the number of families with no children increased dramatically. A growing number of Soviet families are childless, a fact that frightens both Soviet demographers and the authorities (Shlapentock 1984).

The number of illegitimate children increased too. It can be said that between 10 to 15 percent of all children in the Soviet Union were born to single mothers (Larmin 1974; Tolts 1974). This figure can be compared with another showing that 31 percent of the women giving birth between the ages of 40 and 44 yearswere unmarried. Yakovleva (1972) showed in her research that in 1970, in Minsk, illegitimate children constituted 6.7 percent of the total number of children. This rise in illegitimacy could be traced primarily to men's irresponsibility regarding marriage and fatherhood.

A high divorce rate and its annual increase were other responses to the social policy on family stabilization. Even in 1953 when it was almost impossible to obtain a divorce, about 10 percent of all marriages ended in divorce. As soon as the legislation was changed, and the divorce procedure was not so complicated, the number of broken marriages increased steadily.

Perestroyka, glasnost, political freedom and the family

The socialist economy was built on compulsory work. For decades the Soviet population was conditioned to do depersonalized work and to distrust government policies. Not only were individual efforts virtually unrewarded, but any display of initiative could be dangerous. Total control over the economy and decision making resulted in economic dependence and social helplessness when work problems were dealt with.

With the abolishment of the Communist Party a rapid transition from complete obedience to the absence of any direction took place. On obtaining sudden economic and social freedom both managers and workers were at a loss. Previous fear and uncertainty about the political situation led to people being afraid to take any steps. They were afraid of taking any responsibility and preferred to wait.

As a result of such *doing nothing*, productivity rapidly decreased. Enterprises could not cope with facing problems; they had to fire more and more workers because they did not have the money to pay salaries. Many of them went bankrupt. Relaxing economic control did not produce a commercial gold rush; instead there was an extremely slow start—up of the small and medium—sized enterprises that had been expected to boom. Liberalization had led to much buying and selling of State property but to no significant growth in the artisan activity that could create self—employment for workers with initiative (Tidmarsh 1993).

Shortage of goods and food reached incredible heights. Automatically all prices kept increasing daily. Hyperinflation took place. The Central Bank reported that inflation was running at an annual rate of 36 percent. While higher prices alleviated the most acute shortages, they did not dramatically improve the quantity, quality or distribution of food and goods.

The ruble virtually collapsed, and the economy declined. Massive unemployment still threatens the already dispirited work force. Closed enterprises, the non—working military industry, destruction of the huge former communist and comsomol apparatus, with its great number of people who used to be engaged in administration, produced unemployment on a gigantic scale.

Under such conditions the family changed its functions. Its main preoccupation now became the struggle for survival. For most Russians, physical survival is the major goal, and the solidarity of the family is their greatest resource. This struggle has required the mobilization of almost all family assets (Shlapentock and Marchenko 1992). Time spent on leisure—time activity in the past has been transferred to time spent on an additional job. Money earlier spent on service and goods is now spent on food. The total hours the family spends on all kinds of work, including housework and work outside the family, has increased dramatically.

Disillusionment with the family as an institution

Hard economic conditions made it impossible for many Russians to support their family. The realization of the fact that to have a family nowadays is a double responsibility and that no help can be expected from the State resulted in an increased number of people giving up their family. The number of marriages decreased from 2.7 million in 1987 to 2.6 million in 1991.

People are afraid of having a family, they do not want to have either a family or children because they cannot even make enough money to support themselves. They have found that it is easy to live without a family in all respects. The new fear of having marital duties has become stronger and more important than the natural desire to raise a family. At the same time the number of single people who want to get married but cannot do so rapidly has also increased. It has become harder and harder to find a husband or wife and to set up a family.

Not only men, but also women, experience the same feelings and the same concerns. It is more and more difficult for women to support themselves, and, at the same time, they realize that to find a proper husband or someone who can support them is even more difficult and practically impossible.

Somehow, however, the desire to get married and have a family is much stronger for women than for men, and women still dream of getting married. They have simply changed their preferences. Now they dream of marrying a foreigner. A great number of young women have rushed to learn foreign languages merely for the purpose of being able to communicate with a possible foreign partner. Many of them spend much of their time walking around international hotels and restaurants — the places where they can meet a single male foreigner.

For them marriage is an ideal alternative because it is a certain means of solving financial problems without breaking the norms of society. But, if not marriage, then they do not mind settling for all sorts of relationships with wealthy newcomers. Being unable to find a job and to support themselves, women consider such relationships a new way to obtain goods and money and also increase their standard of living.

Many women think about more simple relationships. Money for love seems to be acceptable. In Moscow, teenage girls consider prostitution a glamorous career opportunity. According to the Moscow daily newspaper, *Komsomolskaya Pravda*, more than half of adolescent girls, rated hard—currency prostitution as highly attractive work when they were asked about potential careers. Not only young and single women think about prostitution as an attractive profession. Even older and married women have tried it. *Nothing to lose* is their answer. Prostitution became a major problem at the very beginning of the perestroyka period. Neither the police nor the authorities could cope with it. Prostitution assumed an incredible scale when, for the first time since the Revolution, glasnost allowed articles devoted to this problem to be published. Despite all efforts of journalists to describe a prostitute's life as humiliating and unattractive, thousands of women rushed to prostitution hoping to get something they could not get in any other way.

Decline in the birth rate

People try to adjust to new ways of life, to new conditions and situations. This adjustment expresses itself in many different forms. One of the most vivid indications of people's adaptation in Russia is the drop in birth rate. In 1992 the birth rate in Moscow decreased fourfold when compared with that of 1991. In 1993 Russia's birth rate dropped 12 percent, and it is expected to decline even more sharply this year. The birth rate decreases mostly because more and more families refuse to have a second, let alone third, child. In addition, the number of childless families has reached enormous proportions. Russia's death rate now exceeds its birth rate, and the country's population is actually shrinking.

Of course, the main reason for not having children is the loss of opportunity to support them. People cannot make enough money to provide a minimum standard of living for their children, and children's food and children's clothing are still hardly available.

On the other hand, more and more Russians are afraid of a possible civil war or even a new revolution. They are uncertain about tomorrow, and this situation can be viewed as a second major reason for people's rejection of having children. Even those who are doing well (most of them are involved in some kind of business), are not sure that they will be doing so well in the future. Nevertheless, people prefer not to take risks, in other words, not to have children. As recently reported, there are some days in maternity hospitals when not one baby is born.

Still one strong factor influencing the dropping birth rate is the deterioration of medical care. Medical care in Russia was always extremely poor. Since the decline in the economy and the appearance of all kinds of shortages, clinics and hospitals have not been able to obtain either medicine or equipment. Medical care, which was earlier free, has become very expensive, and only a few people can afford it. In addition many doctors are leaving medical practice because they cannot earn enough money to support their families.

Women's and children's health is in desperate shape. The number of stillborn babies in 1991 reached 20.7 out of 1,000 live births. At the same time even though Russia has always held the leading position in the number of abortions the number keeps increasing. As statistics have shown, every fifth woman of child—bearing age undergoes an abortion annually. Last year the refusal to have children coupled with the unavailability of contraception added to the abortion rate dramatically. In 1985 when perestroyka began, the number of abortions in Russia reached 4,552,000. In 1992 there were 200.7 abortions per 100 births.

The performance of abortions is incredibly poor, and, as a result many women suffer different forms of complications, and become naturally sterilized. There are millions of women who have had an abortion and can no longer have children, even if they want to. This fact also plays an important role in the decline in birth rate.

Perestroyka and divorce

The unfavorable political and economic situation has also affected the divorce rate. As has already been mentioned, the divorce rate has always been on the increase, but the increase has become even more noticeable in the last few years. In 1990 it climbed to 38 percent of all concluded marriages, and by 1992 it reached 43 percent. In 1991 the maximum number of divorces (970 000) was registered in Russia. The greatest number of divorces took place among men and women in the age group of 25 to 34 years. The length of their marriages was from 5 to 9 years.

The deterioration of the economic situation has sharpened the earlier problems at the Soviet families. The dissensions and disagreements that were somehow worked out earlier have suddenly reached the breaking point. More and more often, people do not find any advantage to continuing to live together. In most families a husband can no longer support his family. At the same time he still requires to be served. Thus many women look at their marriages as additional housework or a burden. Even the presence of children does not stop them from leaving their husbands. According to the census population of 1989 the number of one—parent families rose to 8.5 million. It is two million or 30 percent more than in 1970.

In addition the removal of the Communist Party's control over the family has provided people with unlimited freedom in their personal relationships. They have finally received the opportunity to do whatever they want with their personal lives. They are no longer afraid of the Communist Party. They are not afraid of God's punishment either since religion was taken away a long time ago. Divorce, adultery, and extramarital relationships had already become a solid factor in everyday life.

The increase in the divorce rate was also due to another reason. Since people cannot find a job, or in many cases; they are not paid enough to support themselves, they try to immigrate. Immediately after perestroyka countries like Germany, Israel, Australia, and America offered immigration opportunities to certain categories of the population. More and more people wanted to leave the country. This situation set the stage for a greater number of divorces because many couples had a disagreement in principle on this matter. A husband wanted to immigrate, a wife did not. Or the wife's relatives had already immigrated, and she wanted to join them but the husband did not. They divorced merely because one of them decided to stay and the other decided to leave.

Immigration or the desire to immigrate spread all over the country and broke up a great number of families.

Social problems around the family

The deterioration of the economic situation in the country in general sharpened and worsened all social problems in particular. The alcoholism problem has assumed a threatening scale. Yet the total number of alcoholics, let alone the number of heavy drinkers, still remains unknown.

Alcoholism contributed to the degradation of a considerable part of the male population in Russia. Feeling miserable because of the role a man has to play in his family —he is not the real head of the family any longer, he cannot support his family, his income is very low, he cannot protect his family, he is not the only one who can represent his family in outside institutions— men use alcohol to increase their self—esteem. They need respect they cannot get either in their family or in their workplaces.

Not only the men but also the women and teenagers have a problem with alcoholism. Since Party control was removed, and no—one can stop black market sales, alcohol has become easily available for everyone willing to pay for it. Unfortunately teenagers are no exception.

In the last few years alcohol has become the only available way to spend free time and the only remedy people use to solve medical and psychological problems.

An anti—alcohol campaign undertaken by Gorbachev rapidly increased the drug addiction rate. Later on it too kept increasing.

Alcohol and drug addiction has made a contribution to the increase in crime. According to Russia's Ministry of the Interior, there were 32 percent more murders and attempted murders during the first nine months of 1992 than in the same period in 1991. In addition, there were 60 percent more armed robberies and 51 percent more burglaries of homes (U.S. News & World Report 1992).

A general depression and psychological oppression has taken place. According to statistical data about a million Russians attempted suicide in 1991, twice as many as in 1990. Since there is no control or even proper administration, anarchy and chaos are evident.

Russian women in the 1990s

The women's situation has worsened. As Rimachevskaya (1993) noted *a feminization of poverty has been observed*. It has mostly been women who have lost their jobs and thus lost their social positions; it has been women who have become more dependent on their husbands economically and psychologically; it has been women who's situation is always worse.

The deterioration of women's situations has also influenced families. Making less money in their workplaces, women have had to come back to their domestic chores and their role as a provider of services for their husbands.

At the beginning of perestroyka, when the situation with the labor force changed, Gorbachev suggested that women would come back to their traditional role. As Rimachevskaya noted, depending on the economic strategy chosen, women are either called upon to *mobilize themselves* and take an active part in social production or to return *into the fold of the family* and preform their maternal duties (Rimachevskaya 1993).

It should be pointed out that some women have wanted to stay home as housewives. Now, since salaries are so small a pension does not seem to be a sensible goal, many women have returned to the home. Some of them had to do it because they lost their jobs and there was no way to find another one.

Therefore, as more and more women are being involved in the labour force in the West and in the United States, an opposite trend is taking place in Russia. More and more women are leaving paid jobs to become housewives.

Even single women who do not have a husband to support them have to stay at home if they lose their job, at least for a certain period of time. They usually try to find a boyfriend who can either support them directly or give them a job. At the same time women who do have a job, and who are afraid of losing it, try to sleep with their managers and thus to protect themselves. Managers, on the other hand, do not hide their preferences about possible employees. Sometimes they openly advertise them. Women have to please their managers, who often openly require a sexual *service. With declining chances to find employment, women are now more exposed than ever to various abuses* (Shlapentokh and Marchenko 1992). Sexual harassment, which always took place, has assumed enormous proportions. Sex has become a tool for sale and purchase in all respects. There has been an explosion of sex shops in the cities, pornographic magazines, sex on television, payphone sex and related activities.

Along with decreasing opportunities to obtain a normal job, new possibilities have appeared for women. The porno industry began to develop and has enticed more and more women to work for it. Of course these career opportunities are available only for young and attractive women.

Sex has also started to play an important role during leisure time. If, before, the main leisure—time activities in Russia were watching television, having guests or talking with friends, they are now sexual relationships. As it also occurred after the Revolution of 1917, the idea of freedom is being embodied in sexual expression.

Conclusion

All the social and economic changes that have taken place during the last several years in the former Soviet Union have had both positive and negative aspects. We cannot reject the fact that the political and personal freedom the Soviet people now have is an incredible positive achievement. The fake socialist system was finally destroyed; people obtained the right to talk openly, to handle their personal life in a way they liked, and to have their own ideology.

On the other hand rapid transition to a market economy from a completely different economic system and way of life has led to many negative effects. The general poverty of the population, unemployment, and hyperinflation have grown.

It may seem strange, but all the changes that occurred after perestroyka almost without exception influenced the family negatively. Even positive changes like personal and political freedom resulted in the growth of extramarital relationships, various kinds of liaisons, and open sexual relationships in the workplace.

Women who were earlier equal at least in the social sphere, lost their independence. Sexism and gender inequality became even worse. Earlier a woman was protected by her husband, and her husband could and, in fact did, provide enough money to support his family. Now a woman's position is insecure from all sides. A woman can no longer rely on her husband. Often it is the wife who is thinking of how to support the family and a husband. During the many years of socialist administration men felt helpless and worthless and finally lost their feeling of responsibility. With the advent of perestroyka they could not suddenly regain it.

Being affected from all sides — alcoholism of most of the population, adultery, hard economic conditions— the Russian family lost its main functions. In most cases it became a fake like the socialist system which developed this family. Spouses lived together in many cases just because they shared the same flat and because there was no way to obtain another one. Spouses lived together in many cases just because they were too lazy to change anything in their life. Finally there are some spouses who continue to live together for the sake of children or relatives.

Nowadays Russian society is going through the break up of norms, values and attitudes, and the Russian family is undergoing the same. It will take time for the people, and particularly the family to develop or adopt a different way of thinking.

7 Gender and rationality: The case of Estonian women

Anu Narusk

At the outset, I must confess my dual feelings about writing this chapter. On one hand, it has been really interesting to discuss the general (and personal) unresolved dilemmas within women's work—family nexus in times of rapid social changes around the world. On the other, it has brought with it worries and doubts, as can any other attempt to deal with such subjects as women's issues or rationality, especially within the chaos caused by the collapse of a totalitarian Soviet regime, characterized by its officially claimed but non—existent gender equality. The reality behind the *Soviet purdah* has been a subject of great surprise for some and a real shock for many researchers.

As an aftermath, many similarities have been found in women's positions in society and employment in comparisons between Western and Eastern European countries. Primary among these, as summarized by Sutherland (1991) are

1   the pyramid structure (women are few in top positions and many in lower ones);
2   the grouping of women in the certain occupations;
3   the tendency for women to be paid less than men, and
4   the greater work load of women in comparison with that of men.

In the same way, women's *unresolved dilemmas of combining employment and family life* have become similarly visible both in the East and in the West in that women are seen mostly as oppressed victims of patriarchal, male—oriented social systems.

More rarely the question is posed of *What role do women themselves have in preserving women's special situation and traditional gender roles in changing social conditions?* Although little about this question is found in the literature, some examples exist. According to Bestuzev—Lada, *the historically formed division of housework into 'men's work' and 'women's work' has turned into an anachronism and family splitter today.* He accuses women of releasing their husbands and sons from housework, as well as of expecting such behaviour to be natural without understanding that more equally shared responsibilities make the family stronger.

Some other analogous arguments like — *a breakdown of obsolete stereotypes is delayed not only because men have low level of consciousness, but also because women are insufficiently demanding* — are based on the evidence of a strong female influence in family life and child rearing in former socialist countries (Kohn et al. 1986; Narusk 1988, 1992).

Dealing with the question of women's choics, I proceed from the main postulate of rational choice theory, presupposing that, from the behavioural alternatives given in a specific situation, the alternative with the highest expected utility is chosen. The expected utility of an action is interpreted as a function of rewards and costs as a consequence (Wippler 1986 p. 2). Both the rewards and costs are considered to be socially determined — the same behaviour under different social and ecological constraints results in different rewards or costs to an individual.

We can deal with the problem of women in the same way — women have to weigh the expected costs of chosen behaviour against the expected rewards. It does not mean that all women are expected consciously to calculate both the costs and rewards one by one, but as Wippler expounds *it is simply assumed that people display certain consistent and predictable patterns of response to positive and negative incentives, or stated more generally, to changes in their environment, i.e. that people act 'as if' they weigh costs and benefits* (Wippler 1990 p. 188).

Estonia is one of the East European countries in transition, and the calls for preserving traditional gender roles and values are being supported by the men and women themselves.[1] Traditional in this instance means legal, life long, sexually exclusive (for women) marriage in which the home—oriented (employed or not) main responsibility of the wife is to take care of her husband and raise their children.

To start such an analysis, I try to determine *what the expected rewards (utilities) and costs (disutilities) that accompany the support of traditional gender socialization for women are.* In addition I consider the question *Under what conditions do real rewards and costs correspond to expected ones?*

Social prerequisites for women's choice of traditional gender roles and the expected rewards on a social level

For the choice question, reference should be made to the processes wherein resourceful actors attempt to *produce* positively valued states (goals) under constraints particular to their social circumstances (Wippler 1990). Then the rewards or costs weighed are strictly connected with social constraints and resources in an intertwined manner that makes it often difficult to distinguish one from the other.

Assuming survival as the main goal all human beings strive for, let us analyze the mutual influence of social constraints and individual (familial) resources.

Scarce economical resources and survival strategies

A deep economic crises is the current situation faced by the former Soviet Union and the other East European countries. For example, in the beginning of 1993, every 10th Estonian woman reported that there was not enough money for everyday eating, almost every second woman stated that their income was spent on food and rent for housing, every third woman was able to buy necessary clothes in addition to supplying food and housing, and the rest (11 percent) felt economic difficulties only if expensive goods (furniture, car, house, etc.) were an issue (Narusk 1995a).[2]

As family historians have shown, in times of deep economic crises, it is the traditional *strong* rural families that survive better (Thomas and Wilcox 1987). Given the poor economic situation, Estonian people keep close to a rural way of life[3] and, to a great degree, depend on the agricultural products produced on their own plots. The share of people trying to grow vegetables on plots of their own or those of close relatives rented from the State increased by a little over half in 1985 to almost 70 percent in 1993. Estonians today also wish to revive the once violently interrupted (during the World War II and Soviet occupation) development of small private agricultural farms. It is hoped that such a revival of a rural life—style will help to overcome both the identity and economic crisis in times of deep social change.

Cultural traditions and the 'Soviet heritage'

In addition to the strong impact of values connected with a rural life—style, the Puritan, Lutheran life values and living styles with emphasis on the *good mother* have been the main cultural orientations transmitted within the family over generations. As for the transmission of cultural traditions, the *Soviet admixture* has to be taken into account.

First, the pressures caused by the disruptive effects of forced industralization, collectivization, political terror, purges, and war often left the family to be the only place providing a *refuge, a temporary escape* from these pressures; it preserved and transmitted important residues of earlier cultural orientations and life—styles (Lapidus 1978, 1992).

Second, the war and political deportations caused an abnormal scarcity of men, thus transforming women into heads of households and forcing them to care for all other (too young, too old, too ill, etc.) family members.

Third, the lack of reliable social information has had a strong influence on the transmission of cultural traditions. The more closed to information the system is, the stronger the impact of cultural traditions on people's behaviour. And this has been exactly the case in Estonia for the last 50 years. People's possibilities to obtain objective, reliable information on factors both inside and outside the system were strongly warded off.

The ideologically restricted social studies and deformed statistics served as pillars for the totalitarian system. And now, in spite of the breakdown of Soviet rule in Estonia, the influence of the *Soviet heritage* is still evident. The long period of living in closed information system has caused for a majority of people a kind of *learned helplessness* in the gathering and use of reliable and operative information for social rearrangements. Such a shortage of information often influences the decision processes, both for women and men: if they simply do not know about different alternatives, they can not make choices.

Closely tied to the shortage of information remains the *problem with words available* (Baalsrud and Fougner 1992). To understand why women's striving for equal opportunities is met by such strong opposition in post—Soviet countries it underlines the fact that the same rigid Soviet system that the people in these countries have revolted against has claimed equality between women and men (although only in words). Consequently, those who want to speak up for the well—being of women in these countries today, have serious difficulties with the words available. *The very word 'rights' has a hollow ring to it . . . The word most closely resembles 'demands' — the demands that women should work hard and give birth to many children* (Baalsrud and Fougner 1992 p. 103).

To understand the situation of post—Soviet Estonian women, we must consider that the Soviet system of obligatory full—time employment, its economy and social policy, including the low average wage levels, have forced women into a worker role outside the home even in the situation of scarce child—care facilities. For example, in 1988 in Estonia 75 percent of urban and 51 percent of rural children had places in kindergartens or *creches*.

Women were left without the freedom to choose not to work or to reshape the terms of their employment to suit their individual needs. At the same time, despite the fact that women entered many scientific and technical fields, sexual stereotyping of occupations was maintained and sustained by both official policies and public opinion. The distinction between *men's work* and *women's work* — based on biological and psychological stereotypes — remained unchallenged. The household responsibilities that remained unbearable for an underdeveloped social service system were treated as the main domain of women. Thus the *fundamental assumption of Soviet economic and family policy — that women and women only have dual roles — effectively assigned women a distinctive position in both the occupational and the family systems* (Lapidus 1992 p. 150).

In addition Estonian women could not count on the husband's active participation in housework and child rearing. There was no legislation broadening men's rights or responsibilities at home and in child rearing — no paternity leave, joint custodial laws, no father's rights for assistance at birth or even for a visit to see his newborn in the hospital. The impact of this *Soviet heritage* is still visible —

although paternity leave and fathers' assistance at birth (the latter more in principle) have been accepted by legislation and health institutions during the last several years. Public opinion does not accept this kind of behaviour as suitable for a *real* man. Instead, longer maternity leave and other provisions for better *mothering* are largely appreciated without the reasoning that special protective arrangements for women only reinforce patterns of occupational segregation and obstruct the achievement of equality between the genders (Haavio—Mannila and Kauppinen 1994).

Today, the word *equality* is condemned in Estonia, as well as in the other post—Soviet countries. This is done without realizing that there was no equality between genders in Soviet times. The same applies to many other words formally used in Soviet ideology, for example, words like *solidarity, internationalism, socialism* or *communism.* Analogously the *problem with words* was also faced by some Western researchers not able to realize the unreasonability of speaking about post—communist countries, because no communist countries existed anywhere. Moreover, it is understandable that now, while officially *misused* words are *out* and the necessary information for their redefinition is missing, the *comeback* of *old* words and traditional values is welcomed in Estonia.

Estonian's national anxiety of becoming a minority people in their homeland

The simple statistics make the fear of Estonians, that they will become a minority in their own country, understandable. Since 1940 when Estonia first became a part of the Soviet Union the continuous decrease in the share of Estonians shifted from about 90 percent to 75 percent in 1959 to 61 percent in 1989. The neoconservative social movements with slogans such as, *To fill the Estonian land with Estonians!* brought together people frightened by the decrease of Estonians. They wished to save the Estonian nation, nature and culture. This hope — not to become a minority in their own homeland — has (until the beginning of the 1990s) favored the relatively high fertility of Estonians compared with that of the non—Estonians living in Estonia, especially for the more educated and socially active Estonians.

This hope becomes even more understandable if we consider that, despite the relatively high fertility rates of Estonians until the 1990s, high rates of immigration, the mechanical increase of the non— Estonian population, was continued. From 1980 to 1988 the migrational increase was 60,000; the natural increase of the whole population was 49,000 and the natural increase of Estonians was 6,000.

Expected rewards on an individual level

The expected individual rewards to be gained by preserving the traditional gender pattern in Estonia can be divided into two main groups.

The *first group* includes rewards for *all family members*. These are the rewards accompanying the higher evaluation of such traditionally *feminine* values as efficiency, hard labour, responsibility for others, and sacrifice. These rewards become especially visible in everyday life, which has not changed much in comparison with that of *Soviet times*. The latter has been very illustratively characterized by Kalns— Timans:

> Within Soviet research and the popular press it has even been stated that women should tolerate bad husbands, their drinking, and affairs, and that women should be weak or indeed play at being weak so that their men can be strong. Men should be cared for almost like children, food cooked, clothes washed, the toilet cleaned and if he does do anything to help this should be achieved by manipulating the situation till he actually does some task almost without realising. (Kalns— Timans 1992 p. 40.)

Some parallels to the latest discussions about the care functions in the literature of the 1980s can be drawn. Some current feminist movements exalt femininity and the gentle, maternal, sensitive traits that can be encouraged in everyone. They emphasize these qualities, not only because they are intrinsically valuable (indeed necessary for survival), but also to help restore women's self—respect and dignity (Saarinen 1992). The concept *care rationality* has been introduced to

118

signify female values as a main basis for action. The *new everyday life* as a concrete utopia for the rationalisation of everyday life has been elaborated accordingly. A reduction in care is seen to lead to the disappearance of female values, the female counter argument has been not to eliminate housework and care functions, but instead to expand the scope of activities, implying the integration of socialized men also into these activities care rationality.

The *second group* includes rewards generally considered beneficial for *women as females*. They are as follows.

1. A *woman can 'lean on a man's shoulder'*; she can consider the economic, physical and intellectual help of a man as *natural*, as *determined by nature, by human biology*. All she needs is to be a *good* wife to her husband and a *good* mother to her children.

2. A *woman can avoid the burnout and distress* caused by the unbearable dual burden. Estonian women assume that in their situation it would be better to choose the family—oriented life—style and put more emphasis on creating, maintaining and developing social networks for warm relationships both inside and outside the family, all needed for providing mental and economic resources for themselves and their family. Slogans limiting women's responsibilities to home and children are enticing when work outside the home often means physically hard, health hazardous, monotonous, urgent, and poorly paid activity. Every 14th employed Estonian woman considered her work well—paid; every sixth saw possibilities for career—making; every second estimated it as urgent; every fiftth believed it unhealthy; every third claimed it to be physically hard. Only one in five employed women would continue full—time work if there was no economic need for it. (Narusk 1995a)

In other words, the compensation effect for some women becomes evident — because of their dissatisfaction in the spheres outside the home they search for greater gratification in family life.

3. A *woman can avoid or at least diminish identity problems*. Leaving the determination of their identity to others, as generally happens in conditions of traditional gender—socialization, seems to bring for some women. According to Marcia (1980 pp. 174—175), boys are more often encouraged to make decisions leading to conflicts either within the family or with other possible authorities; such conflicts mostly strenghten their identity. Quite the opposite occurs with girls, who are

spurred on to deal, develop and maintain good human relationships. Such conflicts may weaken their identity because the pressure put upon them to accommodate others is too hard. In addition, as Miller (1986) suggests,

> Women's sense of self becomes very much organized around being able to make and then to maintain affiliations and relationships. Eventually, for many women the threat of disruption of an affiliation is perceived not as a loss of relationship but as something closer to a total loss of self.

Concerning the positive effect of social approval on women's self—esteem, both types of social conditions favoring the production of social approval in the form of behavioural confirmation can be found nowadays in Estonia.

4. A *woman can enjoy maternal power* within the family. The fact that the maternal, compared with paternal, influence prevailed in Soviet families (Mozny 1985, Kohn et al. 1986, Narusk 1988, 1992) can be explained by women's high level of education (i.e., the average level of education of women is higher than that of men in Estonia) and their continuously broadening number of roles and responsibilities both inside and outside the home. Defining the exchange between men and women as Bimbi does, *the man benefits from an asymmetry in the division of household tasks, whereas the woman benefits from her greater authority in the performance of maternal duties*, we have to agree with her conclusion: *Women seem to want to maintain maternal supremacy within the family while at the same time moving towards equality* (Bimbi 1992 p. 12). Perceived maternal power and formal equality must be considered as factors partly influencing the fact (often striking for Western researchers) that only few women report direct experiences with discrimination at school or on the job and even fewer attribute the discrimination to their sex.

5. There is *perceived social approval* and an avoidance of the labels of *overemancipated* for women. Overemancipation is blamed for social problems such as divorce, men's drinking, juvenile delinquency, the decline in morality and so on. Although a great deal of these perceived rewards can be called into question, they can help us to understand why Estonian women give their support to those speakers

openly resisting *equal rights* movements. This is the case particularly because many costs of behavior stay invisible. There are two main reasons for the invisibility of costs of preserving traditional gender roles for Estonian women. They are first, that there is no economic possibility for most women to stay at home (and see the real concequences) and, second, that there are no reliable statistics and research evidence (as well as interest in it) reflecting the real costs of supporting traditional gender roles for women who are employed themselves.

Invisible costs of supporting the traditional gender roles for employed women

Invisible costs on a social level

According to the 1989 census, women in Estonia made up 53 percent of the total population, 54 percent of the working population, 57 percent of the working population with higher education, and 62 percent of the working population having secondary vocational education. The active participation of Estonian women in the sphere of paid work is accompanied by severe horizontal and vertical sex segregation of the Estonian labour market. The *perestroika* period removed the curtains from the inequality between men and women, also in decicions of social matters. After the fixed quotas were dropped, the participation of women in politics decreased to a minimum. Now there are, for example, 13 women among the 101 members of the Estonian Parliament (Riigikogu). The same situation has been observed in all East European countries.

Notwithstanding the relatively high average level of education of women in Estonia (higher than that of men on the average[5]), the average pay of women is considerably lower than that of men. An interesting fact is that, in the middle of the 1980s, Estonia reached a situation in which men with primary education received the highest average pay. At the same time the average pay of women was 58 percent of that of men among workers with (up to) an eighth grade education and, respectively 78 percent among workers with higher education.

121

Most women do not know and do not care about such segregation because they still believe in *official declarations* asserting complete equality between the genders. In 1993 over half of the employed women believed that men and women had equal possibilities to get on in life (44 percent believed that men's opportunities were better and 2 percent assumed that women's possibilities were better (Narusk 1995a). In the same vein, most Estonian women proclaimed that *we have had our equality already, and it was bad, so we do not want it any more* — as do women from the most popular organization of Estonian women (Estonian Women's Union) nowadays.

Invisible costs on an individual level

Women experience strains and overload. Compared with that of women from Western countries, Estonian working women's time off from their professional work is more involved with matters connected with their tasks as wives and mothers, and they do not have enough time for hobbies or any other kind of leisure (Narusk 1988). The huge losses of women's time are connected with the underdevelopment of public services and a scarcity of affordable food and consumer goods, including household machines, not to mention the quality of what exists.

Generally then, this situation leads to women being involved in more activities than they can deal with sufficiently (i.e., demands on energy and stamina exceed the individual's capacities). Women are faced with multiple, incompatible demands and situations in which they have to perform several tasks simultaneously and thus experience strain and conflict (Pearlin 1989).

Overburdening leadis to distress and dissatisfaction. Especially the relationships with the spouse and professional work seem to suffer. In general, a woman's marital happiness and satisfaction with her partner are positively connected with her husbands' active participation in housework (Kauppinen—Toropainen and Kandolin 1991; Haavio—Mannila 1992), and traditional, unfavorable attitudes of a spouse as well as a lack of spouse's support, are connected with high role conflict. A relatively small number of families with an egalitarian division of housework can be found among Estonian families when

122

compared with Western ones (Haavio—Mannila and Rannik 1985; Narusk 1995).

The children are also influenced. In conflict—ridden families, parents find less time to spend with their children, and the relationships between children and their parents are less warm and supportive (especially father—child relationships) (Narusk 1988, 1995).

Often the distress and dissatisfaction of women in trying to establish a balance between their family life and work leads to an *accommodation* (i.e., to limiting involvement in either sphere in order to meet the demands of the other, Lambert 1990). Or it leads to a loosening of strong commitment to both (according to the *Estonia 93* survey, almost every sixth working Estonian woman did not rate family or work as *very important* on a 5—point scale) (Narusk 1995a).

The exclusion of fathers from everyday life means losses for all family members — women, men and children. For women, the passive participation of men in family life means, as has already been mentioned, overload, distress and dissatisfaction with the relationship with the spouse (interrelated with the dissatisfaction with the other life domains). For men, it often means a loss in close relationships (especially with his wife and children) as well. The powerlessness of fathers in family life can be compared with that of women both in work and social life, including all negative consequences accompanying the latter. While women lack opportunities in work organizations, men lack opportunities in family life. Men also tend to (1) avoid responsibility and participation, (2) have less self—confidence, (3) look for satisfaction in activities outside of work, (4) be critical of power and management, and (5) be concerned with tangible rewards (Kvande and Rasmussen 1989). The actual results are often, as pointed out by Kalns—Timans (1992 p. 43), that *men currently seem at a loss for a role for themselves. Alcohol seems a way out for many and disrespect for women another.*

As for children, the lack of a close relationship to their fathers has a different, mostly negative impact. While few father—child shared activities (especially with daughters) take place in two—parent families, the father/child interaction disappears in post—divorce single—mother families. In Estonia, as elsewhere in former Soviet countries, a great share of fathers limit their *post—divorce role* to alimony payment, abandoning practical parenting. The costs of this situation are borne by all — both the family, and the society.

Conflicts between the perceived values and satisfaction in family—work arrangements.

The conflicts between women's perceived values and satisfaction in different life domains becomes evident when the data from *Estonia 85* and *Estonia 93* population surveys of family and work domains are compared (Narusk 1995a). A *socially approved* increase in the importance of family life and a decrease in the importance of professional work (experienced by both women and men) have been accompanied, not by a decrease but, by an increase of work satisfaction.

According to the *Estonia 93* survey (Narusk 1995a), for example, 72 percent of employed Estonian women completely or mostly (on a 5—point scale) agreed with the statement — *I am generally very satisfied with my work.* Moreover, 58 percent agreed with *At the end of workday I have often the feeling of having done something really useful,* and 88 percent *My selfconfidence rises if I manage well at work.* At the same time, only 60 percent of the women were completely or mostly satisfied with their family—life; 53 percent of the married or cohabitating women were completely or mostly satisfied with their emotional relationship with their husband, and 60 percent felt the same about their intimate relationship with their husband.

In this case — when the life domain of lower value gives a higher satisfaction than that of higher value (i.e., when the satisfaction from work for employed women is higher than, for example, that from the relationship with their partner), the evidence indicates considerable conflicts between values and real life. But, to underline once more, these conflicts and their consequences remain invisible, and invisible rewards and disadvantages cannot be weighed.

Conclusions

Estonian women are not only victims of, but also real supporters of, traditional gender socialization. Their actual choices are made under certain social constraints limiting the individual resources they need for choosing alternative behavior. Status and money, time and energy, information available to them, as well as their health and self—esteem have to be considered as the main components of an interrelated system of their individual resources.

Depending on social constraints, determined by the level of economic and political development of society, the expected rewards occur in a rather different form. Many rewards often remain unattainable for an individual by any other means than through another person's activities. These activities of another person can be triggered when an individual expects the result of another person's behavior to be beneficial for him or herself. Therefore, even the most altruistic act can sometimes take place because of the hope of some material or non—material reward. It seems unreasonable to speak about *rational* choice only when economic rewards are weighed. Similarly, it seems inappropriate to speak about instrumental rationality versus care rationality or *rational* versus *normative* choice. In contrast, it seems reasonable to speak about rational choice when the alternative with the highest expected rewards is chosen regardless of the form (economic psychological well—being) of the rewards. For the individual, the form of expected rewards depends on both social constraints and his or her personal characteristics. The better economic conditions and the more democracy we find in society, the more influential the personal characteristics become.

In a situation of economic difficulties, as well as in status—scarce situations, the compensatory function and positive effect of behavioral confirmation become especially evident (Wippler 1990). The feeling of having done *the right thing* in the eyes of relevant others becomes the most important reward. This can be considered as the rational choice of the behavioral alternative that allows mental well—being if economic well—being is lacking. In turn, multiple (and different) behavioral strategies can be estimated as rational in societies with high economic welfare.

Behavioral choices depend directly on the *visibility* of rewards or costs concurrent with the choice of alternative behavior. *Invisible* ones cannot be taken into account or they can be over (or under) estimated. For the individual, the *visibility* of consequences, in turn, is conditioned by the authenticity of reflection of the social environment on public opinion and mass media.

While persons and societies differ, and the gender system is always intimately interconnected with political and economic factors in each society, an increasing amount of different cultural sensibilities exists in the world. One can hardly expect to find a singular ideal of truth or goodness. Therefore choices that are rational for Estonian women today can be rated as unrational for women in other countries. One *rational for all* alternative can hardly be found.

Notes:

1   I do not expect all Estonian women to have similar opinions. I am well aware of the different groups of women, as well as the different attitudes and behavioural strategies among Estonian women. I only deal with the main one that is most visible as a first response to the breakdown of the totalitarian Soviet system from 1990 onward. Therefore, I try to answer to the question, *Why did public opinion and the new political mainstream in the beginning of the 1990s give preference to the most conservative of the several existing women's movements?* Women were advocated to go back home after they had done their duties during the *silent* revolution that brought independence to Estonia. I try to determine why most of the women remained silent when the voice of the rest was *amplified* through mass media. This voice claimed that real women are mothers who *act like housewives even if employed.* It certainly did not happen because no women acknowledged gender equality as important and searched for the means to improve the real situation of Estonian women. They were there — scientists, teachers, physicians, etc. — and their thoughts were fixed in the program *Women in Estonia Today and Tomorrow.* But, in spite of the fact that this program was accepted by almost 1,000 participants of the congress of Estonian women in 1989, it did not gain popularity.

2   *Estonia 93* and *Estonia 85* are population surveys from 1993 and 1985, respectively, of national samples; they were conducted by a group of sociologists from the Estonian Academy of Sciences (Narusk 1995a).

3   The data from the *Estonia 93* survey showed that, although 72 percent of the population in Estonia lives in urban areas, only 40 percent of Estonians perceived themselves as *principally urban* or *more urban than rural*. Thirteen percent had difficulties to define themselves, and the rest (47 percent) perceived themselves as *more rural than urban* or as *principally rural*.

4   According to the 1989 census, the percentage of women among the workers was 87 in commerce and catering, 82 in medicine and social services, 79 in education, 76 in culture, 72 in postal services and communication, and only 20 in construction. The proportion of female top managers in the national economy of Estonia in 1989 was about 3 percent.

5   According to the 1989 census, 16 percent of the employed women had a higher education and 27 percent had a secondary vocational one; the respective figures for the men were 14 and 22.

6   For example, in the survey of 921 employed women in 1990 in Estonia (carried out by the National Statistics Office, unpublished manuscript), the women were asked to point out three of the most important sources of satisfaction for them. First among these was *dealing with the children*, and *leisure at home* (both were mentioned among the three by 53 percent of women). Before the *relationship with one's own husband* (17 percent) came *friends* (27 percent), *hobbies* (21 percent), and even *work in the garden* (21 percent).

8 Changes in social structure: Change in the self

Cynthia Fuchs-Epstein

What does it mean to have a self? To what extent is the self lodged in an identity as a woman or a man? Does the self change or is it fixed in its fundamentals? How do social roles as mothers and fathers, citizens and workers affect people's sense of themselves?

Different theories inform us; they can be found in everyday discourse, in popular culture, and in the social and physical sciences. But whether based on scientific inquiry, on philosophical or ideological logic, on theology or on folk wisdom, there is no consensus on this issue. Today, no less than before, researchers disagree on how people derive identity, what it is composed of, how lasting it is, and to what extent it is anchored in the physiological characteristics that determine sex or in the socially created categories of gender.

Some analysts assume that deep—seated differences between the sexes make for male and female selves that have fairly consistent regularities. The school of Cultural Feminism, for example, offers the view that women's selves may be characterized in particular ways — as having an orientation distinct from men with regard to moral issues, for example. This perspective, with roots in psychoanalytic theory, proposes that women and men possess highly differentiated and persistent identities — selves — that arise through their early experiences in the family.[1] Other analysts characterize the self as a product of the uniqueness of every individual, stemming from the person's distinctive background and history. And there are views that the self is rather more interactive, affected by personal background, but responsive and changeable with alteration in social experience and social environment. Even then there is disagreement. Some analysts

128

think it takes involvement in major upheavals such as war to effect change, and some think the self can change because of less dramatic events — marriage or other life passages, relocation (Hormuth 1990), change in job or the content of the work.[2]

This chapter explores the impact of social factors on the construction of the self. I suggest that there are social mechanisms that contribute to — and enforce — conceptions of the self, that produce gender—related identities, and that contribute to a person's sense of an empowered (or disempowered) self. Drawing on the self—reported accounts of persons who have undergone changes in their work and family lives and thus experienced a change in their self—concept or avoided change in a situation because of concern that they would change, I support the models that pose the self as not necessarily unitary, as complex (in that multiple selves combine in an individual's *self*) and amenable to change. Therefore evidence is offered that undermines the theory that the self is set early and that gendered identity established in the early years will necessarily determine how the adult self is determined. The data are drawn from a study by Epstein and Kai Erikson in the mid—1980s of organizational and technological change and its meaning to several hundred male and female employees of the American Telephone and Telegraph Company (AT&T) and several Bell system telephone companies, from my research on female attorneys over the past decade and on their current advancement in large firms, and from Reed's current study of women entrepreneurs who have founded their own small businesses.

In a sense, the studies report on natural field experiments in which women and men have experienced the impact of change brought about by their own choice, or by the decisions of others, or have been prevented from experiencing change because of their own concerns, or the pressures of salient others. Although I focus on the microinteractions of particular people in family and work situations, I also note the impact of macro processes such as the division of labor by sex in the workplace and the family and its accompanying cultural legitimation (gender ideology, for example) as affecting the possibility of change in people's selves.

This work is in the tradition of William James [1890] (1983), George Herbert Mead (1934), and more recently Kay Deaux (1992), S. Rosenberg (1988), Faye Crosby (1987) and others who see change as a lifelong process and who suggest that people may have multiple selves or selves composed of multiple components or selves that become activated through interaction with *significant others*. As Mead noted, *We divide ourselves up in all sorts of different selves with reference to our acquaintances . . . a multiple personality is in a certain sense normal* (p. 142).[3] The notion of multiple selves recognizes that the various selves possessed by a person are not necessarily homogeneous, that the self may change through both large and small alterations in its social environments, and that there may be differential focus on one self or the other at different periods in one's life, or even in the day. For example, Deaux (1992) has shown that salient selves (Stryker 1987), linked to particular statuses such as ethnicity, may change in different social contexts. She also shows that critical life events can alter the hierarchy one assigns various identities (such as gender or marital status), to make them more or less central at different times.

I realize that it is difficult to assess change by asking people to identify it in their lives. Some of the people interviewed in this study view their selves as complex and changeable, but, paradoxically, others who find themselves changing or handling many roles do not recognize the process. Of course, some people do not change very much, and their selves reflect that fact, perhaps by remaining less complex.

But aside from the individual accounts that I report, I note how Melvin Kohn and Carmi Schooler (1973) have documented how job characteristics affect the personality in large samples of workers in the United States, Europe and Japan, for example, how complex work tends to develop a person's intellectual flexibility, and how dull, repetitive work reinforces more rigid personality traits. My own research (1981 and 1993) has shown that as discriminatory practices against female lawyers in the United States were curtailed over the past two decades, those who assumed demanding and responsible work as attorneys developed new self—images as they achieved competence in business and courtroom settings, resulting in *new selves*. Rose Laub Coser, too, has proposed in her book *In Defense of Modernity* (1991) that, as people take on multiple roles in urban life, they develop intellectually and exhibit identifiable changes. We do not know too much about the circumstances under which new roles are translated into new selves, but we do know that people experience these transformations at a level that transcends mere conformity to normative prescriptions attached to roles. In fact, people may be quite self—conscious about the difference between their roles and selves; some, for example, experience a mismatch between the roles they play and their sense of self, and this mismatch may cause them to take on or discard roles that they regard as disharmonious, while others may easily assume the self that playing a role may entail (if even for a limited time).

If people do develop multiple selves, what consequences develop from the interplay between varying facets of their persons? The selves one has may or may not be in harmony, the roles and statuses one has may or may not be integrated or complementary, and there may or may not be complementarity between the roles and the *selves* that develop. Both Robert K. Merton (1957) and William J. Goode (1960) have addressed the problems associated with the strains that can occur when the various statuses and roles one acquires are at odds with one another and the structural mechanisms that are available to resolve strain. The conflicts women face as a result of contradictory demands of the norms governing work roles and family roles have been specified and examined a great deal in scholarly writing and in public discourse in the past 25 years (although men's problems in this regard have received scant attention). Individuals and institutions respond to these presumed tensions quite differently. For example, many people find gratification in being able to express very different selves in the course of a day or in the course of their lives (Thoits 1986; Epstein 1987), for example, managing to be tough at work but tender at home, or even both tough and tender both at work and in the home. However, cultural themes stressing unity of self often make people uncomfortable with the idea of multiple selves, especially when they appear to be inconsistent or in conflict.

Ideological and political commitments often determine whether multiple roles, especially diverse roles (and particularly those seen as inconsistent), are approved or not and whether particular persons may assume them (Epstein 1970). Such views have made it difficult for women to take jobs that are higher in rank than their husbands, for example. Formal opportunity structures (Merton [1948] 1968) may change because of legislation banning discrimination or economic pressures, but popular views about the appropriateness of specific opportunities for persons of certain backgrounds may set limits on their ability to take advantage of them.[4]

I explore how people enter into the process of changing themselves or limiting changes in themselves because of structural opportunities or constraints and because of cultural views about who they may become. Cultural change occurs with structural change, such as economic fluctuation. There is interaction between the processes that has an impact on the social psychological perceptions of possibilities for the self.

Cultural modes include folk wisdom and popularizations of models from the social sciences and humanities. Such concepts as *masculinity* and *femininity* and *socialization* affect people's notions of what Hazel Markus and Paula Nurius (1986) call *possible selves*, the views people hold about what is possible or impossible for them to be. Social psychologists have theorized that people contemplate *possible selves* and define imaginary selves as motivational resources; they can make decisions about what to do and what not to do based on images of what their *new* identity might mean. Statuses such as sex, age, ethnicity or occupation determine possible selves according to the rules set by the culture.

Certainly ideas (as well as more formalized rules) about what is appropriate for a man or woman to be limit and edit the development of different selves. This activity may differ across cultures, however, according to how a particular society defines gender roles. Haavio—Mannila's (1986) cross—national research reveals how sex—role definitions contribute to anxiety. She found, for example, that working women in Denmark, Finland and Norway score high in rates of anxiety, but that in Sweden, home—staying women are more anxious than working wives. She explains these differences by the amount of social support working women receive in Sweden contrasted with the other two Scandinavian countries. Social definitions make the women feel they are doing the right or wrong thing by choosing certain roles, and social approval or disapproval is usually infused in the internal discussions one has with oneself. I have noted elsewhere (1988) how researchers have neglected the coercive elements that are at work in limiting the choices people have in their selection of selves. Conformity to culturally acceptable models is demanded by gatekeepers — salient others, such as families and employers. The demand is backed by moral claims and by social controls. For example, women are supposed to be altruistic; thus women who are self—seeking and work—driven in their occupational lives are defined as conforming to a *male model* or as not being true to who they *really are*. Men may in fact be nurturant, but, when they act on such tendencies, they may face disapproval that comes from not acting like *real men*.

Thus, people whose selves do not conform to social expectations or prescriptions, or whose personalities seem inconsistent, disorderly or heterogeneous, face disapproval from others and from within themselves. Such people are often regarded as psychologically impaired, or hypocritical. Some people label themselves in accordance with acceptable norms in spite of behavior not consistent with the label.

Of course, people differ with regard to their vulnerability to constraints on change. There are, after all, highly gifted adapters who are able to change themselves and create new selves, and there are leaden social actors who cling (or are forced to cling) to identities that are set early.

In the next section I use from the studies of telephone company workers, lawyers and entrepreneurs to illustrate some of the ways in which people change or fail to change in the context of their work lives, how notions that they can or cannot change act as constraints, and how changes in social position open them to new selves.

How jobs change people

Some people are aware of how changes in their work lives have changed them, and they are reminded by others that they have changed.

Among a sample of small business owners it was common for women to acknowledge changes in themselves that they regarded as positive. Most referred to some kind of *take charge* elements in their *new selves*, such as *more authoritarian, more positive, bossier, a lot bossier, a sense of power*, and *confidence*.

These responses were similar to those of female attorneys employed in large firms in New York City. Like the small business owners they referred to becoming *less emotional, more analytical, and more in control,*

133

as one young lawyer put it. She further noted that these qualities spilled over to her private life so that at home what seemed like work—generated attributes — such as unemotional analytical thinking — became the way she thought through problems in her relationship with her husband and that the emotional distance made her less nurturant. In her words:

> As I went further in my legal career I became a lot more analytical. I analyzed the family problems as I would a legal problem and I really didn't want to have a lot of . . . complexities in my home life.

Telephone company workers also experienced a change in self with a change in job. Dick, an operator observed:

> You learn to talk to people; . . . I enjoy talking to people. It's opened me up.

And Hank, who took on the job of splicer, regarded as highly *macho*, noted how the job created distinct personality types:

> It makes [us] . . . confident people. People that know their direction; [who] have particular goals in what they want to do . . . they give you a job in the morning and they say, o.k., go do it and when you finish they call for another one. So these people that are into that, they [gain] . . . a lot of self— confidence.

Yet the strong identity splicers develop is linked to what they do, and their sense of collectivity makes it difficult for them to acknowledge change. And, following theories of the self in popular culture, they see themselves as unchanging. George, a former splicer, who has been a foreman for many years (which means he is precluded by union rules from engaging in hands—on work) laments the change in status because the former job defined his identity. As he insisted, *In my heart I'm a splicer, that's who I am.*

But people do get promoted, and there are many first line supervisors who are pleased to move up the ladder. I found this particularly dramatic with women. Joan, who was an installer, a non—traditional job for a woman, felt she changed for the better when she was made a foreman (the term she used). She became more outgoing and added:

> I'm not afraid of men anymore... I realize they are no different... they're human... I can talk to them in the same way.

Some workers accept a notion of change that comes about not from any specific job but from the simple fact of becoming a worker. Epstein encountered many craft workers who reflected on who they were as young men — often they characterized themselves as wild and undirected. The mere fact of having a steady job had altered them. As one put it:

> Working has changed me, and having different friends has changed me.
> ...I was a bit of a hell—raiser when I was young but now I have a wife and a mortgage.

Or a woman who sees change in herself because she is a worker, different from her friends who are housewives:

> I would say I'm more mature now ... I think I've changed a lot. I feel I can do better for myself now and for my son ... I don't have the same friends I had when I grew up ... it's different when you have friends that don't work and friends that work. The friends that work can understand you better, you communicate better with them ... The ones that don't work, they don't know the working world, so you really can't communicate with them about going to work, getting up in the morning and coming home, having to cook dinner and up again the next morning, when they could be home all day looking at soap operas when you're out working. I think I have matured more now that I'm working.

Amy thought that becoming an operator for the phone company changed her:

> It gave me more confidence in myself as a person. Because before I would work . . . at all sorts of odd jobs . . . two or three jobs at a time. I felt good I was working. But, you know, just to say *I'm a cook at a diner* or *I'm a health aide* or something —it wasn't going anywhere. Now I feel that I'm in a company where I can go somewhere.

Reed found that women entrepreneurs often experienced a high degree of identification with their businesses. For example, a cleaning franchise owner noted how personally disturbed she was when an employee acted in a way that violated *the way you want your company to be represented,* a feeling very different from just working for *corporate America.* As an owner, she reported, *it really kills you . . . because your identity gets all wrapped up in what you're doing.*

There was recognition that age interacted with work roles in the experience of a changing self. This may be because prescriptions around gender norms become less restrictive after courtship, marriage and early child—bearing periods have ended. When asked about the decision to go into business for herself, a woman in the export business spoke of her decision *to take control of my own finances and my own future . . .*

> I don't think it was just the business, it was also the age. I was probably in my early 30s and I think at that time most women change anyway; you become more secure or confident. The more you do the more you know, the more aggressive you can be . . . a combination of . . . having the responsibility of making a business work and also maturing.

Restrictions on change

Gender ideology

I have explored (1989, 1992[5]) how gender ideology causes women and men to sanction themselves and others when they contemplate nontraditional work or when they are recruited to these jobs within a company. Of course, whether self—inflicted or imposed on others, such sanctions structure choices so that sex segregation is reinforced. In this report I only briefly consider this point, although gender identity is an important component of self and work assignments universally are related to sex role assignments. I begin with the interactive relationship between cultural norms and telephone company workers' ability to contemplate taking certain jobs.

The *maleness* of a job has an impact on both the women who avoid taking on such work or who are made to feel they somehow violate themselves when they do, and men who have a stake in preserving the definition since it roots their identity. Similarly, the *femaleness* attributed to a job causes discomfort to men who choose such work. The following examples illustrate these mechanisms at work:

Sandra, a member of a suburban repair group in New York, commented on why she would not take a job in construction:

> Because I don't believe a woman is equal to a man doing that. I don't see myself going into a manhole . . . I don't see myself. I don't see that.

Female workers who worked as frame attendants, a job just recently opened to women, reported how friends made them feel self—conscious and *wrong* for taking a job not considered traditional for their sex:

> I've noticed with a few friends, either from school or boyfriends, men, they say *yes, you wear a tool pouch, you lift wire bags and stuff,* and they look at you like you're not a girl anymore, like you're super tough . . .
>
> . . .basically they think I'm not feminine anymore if I'm cutting my hands . . . getting dirty and carrying tools and so on; its a man's job and what . . . you want to be like a man?

Some women worked to retain their female identity while doing a *man's job*. As one said:

> I don't think I could run around slapping boys on the back and trying to be like a man. I'm not trying to be like a man. I'm being myself, doing a job which I feel I can do.

Fear of not being attractive to men in their age group is a powerful inducement for many women to conform to conventional gender roles, to keep their *feminine* selves.

Roy, a man who seized the opportunity for employment in the telephone company by becoming a service representative, a job traditionally occupied by women but open to men as part of an Affirmative Action plan, had difficulty finding ways to shore up his masculinity and found his work identity a threat. As he recounted:

> I think being in this job has done more harm than good in that respect (his sense of self) . . . I don't like the job, . . .I don't like it . . . [customers and outsiders . . .] they'd tell me its a girl's job.

Similarly situated, Andy, found the job of service representative in an office too threatening to his male identity, because he assumed that the other male reps were gay, working in a *woman's job*. He sought a transfer back to a lower level *male* job, because, he said, [the] mode [on the job] was . . . feminine. A product of working—class culture, Andy associated masculine identity with hard hats. The social environment and ethos of an office made him uncomfortable even to the point of refusing a promotion because a *desk job* implied working in a less *masculine* environment.

But some people have given up opportunities because of peer pressure not to change and move beyond others in the group or the pressures on them by family members not to change. This process is clear to many women whose husbands find it difficult when wives demonstrate qualities that run counter to traditional gender roles. A lawyer reported that her husband, also an attorney, appreciated her toughness on the job, but, as she described, at home he needed more of the nurturing, *let me take care of you* sort of motherly type.

Marlene, a first level supervisor, found stereotypes about appropriate women's traits in the disapproval of her friends who perceived changes in her personality after a promotion:

I had a friend ... a guy who I was dating who said to me, *I don't work for you ... you act like you're at work* because I was taking the initiative.

Peer pressures to conform

Restrictions on change that are exercised by *significant others* are not necessarily focused on gender issues. Two people, a woman and a man, in a southern city telephone company office described peer pressure to remain at the same status level as the rest of the group:

> I'm sure I was like a lot of other people when I started with the company, being an ambitious person ... I wanted to go far with the company ... trying to work as hard as I could to do a good job, [but] the people who had been around a while [worked on me giving me the message] ... it was like *all right kids, slow down, you're making the rest of us look bad*. My aspirations have been bashed. I've come to accept it.

And George, who described pressures on him from his co—workers to be *one of the boys* and not assert the authority required of him in his role as an acting supervisor:

> ... They would always break chops, they would break your shoes. they'd say, *heh, what are you doin, c'mon, what's the act all about, you know, you're acting.*

Not peer pressure at work, but the subtle pressure of his ethnic group made Larry, a switching technician, cut off his education at high school; his identity was bound up in the model set by his parents. As he described it:

> If I had to say I had one regret, it would be not having the motivation towards a degree at the time ... But coming from parents of Italian ethnic background ... you go to work after you get out of high school and you get a job and you make a living, and you buy a house and you have three kids ... that's it.

But marriage to a woman with high aspirations made him reflect on this identity:

> I married a woman whose family is totally all upwardly mobile professionals. Which is unusual for the Italian background, doctors, lawyers . . . They provided some good role models for her and me now . . . my wife has been tremendously influential. I make no bones about that, her influence on me has definitely motivated me . . . this feeling of wanting to succeed or change my thoughts of what success is . . . to that extent I've become [a] bad guy with my family now because I've changed my ideas on not being like what my family says is successful . . .

He has tried to change and become a new self, but he has not yet overcome his ambivalence about who he is or who he should strive to be.

Weighing changes in the self

The changes in the self resulting from a new job, one that carries a change in rank, is of particular significance to a person and the community from which the person comes. Promotion is a vehicle into a new status with its attendant norms prescribing new behavior and often companion emotions and personality traits. People possess information about the expectations that accompany a new position and can assess whether it will involve changes in the self that match or conflict with the person's view of who they are, or with the expectations of significant others in their families and communities.

Taking a new position in a company may reinforce or change a person's self—definition. The new position may reinforce or conflict with other *selves* an individual has known, or it may alter the configuration of role identities which support a coherent self—concept. Amy, an operator, speculated on promotion:

> It's something I could do . . . I know this girl who came after I did and she's training for supervisor now. I know I have the

brains to do it. I'm not sure I'd like it once I got into it though, because being a supervisor . . . changes your personality.

Promotion to a supervisory position entails new pressures and leaving behind the camaraderie and security of the work group. Workers weigh their experience when they consider limited choices for promotion. Many workers are aware of the pressures on their supervisors. A switching technician described why he does not want to become a foreman:

> I had considered it, but it's just too much pressure from the top. I'd rather be where I am than where they are because I can go home at night and that's it; I'm finished but they're not. They can get called up and such like that. They have to take the pressure from their bosses more than we have to take the pressure from them. They see what's happening, they don't look only at numbers . . . So the foreman is basically like on the frontline and he's catching it from both ends.

Ramona, an order reviewer, told why she rejected the opportunity to become a supervisor:

> I don't like the person you have to be when you're over people. Your personality has to change and I can't deal with forgetting where I come from and a lot of them . . . their attitudes change. They're very evil and you have to chop down people that you care about. To me, I said that's not worth it . . .

One person knew she would change as a supervisor and got her husband's agreement that it would be all right for her to change. as Effie, a first level supervisor, put it:

> I didn't take the supervisor's position until I got his agreement on it because I knew some days I would come in very upset and I know I'm not the type of person that's just going to change on my way home and be mellow and sweet when I had a rough day at the office, so he was one of my main reasons for taking this position.

Fellow workers observe changes in people who are promoted from their ranks to a supervisory level and some tend to deride the changes:

> Once they become a supervisor they're like a machine.

> With the exception of one or two of them their whole personality changes. One of them is now filing for a divorce. I think that because she got the management job it affected her home life.

Yet Steven, who was promoted to a level one manager, became a new person to his wife. Conforming to a conventional script specifying that a husband take responsibility and become a leader at work and in the home elicited a positive, reinforcing response from her as he reported:

> She said, [now] I feel comfortable with you. I know ... if a problem comes up I feel comfortable and confident that you'll have the solution ... she said, *I have no fear now.*

Other people can acknowledge and support particular choices and behaviors, or they can actively or passively undermine them, thus exerting control over group boundaries and individual behaviour Although this personal growth *feels good*, Ramona, the order reviewer, had to balance her behavior with the expectations of others around her, being *diplomatic* about fitting into the expectations of other workers. She pragmatically accepted the limits or social boundaries that control her behavior in the workplace. While social roles are part of an interpersonally negotiated order, the ability of an individual to change the self depends on the encouragement and tolerance of those around her. Perhaps over time the social boundaries which control self—initiative will lead the person to a diminished sense of self and its potential worth, or the individual may rebel against her status and seek better opportunities for personal growth.

Effie, the woman whose husband agreed to support change that would come from her promotion to first level craft supervisor, described how customary family roles and identities conflicted with her new presentation of self:

> One of my sisters used to complain to me, when you have family gatherings and you're holding a certain type of business discussions or whatever, they used to tell me I was very domineering. In other words, they thought I was really thinking I was talking to my people that work for me and even my husband called me down. He said, *wait a minute, you're talking to your husband*. I really catch myself in that authoritative position . . . I try to watch it because for me its kind of embarrassing.

The active interpretation of these identities, sister, wife, are continuously reinforced by her family. They did not wish her to take on a new self. Through interaction the family members attempted to control and modify the individual's behavior.

Some people find their *new selves* violate a concept of who *they are*. Herbie, a frame attendant tried making the transition to supervisor/management when co—workers encouraged him to do so, but he didn't like it.

> . . . I didn't particularly like it . . . I missed my tools, . . . and I didn't like sitting in an office, I didn't like telling people what to do and it just wasn't for me.

Herbie had trouble *acting* as management, and went back to being an attendant. Herbie saw himself as composed of several selves:

> Only parts of me [would go back to managing] . . . only a bruised ego or . . . a part of me that feels it could do a better job or that I know of some problems here... and that part of me, but when all of me would come together for a decision, no, no I wouldn't. (What would that part say?) You won't be too happy; you again will have to tell people what to do; you may have a lot of paperwork which I can't stand.

It is by now a well supported finding that workers who become supervisors have serious problems establishing an identity consonant with their new posts. The first level supervisor has to negotiate between two different *selves* supported by two different sets of role behaviors tied to two different social contexts of status. The self that is rooted in the working—class status manifests itself in a set of attitudes at odds with those of the manager who must demonstrate authority and assertiveness. The person often feels he is neither the worker he was nor a manager. I use the pronoun *he* here because I believe men suffer more than women from this change in role, although there are cases that show that women too have their problems. But women do not have to jump from a *macho*, hands on, sports—oriented ethos to a white—collar ethos, although they face stresses changing from a deferential, subordination ethos to one of authority and command. For example, the statuses of the workplace supervisor and the status of the deferential wife and cooperative sister clash. Both the customary deference and the progressive assertion of a new authority are tied to the cultural definitions of place and status.

But people do get promoted and there are many first—line supervisors who are pleased to move up the ladder. Joan, who was an installer, a non—traditional job for a woman felt she changed for the better when she was made a foreman (the term she used). She became more outgoing and added:

> I'm not afraid of men anymore... I realize they are no different... they're human... I can talk to them in the same way.

Multiple selves

People have long assumed that women's home roles have been their primary source of identity and that men find primary identity in their work roles. This assumption reinforces a dichotomous pattern of identity priorities according to gender norms. However, I found, as did Kay Deaux (1992) in her work on Hispanic Americans and other groups, that people's self—identity priorities varied. Some persons weigh their options and experience when assigning priority to one self or another, and do not rely on norms linked to gender ideology.[6] The assumptions that women focus on their traditional identities outside of work — as mother, wife, or family member — while men focus their primary identity on who they are in their job, and only after that on their family, are part of larger social patterns controlling men's and women's behavior. Epstein and Erikson in their study of communications workers, found the decision to emphasize roles and identities in different contexts depended on a person's perceptions of possibilities for recognition, status and value. Men were as likely as women to respond to limitations in the workplace by emphasizing and enhancing their roles and statuses outside work in the community, or among friends and family. As has been observed, no one talks about a glass ceiling for working—class men and women because it is assumed that their mobility and opportunities are limited. Concepts of multiple selves or clusters of identities help in understanding certain paradoxes. The theory of alienation is one example. A perplexing question for sociologists studying work is why some people accept boring and routine work conditions without feeling alienated. As will be seen, some persons may feel a sense of detatchment in one aspect of their lives but feel very much connected in another; they may dislike the work they do but enjoy the companionship of their co—workers. My study of attorneys revealed that women with families could often deal with frustrations of career because work only constituted one part of their life and that the satisfactions of family life diverted them from feeling too intensely about work problems,[7] a not uncommon condition for many female workers.

Wilma, a telephone worker, showed another aspect of the alienation—satisfaction equation by noting that monotony of work may be balanced by the job's significance to one's self in the outside world:[8]

> [Being an operator is difficult] I am not thrilled with my job . . . [but] I'm proud of the fact that I've gotten to this point in my life [working for such a good company] especially [considering] where I came from — my mother raising four kids alone and never really going anywhere.

Men also negotiated the interplay between selves. In the following examples we see how personal limitations or limitations in the structure of opportunity affected telephone workers' sense of self and how multiple sources of identity may be salutary to an individual in the process of maintaining a positive self—image.

One installer/repairman named Bill was considered to be a mediocre worker by his supervisor, because he was not committed to doing a good job, just an adequate one. Bill looked for satisfaction and recognition outside of the workplace:

> I enjoy my couple of beers after work, playing darts with the guys and stuff like that. My work is my work. [In order to] go on vacation, I've got to keep this job.

Bill's work did not provide him with a primary identity; his *real* self came to life after work and on vacation. He was not unlike Dick, an unmarried maintenance administrator who chose to focus on his identification as a volunteer fireman, an important identity for many blue—collar craftsmen we interviewed for this study. As he said:

> It gives you a place to go and it's like a whole other family . . . the only people I hang out with are the people in the firehouse . . .

For many working—class men the sporting activity in their communities (after work) was the focus of friendship and kin and determined who they were; sports were not simply leisure time activities, they were core activities. Many men also value their life in the family; fatherhood, marriage, and the contentment of good relationships were primary themes of self—definition for many.

People don't ordinarily think of having *multiple selves*, but they tend to observe their own behavior in different spheres of their lives and to recognize how in or out of character these may be. We saw this earlier when we looked at how people assign priorities to their different selves. Here we see how they identify their separate selves:

Joyce, an operator, described her change from work to home:

> [on the job, I] really have patience . . . you really try when you're in there . . . [but] you're different with your family.

or Jean:

146

> On the job I'm as sweet as can be ... but outside of this job, if anyone says something to me that I don't like ... I let them know ... I'm much more assertive ... I do not take crap from anybody ... Somebody's rude to me, they find out very quickly.

Workers who were active in their unions and served as stewards or in a higher union office also found gratification in the two workplace roles. They did not find it discordant to have a subordinate rank as a craftsperson, for example, and to hold a post as an official in their union. In fact, many union officials were tapped as management material by the company but frequently refused promotions that would cost them their union posts because they felt that holding the roles of worker and union official gave them more freedom.

Organizational and technological change and changing self images

The development of skill is a continuous social process, linked both to the social and technical spheres. Earlier we saw the ways in which people noted changes in themselves as they developed social skills. Developing technological skills change people, and working at jobs that become de—skilled also changes people's sense of self.

People often tie social recognition of the self and the valuing of their workplace identity to the quality of their work performance and to the job itself. Technological or organizational changes imposed by the company can disrupt worker roles and identities and produce anxiety and dissatisfaction. An installer/repairman described changes in his work that affect his satisfaction and identity:

> ... They're watching production. Where years ago it was quality. I think there are a lot of guys who couldn't do a quality job... but that's the way I was trained ... (The phone company is changing?) Get in and get out ... get the phone working and get out ... (And then?) ... if you have a nice customer, ... I'll talk with them and rap with them ... that's part of being a telephone man, I feel ... the company doesn't want that.

147

The technical content of this job did not change, but the social content of the job was forcibly altered by changes in work rules. It was the social content of the job that defined *being a telephone man*. The result was anxiety and dissatisfaction.

A frame administrator does not like the new computerized system, in part because he was not recognized as an individual in his old role as a tester. The decisions were no longer his alone to make, and the computer operator who handled many calls could not spend time talking to every single line tester:

> I find it very frustrating, like you're not even a person there because you're waiting and they're talking to other people ... Whereas with the old test and the old ways of testing without waiting for all this equipment and computers, you just tested it ... [the tester] got it done and knew what he was doing and that was the end of it ...

But technology has the potential for establishing new roles and can also offer opportunity to people — often younger workers and women — who are not wed to old images of what a particular job entails or who should be working at it.

A switching technician explained that her opportunity to work in the Switch Control Center came about because men who had outside jobs couldn't see themselves working in an office environment:

> When they decided to have a control center, they asked the senior man would he want to go ... Naturally, none of the men [who] were out in the field wanted to ... they wouldn't want to be in an office environment. So they all turned it down, so it got down to the junior person ... They like being out there. It's kind of confining when you're confined to a desk. If you're out there trouble shooting, you're walking around and you're using your own knowledge that you've accumulated ... you're kind of tied down here.

In this case, a junior woman employee ended up with a job that was first offered to senior men. Even though technological changes made outside jobs more vulnerable because fewer workers were required, the senior men were less flexible because they were culturally invested in old work forms that supported their identities as masculine, autonomous, skilled workers, trusted to get the physical job done outside the confines of an office.

Younger workers probably have an easier transition to new work forms caused by technological change, and age, more than gender, may determine the perception of new opportunities.

Thus, studies that focus only on the structurally generated interests of groups of workers, who are divided by class, skill or gender, overlook the dimensions of human interaction and the revision of cultural meaning as they intersect with structural conditions and changing patterns of social control.[9] Technological changes profoundly alter the old craft culture and the conditions of production workers and thus have impact on social identities, self—image, and the perception of collective interests tied to particular jobs. The culture of the workplace is a communicative, interactive process that is sensitive to structural reorganization.

Conclusion

I have given an overview of the kinds of social factors, cultural perspectives and technology that contribute to change, or impose limits on change on the *selves* of women and men. I identified the ways in which people develop complexity in their selves (multiple selves) from new roles — especially work roles and the forces that curtail their acquisition. Gender ideology and gender norms attached to work and family roles enable or constrict people's choices and opportunities to change their lives. Thus women and men experience pressures — both anonymously, as expressed in the culture, and through the voices and sanctions of intimate and casual companions and management — that prevent them from expanding or permit personal growth. Evidence from the studies reported show how stereotypes about women's and men's work diminish options as they make women and men uncomfortable when they transgress gender role boundaries. In addition I have shown how gender definitions affixed to certain jobs are not only internalized but provide rewards which make women and men so invested in them that it is difficult for the *wrong* gendered person to move into them.

I have also pointed to a process in which structural changes create changes in identity. There are many positive effects of taking on new tasks, most dramatically for the women whose moves into professional, supervisory and entrepreneurial status create changes in their self—concepts. This work also suggests that social policies which break down stereotypes and remove boundaries imposed by tradition or the self—interest of particular groups can be instrumental in helping women and men to lead more productive and meaningful lives.

Notes:

1   For women, it envisages a cluster of traits encompassing a focus on relationships, caring, and nurturance; for men, it is a cluster of qualities that might be conceptualized as abstracted and individuated (Chodorow 1978; Gilligan 1982). Cultural feminism has roots in common stereotypes about men and women which relate men's and women's prescribed activities to their presumed characters. In other words, an assignment to such roles as care givers (for pay or without pay) is correlated with a propensity for such roles. Yet, as Arlie Hochschild has so aptly shown in her study of airline attendants (1983), training (*emotion work*) is necessary to produce the nurturant behavior required for job performance.

2   I discuss in more detail various models of the self and their implications for social science analysis in *Deceptive Distinctions: Sex, Gender and the Social Order* (1988).

I note in this context that Elina Haavio—Mannila is among the social scientists who have noted the importance of social structure in determining the self. She was among the first feminist scholars to study the impact of social structural variables on men's and women's behavior and on their sense of who they are. Her various studies, which have examined behavior ranging from work—force participation to erotic attachments, provide many building blocks for the theoretical

framework that suggests a changing rather than static self —
one determined by social factors rather than by innate qualities,
one affected by sexual characteristics but not determined by
them and one that is multidimensional, with various
components activated in different contexts.

3   I am grateful to Kay Deaux for her retrieval of this quotation.

4   Elina Haavio—Mannila and Raija Snicker's (1980) study of
afternoon dancing, a relatively recent practice instituted by
restaurants in modern Finland, is a good example of a changing
practice which has multiple meanings to the people who
participate in it. In establishing *women's dances* in their
restaurants, managers encourage women to ask men to dance,
contrary to traditional practice. But while working—class men
and women were willing to step beyond social conventions
(expanding their selves), upper—class men experienced the
change in etiquette as a violation of self. Haavio—Mannila and
Snicker conclude that such men have a stake in being assertive
and resist reversal to a more passive role. Yet, while resisting
change to one aspect of their persona, they were in fact engaged
in a new practice (dancing with strangers in a public setting) that
redefined them.

5   These papers were also based on the study of communications
workers.

6   Kay Deaux, *Incipient Identity*, Carolyn Wood Sherif Lecture,
American Psychological Association, Atlanta, GA., August 1988.
Also see Kay Deaux and Brenda Major, *Putting Gender Into
Context: An Interactive Model of Gender Related Behavior*,
Psychological Review 94 (1987), pp. 369—389.

7   See Epstein (1987) and other papers in this volume.

8   In the article *Positive Effects of the Multiple Negative: Explaining the
Success of Black Professional Women* (1973), I pointed to the way in
which the perception of traits associated with different statuses
by gatekeepers lead them, under certain circumstances, to be
more hospitable to black women than white women or black
men in professional jobs.

9   A study by Ruth Milkman and Cydney Pullman (1991) of an Edison, New Jersey, Ford plant reports that technological change is linked to changes in organizational structure, but that these changes did not cause a reconfiguration of work roles between skilled and line workers. Production workers remain subordinated to the equipment, while the role of the skilled trade workers is to maintain and manage the machinery. The shift to new, more complex technology magnified the preexisting skill differences between the two groups of workers. The job content changed slightly, but remained divided along lines of skill. This finding seems to suggest that this culture of the workplace would not change much, because the division of skilled and operative work roles did not change.

9 Women's changing lives and the emergence of family policy

Janet Zollinger Giele

Just since 1990, a new paradigm has emerged for understanding the development of the welfare state and women's place within it. This research both builds on and replaces T.H. Marshall's (1963) classic statement that social rights of citizenship expanded with industrialization and modernization. In place of Marshall's unilinear model of progress, the new and more complex theory of the welfare state discovers major variations in citizenship rights among nations. As Esping—Andersen (1990) and others have shown, different state—market—culture combinations produce welfare states with different types of work and family policies.

Feminist scholars have further elaborated the model, first by criticizing its male bias and then by spelling out the conditions under which a welfare state can be *woman—friendly*. Beginning with Pateman's (1988) work on the patriarchal nature of the welfare state, feminists contend that the classic theories presume a male breadwinner in the workplace and a female care giver in the home. Thus, according to Nelson (1990), *welfare* is sex—typed — social insurance and unemployment compensation going to families to replace men's wages and social services and dependency allowances going to widows or single mothers when no husband is around. Anttonen and Hobson (in this volume) suggest that the welfare state is woman—friendly only when citizenship transcends the gender divide between public and private and work and family and considers motherhood as well as work and breadwinning a basis for citizenship. The Nordic countries' welfare states are woman—friendly precisely

153

because they not only encompass work—related income programs, but also family—related social services such as child care.

What has led to these feminist critiques and insights about the welfare state? I believe it is the actual experience of women in bridging the work—family divide or *dual—role* dichotomy that has shaped the social policy of the past century. Not only have the historic women's movements of Great Britain, France, and the United States pushed for equal pay and the desegregation of sex—typed jobs, but the changing personal life experience of thousands of women has called into question the traditional bases of social entitlement. Current debates over child care, parental leave, and family allowances are the result of massive life—course changes in which more women are combining paying jobs with family duties. Virtually every modern nation displays this major trend, despite very different conditions in national cultures. Thus state—market—family models of the welfare state need to be revised to reflect the important impact of women's movements and the actual changes in women's lives. The multiple—role patterns that women have already discovered are the first way to transcend the duality of women's work and family roles. Next are feminist family policy proposals which are essential for a welfare state that is friendly to women.

Theory of gender and the welfare state

Over time the theory of the welfare state has become more differentiated and complex, taking into account an additional set of variables — economic, political, and cultural at each new stage of the analysis. First, T.H. Marshall in *Class, Citizenship, and Social Development*, linked workers' expanding rights to economic and social development. Next, Esping—Andersen (1990) introduced the variable of the state's political tradition. Among capitalist economies, for example, the liberal Anglo—American type accepts class inequality and focuses on work as the basis of entitlements. At the other extreme, the Scandinavian social democracies play down class differences and base entitlements on social rights regardless of work or earning status. Intermediate between these two are the corporatist or conservative regimes in Europe, such as France or Germany, which accept status

154

differences but provide for social needs somewhat more generously than the Anglo—American countries. (See also Peattie and Rein 1983; Gordon 1990; Skocpol 1992; Kahne and Giele 1992).

Finally, several feminist scholars have focused on prevailing gender relations as a factor that has shaped social benefits such as family allowances and supports to working parents. Barbara Hobson (1990) shows that the labor—force participation and economic dependency of married women and single mothers affect the ways in which the political economy of a nation bears on the actual lives of women. Building on Hobson's work, Orloff (1993) suggests that the three—variable state—market—culture model should include two other variables that describe women's opportunities: access to paid work, and capacity to maintain an autonomous household.

The resulting model of gender in the welfare state is impressive. It contains a macro level spelled out by Marshall and Esping—Anderson and a micro level spelled out by the feminist theorists. But it lacks a dynamic picture of how social change actually occurs, or it implies that change occurs solely from the *top down*. Most theorists and scholars have focused on how national social policies have shaped individual behavior (poverty, labor—force participation, family structure). Much less attention has been paid to the potential for women's and men's changing work and family lives to affect the child and family policies of the future, or to change the state from the *bottom up*. Figure 9.1 depicts the expanded model of social policy and life pattern interaction that is needed.

In this chapter, I present evidence of the two connections between women's lives and social policy that have been left relatively undeveloped by previous scholars:

1   the link between women's lives and women's movements and
2   the link between contemporary changes in women's lives and current efforts to expand family and children's policies.

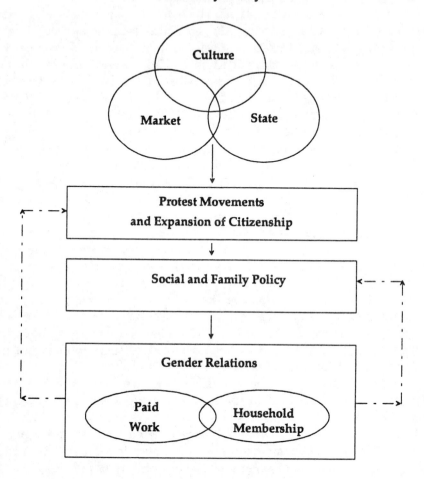

Legend:

—— Connections described in literature on welfare states
- - - Connections which need further investigation

Figure 9.1 Interactive model of change in life patterns and family policy

First, using my own research on women's temperance and suffrage movements in the United States, I show that protest movements are themselves propelled by changes in the lives of their proponents. Such connections can be found in Great Britain, France and Finland between the prevailing pattern of women's lives and the gender ideology which shaped the social protection system. The modern United States women's movement which reached its peak in the 1970s is also a product of the changing life patterns of women born in the 1920s, 1930s, and 1940s, who protested the *feminine mystique*.

Second, drawing on age cohort comparisons of women's changing life patterns in Germany and the United States since World War II, I document what appears to be a nearly universal trend toward women's multiple work and family roles. These trends seem to be due to global economic change and rising uncertainty which may attenuate cross—national differences. It is thus vital in the model of welfare state formation to include the micro level life pattern changes which shape the system from below as well as the macro level market—state—culture matrix, which shapes it from above.

Life pattern changes and the origins of feminist protest

Feminist scholars of the welfare state have already glimpsed a connection between prevailing patterns of women's lives and the nature of women's activism. Strong middle—class women's movements appear in countries with a well—established tradition of the male breadwinner and woman homemaker who devotes herself to arts, charity, and the uplift of poorer women. Under these conditions, state provisions for women and children are likely to focus on earnings—based entitlements which make up for an absent or disabled breadwinner, a pattern typical of the United States or Great Britain. Where there is precedent for women's combining work and family duties, as in France at the turn of the century, social benefits are more likely to focus on the needs of family and children regardless of household composition or employment status of the parents (Pedersen 1993).

So far, evidence for a connection between male breadwinner ideology and social protection has been based on historical examples and aggregate statistics. More attention should now be given to the *connections between women's actual lives and the ideology of women's movements*. I have done this in a comparison of the United States women's temperance and suffrage movements which flourished between 1870 and 1920. These movements were a response to the rapid change in women's lives which gave them an education but denied them property rights and a voice in public affairs. Leaders of both movements were from Protestant middle—class families and had education and professional experience far above the average of the day. The leaders of the two movements differed from each other, however, in ways consistent with their reform ideology. Temperance women, whose primary goal was to protect and improve home life by removing alcohol from men, were more likely to have experienced some loss or tragedy in their family life than were the suffragists. On the other hand, suffrage leaders, whose reform goal was to lift women into public life, were more likely than their temperance counterparts to have been denied access to education or a profession because they were women (Giele 1995).

A close reading of feminist works on protest and the welfare state suggests a parallel dynamic in other nations. In her comparison of family policy in Great Britain and France, Susan Pedersen provides figures on women's percentage of the economically active population from the 1860s to 1911. The evidence suggests that it was more *normal* for a woman to be employed in France than in Great Britain. French women made up 30 to 40 percent of the labor force in all sectors — agriculture and fishing, industry and transport, trade and finance, and services. In Great Britain, by contrast, women contributed less than 10 percent of agricultural workers, less than a quarter of industrial workers, and fewer than a fifth in trade and finance. Only in services were women the *normal* worker, constituting 55 to 60 percent (Pedersen 1993 p. 37). In 1911, across all sectors, the labor—force participation of women in England and Wales was only 24 percent of 35 to 44—year—old women compared with 52 percent of French women of the same age. Such a reality laid the foundation for treating women in France as *both* workers and mothers, whereas in Great Britain, employment and motherhood were more likely to be seen as mutually exclusive. No wonder then that British social welfare policy articulated a male breadwinner logic whereas the French policies were *parental*. The French were able to avoid a presumption that women were dependent on men to take care of them and their children. According to Pedersen (1993 p. 17), the French were able to *presume the dependence of children alone and hence, redistribute income primarily across family types and not along gender lines.*

Anttonen's chapter in this volume suggests that the Finnish experience was not unlike that of France. The woman—friendly state of modern Finland is based on the acceptance of both citizen mothers and citizen workers. How did this happen? Modernization was late in Finland. The society was predominantly rural up to the 1960s. Like France, Finland lacked a strong bourgeois housewife tradition. The agrarian model which did not differentiate work and family life or separate the home from the workplace thus laid a foundation compatible with the demands of modern society to combine work and family life. Municipal child care and social services were initially made available to help farm women feed their animals and fulfill their roles. Now rising land values, the desire to acquire a home, and higher education perpetuate the need for wives, as well as husbands, to be employed (Rantalaiho 1993). The earlier rural life patterns of women helped to produce policies that support modern dual—worker households.

The emergence of the modern United States woman's movement in the 1960s provides yet another example of the connection between women's changing lives and the emergence of social protest and social policy. Longitudinal studies of United States women born between 1910 and 1950 suggest that women's lives changed as a result of new economic and social conditions. They adapted by entering the labor force and gaining further education, while, at the same time, maintaining a family life. As their new pattern came into conflict with the established full—time homemaker norm, they developed a gender role ideology that fueled the modern women's movement. Personal change preceded political involvement. Commitment to these new roles and policies was closely tied to age group.

United States women born between 1900 and 1930 were likely to have a conservative life pattern and gender ideology. College—educated women of this era were likely to have followed a *long interrupted* or *three—phase* pattern, with early employment followed by time out of the labor force until the youngest child was in school. A woman like Betty Friedan who was born in the 1920s satirized the middle phase of this pattern as the *feminine mystique*, the expectation that women would submerge their intelligence and autonomy in family life.

Women born in the 1930s and 1940s, especially if they had a college education, were more likely to be pioneers in combining paid work and family roles. They were entering adulthood just *before* the modern women's movement, and this timing suggests that their changing life patterns helped the movement to emerge. Although they expected that they would follow a traditional feminine role, in many cases they turned out that they did not. Whereas earlier cohorts showed a brief dip in labor—force participation around the age of 30 years, United States women born between 1936 and 1945 were the first to show ever higher employment rates from the age of 20 years and up (Giele 1993 p. 43). College—educated women in particular were likely to combine motherhood with employment and even graduate school education (Konecko 1982; Giele 1987; Giele and Gilfus 1990; Giele 1993 pp. 45—47).

Women born after 1950, however, took the new multiple role pattern as the norm and sought ways to make it easier by surrounding it with institutional supports such as equal pay, affirmative action, work—family leaves, and child care. They have been more likely to take women's right to combine work and family life for granted. They appear frustrated and embittered if they find the multiple role combination difficult or impossible. Even less educated younger women have not in any way retreated from the dual career model established by older women (Giele 1993 pp. 47—48). Instead the trend to continue work alongside motherhood has intensified or many young women choose not to marry or have children at all. For the first time since the days of Jane Addams and others who eschewed marriage for a career, it appears that the *family claim* may be losing ground to career interests.

A new theme is perhaps taking shape in which highly educated women will consciously decide not to have children because heavier family responsibilities will hurt their careers or, alternatively, they may forego having children because they believe that they will not be able to give their families the time they deserve. For this younger generation a new frontier presents itself: finding success equal to men's in the formerly male—dominated occupations and supporting family—friendly policies for parental leave and child care which will support their work and family roles.

Multiple roles and support for family policy

The trend towards multiple roles which has been documented among American college women has also appeared in the non—college population in both the United States and Germany. Using national panel surveys from both countries, I have found that the younger women are much more likely to have combined work and family during the mid—life period between the ages of 35 and 45 years. Why have these patterns arisen and what are their likely consequences for future social policy? A review of the changes suggests that economic uncertainty and the need for flexibility have prompted changes in the organization of the life course. These new norms have in turn brought new family policy issues to the forefront of current political debate.

A trend toward multiple roles

Longitudinal data from Germany and the United States suggest that there is a cross—national trend toward the restructuring of women's life course to combine work and family roles. This trend challenges existing classic sociological and economic theories of the family division of labor between men and women. These theories have argued that strong specialization and differentiation between men's and women's tasks result in smoother integration of work and family life and in greater comparative advantage for each of the marital partners (Parsons and Bales 1955; Becker 1981).

By focusing on a single aspect of women's life patterns such as the rise in education or employment, or the fall in fertility, scholars have narrowed their attention to specific roles and have thus failed to note the change in *role constellations* or *role patterns* of women. A coding scheme that I developed about ten years ago can be used, however, to note the number and combination of multiple simultaneous roles

161

which a woman holds at a specific age. Four types of activity are of particular importance:
education (E),
work (W),
marriage (M), and
parenthood (P).

When one codes a woman's activity patterns according to effort in each of these four domains, sixteen different combinations are possible:
(no activity)...., E..., .W.., EW.., ..M., E.M.,
.WM., EWM., ...P, E..P, .W.P, EW.P,
..MP, E.MP, .WMP, EWMP.

By comparing life patterns of older and younger birth cohorts at a given age, such as 35 years, it becomes possible to chart trends in single and multiple roles.

The most notable finding from these activity descriptions is that the multiple—role trend which I found among college—educated women in the United States is also present in the non—college United States population and among East and West German women as well. The United States National Longitudinal Surveys of Mature Women reveal a similar pattern among a nationally representative sample of largely *non*—college educated women born between 1923 and 1938, who were surveyed biennially beginning in 1967. Between 1969 and 1974, there was a strong rise in work—family roles among 40—year old women — from 40 percent in 1969 to 50 percent in 1972, and 60 percent in 1974.

What is even more impressive is that reduced specialization by gender appears to be occurring in other societies outside the United States. Longitudinal data from the German Socio—Economic Panel (GSOEP) permit a comparison not only across different cohorts of the same age, but also between East and West Germany. Education is strikingly higher among the youngest cohorts. At age 20 years marriage and parenthood are higher for the mothers of the baby boom generation (born in the 1930s and 1940s) than for the older cohorts (of 1910 and 1920). But there is a striking and regular fall in *single* roles (E..., .W.., ..M., and ...P) from the oldest to youngest cohorts and a regular rise in *multiple* roles (defined as some combination of education or work roles in the *public* world and marriage or parenthood in the *private* world). Even though there are stark differences in the frequency scale for East and West, with over 80 percent of the 1940 cohort of East German women in multiple roles as compared with half that many of the West German women, the rise in multiple roles across cohorts is basically similar.

Using a single— and multiple—role comparison with the United States National Longitudinal Survey data reveals a remarkably similar picture. These data had to be transformed to create retrospective work histories for the biennial surveys conducted between 1967 and 1982 among women who were aged 30—45 years in 1967. Compared with the GSOEP, the age ranges for which comparisons are possible are thus truncated. In addition, I did not weight the responses to assure the representativeness of the sample afterthe the attrition of respondents between interview waves. Nevertheless, the results when superimposed on the West German trends, closely coincide. The early and mid—1930s cohorts of United States women have under 30 percent of their members in single roles at ages 35, 40, and 45 years, as do the West German women of comparable age. Among United States women born a decade earlier, however, about 40 percent occupy single roles (E, W, M, or P only) during their middle years, a pattern which is quite comparable to the West German women born in 1920. The picture for multiple roles is again obverse to that for single roles with an ever higher proportion of younger cohorts combining *public* and *private* spheres. Between 40 and 50 percent of the American women born in the 1930s combined public and private roles at ages 35 and 45 years, similar to the West German women born in 1930 and 1940. But the frequency of such multiple roles among older United States women born in the 1920s was about 10 percent lower, a pattern very comparable to that found among West German women born in 1920 and 1930.

Reasons for women's role innovation

Together these longitudinal cohort comparisons of role patterns by age appear to be striking proof that gender specialization in market and household work is moving in a direction opposite that projected by theorists such as sociologist Talcott Parsons (1942, 1955), who believed that gender specialization led to smoother integration of family life, or economist Gary Becker (1981), who predicted that comparative advantage would lead to strong home and market specialization between two marital partners. Historical and biographical evidence suggests that women born between the late 1920s and 1950 departed from traditional expectations *ahead of time* to prepare for a changing world that they did not know was coming. Women sought more education, had fewer children, and were employed even as wives and mothers more than they ever thought possible when they were young adults.

What appears to have happened is that each woman acting alone made decisions which departed from the traditional expectation of being a full—time housewife. Each woman thought her decision was unique, but taken together these individual decisions added up to a trend. The trend, rather than moving toward greater specialization, resulted in contingency planning on many different fronts — education, work, marriage, and childbearing. In the United States even rather traditional husbands might encourage their wives and daughters to get an education and have a profession as an *insurance policy* in the event that something unforeseen would happen to the principal breadwinner. Women themselves could compare their situation and the society around them with the lives of their own mothers and see that conditions were drastically changed. Less time was needed to perform necessary household tasks. Nor could household production produce much cash income if there was no market worker in the family. Moreover, numbers of children were declining and the time required of a mother in the home was shrinking just as women's life expectancy was increasing. In addition, it was becoming increasingly evident that time out of the labor force worsened chances for later reentry. The upshot was that a woman could see down the road that specialization in housework was potentially not only less rewarding but more risky compared with a broader and more flexible preparation for unknown conditions ahead. These thousands of individual decisions added up to a replacement of the old M—shaped age curve of women's labor—force participation (the three—phase model) with a smoother inverted U—shaped curve increasingly similar to that of men (Kirner and Schulz 1992).

Such personal decisions leading to a new life course pattern appear to have been reinforced by both economic and psychological gains. Despite the frequent explanation that women work because they have to in order *to make ends meet*, the statistics suggest otherwise. The poorest women (on welfare in the United States) are those with the least education and work experience and lowest labor—force participation. The two—earner families, on the other hand, are much better off, with wives' labor—force participation frequently found among the middle and upper middle class, where the woman's income goes toward supporting expensive higher education for children and a more comfortable life—style.

In addition, women with multiple roles in the United States report higher satisfaction with life and better physical and mental health than women who are housewives only. In a survey of Boston—area mid—life women, Baruch and Barnett (1983) found that the women who were most satisfied had outlets for developing a sense of competence at work as well as intimate relationships within the family. In their longitudinal study of Mills college graduates of the 1950s, Helson and Picano (1990) similarly found that women who had maintained involvement in a career were happier and healthier than women who had become full—time housewives. Such findings suggest that the multiple activity pattern represents a positive adaptation to longer life expectancy and economic uncertainty, and not just the *need for two incomes*.

Economists suggest that such flexibility is especially adaptive under conditions of societal or individual uncertainty. Social structures which are too rigidly specialized are at a disadvantage when change is needed. A certain amount of *slack* is helpful for meeting new and pressing needs (Grabher 1993). Likewise, a very high degree of specialization of marital or household partners is risky if one loses a job or the marriage fails. Uncertainty brings out avoidance of ultimate specialization in gender relations (Ott 1992).

Implications for policy change

Despite change in women's *actual* life patterns, consciousness of the change has lagged behind. Women are still discriminated against

165

because it is thought that they will drop out of the labor force when they have children or that they will become less committed to their work. Women still bear the main burden of unpaid family labor. In the Anglo—American countries, there are still serious deficiencies in the provision for parents to combine work and family obligations.

Thus it is only by widely publicizing what is actually happening in women's lives and how they depart from the traditional stereotype that there will be a breakthrough for gender equality or family care. Needed first is a critical phase of showing how current policies disadvantage women. The second phase is to construct positive proposals on the basis of what working parents and other family members actually do. It should be possible to build a family policy that is more in line with current reality than with the male—breadwinner model on which a great deal of existing policy is based. In this chapter I suggest how these role changes could be a useful guide for shaping future policy initiatives in liberal, corporatist, and social democratic versions of the welfare state.

Liberal democracies: the United States and Great Britain

Women's current work and family lives in the United States and Great Britain pose a serious threat to the male breadwinner ideology because so many combine employment with marriage and parenting. In the United States in 1990, 58 percent of all women with children under six years of age were employed. Over half of all mothers with a child under a year old were also working for pay. In the meantime, the use of family day care and other forms of child care for preschoolers has skyrocketed. In 1984—1985, only 8 percent of children under five years of age were cared for in their own home by their own mother, and 15 percent in their home by a relative or other caretaker. Fully 73 percent were cared for outside the home (Hayes et al. 1990 pp. 29, 32). Considerable ferment has resulted in social policy to make parental leave easier through the Family and Medical Leave Act of 1993 and to subsidize child care, especially for poor working mothers (Pleck 1992). Economic recession, however, in Massachusetts in 1991, once known as the *Massachusetts Miracle*, resulted in the loss of 7,000 day care slots. Mothers continued to be employed, however, and a major concern is now that children will be left alone or inadequately cared for.

166

The picture is even more mixed in Great Britain. In 1987, more than two—thirds (68 percent) of married women were *economically active*, but their employment was often available only on a part—time basis, in sex segregated jobs, and with pay levels that averaged only 67.6 percent of full—time male workers. Fewer than half of the places in public nurseries were available for young children in 1990 than were found in 1945. In 1985, there were only nine public nursery facilities per 1.000 children under the age of five years, and private or voluntary nurseries now provide more child care than the public sites. About two—thirds of working women have to rely on other family members to look after their children. The government has resisted demands for some state support of child care and provisions for parental leave after childbearing (MacLennan 1992). But although maternity rights and employment protections for women have been cut, the trend toward women's multiple roles shows no sign of abating. A debate now rages on whether to use the tax system or the benefit system to reduce female dependency.

In both the United States and Great Britain, recent trends to privatize and cut public services in order to rely on individual solutions is increasingly in conflict with families' actual work patterns and the heavy reliance on working women to boost family incomes and to care for family needs.

A corporatist welfare state: Germany

Women's life experience in East and West Germany leads to divergent predictions about the future shape of social policy. On one hand, women in the former German Democratic Republic are being forced into unemployment because of state cuts in child care, as well as reorientation to a capitalist economy (Rudolph 1992; Duggan 1993). On the other, as the GSOEP data demonstrate, the proportion of West German women in the work force has steadily risen among the youngest cohorts. There the school day, which presumes a mother in the home, is a constant source of frustration to working parents. Those who can afford it find schools which will keep their children the whole day. One hesitates to predict how the changing life patterns of women will affect policies for parental leave and child care in Germany. If present trends in women's work continue, however, and especially if frustration with the current system leads to a *birth dearth* among the well—educated, it is likely that current policies will become more friendly to women's combination of work and family roles.

Social democracies: Sweden and Finland

The main challenge to the enlightened work and family policies of the Scandinavian welfare states is their current budget crises, which threaten major cutbacks in child care and bring discouragement to women in dual roles as parents and workers. Is it actually possible that the reduction of government support for child care will turn the clock back to a situation where women will return to the homemaker role? I would be surprised if that happened. It is my impression that women's higher education, emancipation from the home, and experience in self support have been so rewarding that they are unlikely to turn back.

Instead, the policy debate in Scandinavia may have to proceed from somewhat different premises. Citizen mothers *have* been accepted along with citizen workers. Now the question is how to make family support structures pay for themselves. At this point, a new kind of rationale has yet to be developed — not only to argue for family supports on the basis of *citizenship*, but also on the basis of the future well—being of the nation — its *social reproduction*, which is just as important as its economic viability or its national defense. If one adds up the cost of violence perpetrated by children in the United States, who are inadequately supervised by parents and community, the figures are staggering. On the benefits side, the positive result of women's contribution to the economy in the United States or Great Britain are also impressive.

The locus of the family debate should now shift to those real costs and benefits that result from the new ways that women, men and families are actually living their lives. Then the future of nations will truly be seen as flowing from the rights and responsibilities of individual workers and family members, as well as from the protection of their rights as citizens.

10 Inside and outside families
Tuula Gordon

In discussions of unresolved dilemmas of women, the main focus in this book has been on ways in which family and paid work intersect. In this context, the family is often understood to consist of a wife, a husband and children. Married women with children have been defined through wifehood and motherhood. The women's movement has struggled against such a simplified definition and has campaigned for policies and practices that would ensure the possibility of continued participation in the labour market. Such practices and policies are crucial for independence, and the cross—cultural and comparative analyses of writers in this book provide evidence of this cruciality. But what about a woman who is not a *woman* in terms of familial definitions?

At any given time in Great Britain and the United States only about half of the women are married, whereas in Finland less than a half of the women are married. Yet marriage is still culturally prevalent — thus women who do not follow the marriage path have to work at establishing a satisfactory pattern for their lives. Historically, women have been defined in relation to men. Men provide the norm, the normal and the absolute. Women, in this framework, are *the other*; they are the concrete instead of the abstract, they form the subjective instead of the objective, they are associated with nature instead of culture, and they are defined by their bodies instead of their minds. The adult human being is, as the generic *man* indicates, indeed a man, and a *woman* is defined in representations through sexual difference, as *not—man*. Romantic love, partnership, marriage and motherhood form the relational context within which women are located.

Dimensions of women's citizenship have been constructed on the model of being a citizen worker, as Anttonen argues in this volume. Beyond the citizen worker definitions for *women* are implicit assumptions about their dependency, even though there are variations in how problematic such dependency is construed, as Hobson illustrates in her analysis of *solo mothers* in this volume.

In this chapter I want to consider single women who are located *outside* families. Feminist researchers have argued that *the family* is a crucial site in the production of sexual difference, the gendered division of labour, and inegalitarian social relationships (Barrett and McIntosh 1982; Gittins 1985). Thus locating themselves outside families provides possibilities for women. Moreover, the diversification of family forms may have provided new opportunities for women in constructing their life course.

When exploring these questions, one finds interesting analyses of the possibilities of and limitations on single women. If *the family* is a basic unit of society *and* if ideological representations and state practices reinforce the rhetoric around the family, not only may women and children be oppressed *inside* families but also those excluded from families may be oppressed *outside* of families because of this very exclusion. Thus being outside familial structures contributes to the marginality of single women. But if the family is crucial in regulation, it is possible that remaining outside family structures nevertheless provides single women more possibilities in negotiating their *careers*, and more freedom from some aspects of the sexual division of labour. This may be one reason why single women are considered an anomaly. The circumstances of the lives of large numbers of people do not conform to the familial ideology; people live in a range of different types of households. Hence single women, as part of a heterogeneous group increasing in number, may experience a greater degree of scope for constructing their personal lives.

My discussion is based on a study of single women in Great Britain, the United States and Finland (Gordon 1994). Seventy—two women who were at least 35 years of age were interviewed.[2] I included divorced and separated women as well as the unmarried, because, in the context of the diversification of family forms, people move in and out of categories, rather than occupy fixed places. Twenty—three women had children. A majority of these women had not made a conscious decision to be single. Nevertheless, using Stein's (1981) classification, three—quarters of them could be considered voluntary singles, either temporary — that is, interested in marriage but not actively seeking it — or stable — that is, not interested in marriage. This classification enables us to move beyond the traditional stereotype of an *old maid*, who did not get a man, or a more modern stereotype of *city single*, who does not want a man, to more complex and multifaceted portrayals of single women. Singlehood is a result of a complex interaction between structural, cultural and biographical aspects.

Singleness - pulls and pushes

The proportions of single women vary across societies, but there is what demographers call a *European* marriage pattern (which applies to North America, too). In 1988, 23 percent of the women aged 15 years and over in the United States were single; in England and Wales 23 percent of the women aged 16 years and over were single; and in Finland 28 percent of the women aged 15 years and over were single.[3] Traditionally the proportions of single women have been high in Scandinavia. Women's full—time participation in the labour market has increased their options. Because of lower dependence levels it is easier for them to decline to marry or to opt out of bad marriages. However, in Nordic countries cohabitation is also much more common — women who are statistically unmarried or divorced may cohabit in marriage—like relationships.

Structural and cultural patterns can contain obstacles (provide *pushes*) so that women who do become or remain single are more likely to be involuntary singles or facilitate voluntary singlehood (provide *pulls*) (see Stein 1981). For example, in Russia where a great majority of women marry, Yampolskaya[4] in her study of single women found a far larger proportion of involuntary singles than I did in my current study. An example of a push to singlehood given by Yampolskaya is the shortage of housing, which makes it difficult for couples to live together. By contrast, in Japan, where the proportion of single women is very low, recent pulls of singlehood have been more considerable. Singleness has allowed women to engage in paid work and has given them more freedom in relation to traditional expectations of and assumptions about women (Hochschild and Tanaka in this volume).

The singleness of women cannot simply be explained in terms of societal patterns affecting women in similar ways. For example, in the United States the singleness of a black working—class woman and a white middle—class woman can be differentially explained. The singleness of a white middle—class woman can be explained through pulls — she has more options. The singleness of a black working—class woman can be explained through pushes — it reflects structurally and culturally constructed inequalities which frame the problems of black men so that they are not available or are not attractive marital partners (see Staples 1981). However, this is a contentious argument. In my research the subjective meanings given by black women to their singlehood were more likely to reflect pulls rather than pushes. Meanings attached to independence were no less likely to be positive among black women (Afro—American in the United States and Afro—Caribbean in Great Britain) than among white women.

In the *public* sphere

One of the binary oppositions constructed along the axes of *men* as *normal* and *women* as the *other* is the division between the public and the private sphere. The public sphere is seen as the primary location of men and the private sphere as the primary location of women. Such an opposition is not given or historically static, and women's exclusion from the public sphere has never been complete. Feminist researchers have criticized the use of public/private (see Siltanen and Stanworth 1984). I agree that the distinction is not applicable to women and men as a descriptive categorization, but it is useful as an analytical distinction. Men are still connected with the public sphere and women with the private sphere in gender representations. Women carry the *aura* of the private sphere with them when they enter the public sphere; the labour market is gender segregated, and women's work in semi—professions (i.e., teaching, health care, social work) and in service occupations is seen as a continuation of jobs they do at home. Men bring the *aura* of the public sphere to the private; they do less housework and are less involved in child care. The public and private spheres are connected, and the relationship between them is complex and dynamic. Women have not accepted their confinement into the private sphere, and they have sought to challenge the limitations imposed on them.

The main entry to the public sphere is through paid work. Women's location in the labour market is an important facet structuring their lives. For married women their social position is mediated by their husband's location in the labour market as well. For single women their own positioning defines them more precisely. Paid work is thus particularly significant for single women, and in my study three quarters of the women considered work to be important. Work provides financial autonomy, which, when single women discussed different aspects of independence, was usually considered to be its most important dimension. The majority of women liked their jobs because they offered contact with people, expressive and creative possibilities, and intellectual, emotional or political satisfaction. Many women had a strong commitment to work, and most positive descriptions of their jobs were almost overflowing: *brilliant, key to my life.* (See Epstein in this volume.)

The stereotype of a *city—single* does not have as clear—cut a content as that of an *old—maid*. However, one important dimension of it is an assumption that women who do not marry are obsessed with work and their careers and that their lives are one—dimensional. Work—oriented women may have become single because of their primary commitment to their jobs. However, it may also be that the commitment to work is a result of singleness. Such judgements are difficult to make, except in cases of women who made, in terms of their own perception, fairly clear—cut career or partner choices.

> I realized that work was the key to my life. That if I didn't have work, but meaningful work, I would become what women are supposed to be, but which I didn't want to be. And so, from then on, what became my sort of major goal in life was to find work that was meaningful, and relationships were always sort

of secondary to that goal, and I let them go as soon as there was any conflict. (Christine, Cal, USA)

Many conflicts in relationships are connected with a traditional, secondary role that is required of women. Thus women do not prioritise work over relationships as such, but, if they find that the two are in conflict, they opt to give precedence to their work.

Work provides structure and meaning to the lives of these women in diverse ways. The stereotype of a city single hides this complexity. Women committed to their jobs are not best described as *selfish* career women. Many single women work in semi—professions — in health care, social work, teaching — for them the content of their work is important.

Social relations at work

Single women have potential problems when interacting with others at work. Many of them are adept in dealing with their associates, however. When informal discussions at work center on domestic issues and children, childless single women talk about children of friends and relatives. They make efforts not to be marginalized, as social relationships at work are important to them. Lesbian women experience greater difficulties than other single women when struggling with inclusion or exclusion. For many women their workplace was like a *family*, a site of closeness and support, but also of tensions and interference. But they often find that they are the ones making the effort to develop social interaction at work — when they suggest outings and the like. Married women tend to rush home instead, communicating a sense of envy — *it's all right for you*.

The majority of the women do not think that they are discriminated against at work because they are single, but because they are *women*. Women are not as well paid as men, they are bypassed in promotion, and, particularly, women of colour recount experiences of overt discouragement and discrimination. Women complain about the injustice of smaller wages, but they do not talk a great deal about financial difficulties.[5] Because financial independence is so crucial, most women emphasize that they manage with the amount of money available: *I've struggled financially all my life but I've never felt deprived of anything.* Many women, particularly those who have children, have experienced greater financial difficulties previously, and many also anticipate the prospect of retirement and old age. Hence they tend to consider their *present* situation as fairly secure. Nevertheless they are critical of the fact that their work is not adequately rewarded.

Work as 'a rite of passage'

A typical path from childhood to adulthood for women is through marriage (Allen 1989, Chandler 1991). Adulthood defined in this way contains cultural notions of the dependence of women. As the average age of first marriage has increased in Western countries, and young women have often left their parental homes already before marriage, they separate themselves from their parents more definitely by establishing their own family of procreation. They leave salient daughterhood through marriage and motherhood. Many single women I interviewed thought their parents treated them differently from their married sisters. Unmarried women were given more advice, and their life—styles were given more comment.

> It's as if, you know, you are your parents' responsibility until that responsibility is transferred to a partner. (Lorna, Britain)

> I still keep getting advice [from my mother] ... But she never talks — she says herself that it's a point of honour that she has never interfered in the lives of my sisters ... and has not guided them, as they are married and have families. She has never said to them do this or do that. So it has all been channeled so that — yes, I think I have had to struggle and I still struggle all the time. (Anni, Finland)

Divorced women had, however, accomplished the rite of passage into adulthood, though some of them found that their parents became more protective or controlling after they became single again. The single women who do not marry have to use other ways to accomplish separation from their parents, and assert independence. Education and work are important in this process.

> I was very dependent for a long time on my parents I didn't really achieve any autonomy until this last job that I've got now. (Tina, Britain)

Often geographical mobility and thus an increased distance from parents was connected to a choice of place of study or work.

From the 'public' to the 'private'

Research into women and work does not pay a great deal of attention to the significance of singleness. For example, in Finland, where the differences between women in relation to marital status can be expected to have narrowed because the majority of women work full—time, combining work and family has been studied. It is difficult to obtain information on single women. The heterogeneity of single women is particularly important in relation to employment. There are differences between unmarried and divorced women, women with or without children, women of different ages and the like. The significance of singleness is thus difficult to isolate.

The *initial* citizen of modern Western democratic nation states was a man and his household. Thus both single and married women were without a clear footing in the public sphere. In the private sphere single women did not enjoy the advantages the status of a wife and a mother gave to married women. Participation in paid work and their increased entry into the public sphere through paid labour has afforded single women more opportunities to strive towards individuality and autonomy than women in the 19th century had. Paid work has been important in facilitating the striving for an independent status. This is reflected in the way that single women today relate to their work.

In my study work was important for three—quarters of the women. It structured the lives of single women with no small children. For married, cohabiting and single mothers, child care and domestic responsibilities structured their paid work, and placed limits on it. The situation differed, however in the three countries. Finnish single mothers were the most likely to be in paid work, and British single mothers were the least likely. The limits were also differentially negotiated by different women. For childless single women the edges between the public and private **spheres** were more blurred than for married women.

Single women with children usually had to balance **their** work and their family responsibilities and **were** likely to experience stress when doing so. On the other hand, achievement of a measure of financial independence improved the wider pattern of their lives. Establishing a *clear borderline* between their time at work and outside work could be difficult for childless single women.

> If they really need me to work, then I really feel like this obligation to do it. So I have to really remind myself that I shouldn't do it — I don't think it's because I'm single. I think it's because I'm pleasant to work with and ... I'm available. And perhaps they know I can't say no. But I'm willing to help out. I'm not a stingy, selfish person. — And I have this thing where I have to be a good girl so I do it for that. (Sue, Cal, USA)

Regular evening classes helped Sue to protect her non—work time; unstructured activities were not sufficient. Sue continues:

> I'm fully aware that if I had a family to get home to, I'd get out. I would just like [snaps fingers] do it so that I was out of there. But because I don't have anything to go to I don't.

Work spills into other areas of life because time outside work is not shaped by family responsibilities; trying to meet one's own needs can be considered selfish by others.

This situation was evident in one issue frequently raised by interviewed women: the choice of holiday times. Married women were given the opportunity to choose their holidays before single women. This procedure belies the perception of women that, in general, their singleness is relevant to themselves, not to others, and if work and non—work boundaries are less easy to draw, it is because of their own inability to do so. The choice of holidays indicates that others also consider their commitments outside work to be secondary and flexible, while commitments shaped by husbands and children are viewed as primary. If women typically organize their time with reference to others in general, and family members in particular, then those who have no such reference points find that they have to defend their *space*.

In the 'private' sphere

I have argued that the borderline between the public and private spheres tends to be more blurred for single than married women. Work is important in the structuring of the lives of single women because, in comparison with married women, their time is less defined by the needs of others in the private sphere. In the public sphere the achievement of an independent status is a more contentious, contradictory process. Even in the private sphere, outside their own homes, single women can have diverse demands placed on them. Many single women are *support persons* — they offer practical and emotional backing to relatives and friends, but are less likely to be offered, or able to receive, such support from others.

Their homes are typically private retreats; when they are at home they do not have many visitors and do not spend a great deal of time eating and cooking. Housework is kept to a minimum. The significance of their homes is repeatedly emphasized by the women.

> You throw everything away, you know, from the outside world — I mean you disconnect whatever angry dissatisfactions and come home and relax and be yourself. (Amy, Cal, USA)

> It's my independence, it's mine, I can shut the door and no one else is gonna walk in. (Tina, Britain)

> I definitely need time alone. When I say I'm going home, I don't need to solve anybody's problems, and I don't need to take other people into consideration, and there are no demands all the time addressed to me, and I can just be and laze around. (Ulla, Finland)

That homes were such personal areas in the study indicates their importance for women when they are establishing their independence.

But women also left their homes a lot. They attended evening classes, met friends, went to the cinema, the theatre and concerts, and engaged in physical activities and sports. Besides work, so many other activities took them into public places, that the contrast between relaxation at home and busy time elsewhere was considerable. Home was definitely a place of leisure and relaxation. Single women were able to make decisions about how much and when to do housework and what standard to set (see Hochschild 1989). Women with children still living at home did more housework, but they were also more likely to take domestic tasks for granted. Without a husband to cater for, there were no tensions about sharing the housework. It was a necessity to get through, though with older children women had disputes about their contribution.

Being alone

As the lives of many of the single women are active and demanding, they welcomed being alone. That the downside of being alone is loneliness, was for many of them a fact to be accepted. About half considered loneliness a problem. This sense of loneliness was not simply a matter of being or not being with other people. For women who did not want to be single, it was connected to the absence of a partner. More often loneliness was an ambivalent feeling, to do with connectedness to others and separateness from them. There were tensions between these processes. Separateness, in terms of Western notions of individuality, was important in establishing independence; connectedness was necessary to establish relationships of support and intimacy. For some women these tensions were, or had been, considerable. They had suffered from depression and had perhaps sought professional help. Single mothers were less likely to experience loneliness because of their relationships to their children, but some experienced loneliness as a unit *with* their children.

Many women emphasized their self—sufficiency and coped with loneliness in a determined way: *I tell it to go away.* But more typically women had established social networks which protected them from loneliness.

Inside/outside: Families and friends

Social networks of single women typically consist of relatives and friends. (See also Simon 1987, and Chandler 1991.) Most women in my study mentioned one or more members of their family of origin — mothers, sisters, brothers, fathers (in that order). These people provided emotional, practical and sometimes financial support. They helped with children, were available to talk, and were turned to when the person was lonely or in need of intimacy. Being a *daughter* was an important aspect of their lives. This situation had both negative and positive implications, ranging from support to control. (For a more—detailed discussion, see Gordon 1994.) The women in this study were less likely to have looked after ageing parents than previously (see Simon 1987; Allen 1989). Because of full—time employment and geographical mobility many of the women were not in a position to offer help; but many parents, according to their daughters, were also determined that their children should not need to look after them. The development of welfare states has been significant in relaxing the need for unmarried daughters to undertake time—consuming care of their parents (see Allen 1989). However, there were women who had assisted their parents, either because they felt they wanted to or because they were under pressure to do so. Their single status meant that they had fewer familial and domestic responsibilities than their married siblings.

For women with families of procreation their children were important sources of intimacy and companionship, and older children also offered practical support. For some, ex—husbands or partners were also important, particularly if they participated in the care of the children.

Families other than their own did not figure greatly in the social networks of the women. Socializing with married women was thought to be difficult; interacting with their families was even more so. If single women were independent and autonomous, they found the place allocated to women in family gatherings problematic. Married women were occupied with children and domestic concerns; single women had an ambivalent position in such a setting. They had to work at their inclusion and might experience greater loneliness than when being alone. There are generally tensions when people with different life—styles interact, and single women did not necessarily think that they were being excluded. But familial patterns reflect those societal patterns which tend to marginalize single women. The presence of single women reminds members of families that the taken—for—granted familism is not all encompassing; what is constructed as a *normal* way to live, though it is the dominant cultural representation, there is only one way to organize one's life. Moreover, single women were still thought to represent a sexual threat.

> There are women who are married and whose marriages are a bit difficult, and I've noticed a sort of hostility in their attitudes sometimes. They think, for example, that I'm trying to get their husband . . . Other women fear a woman who's sort of free. (Rosa, Finland)

Interaction with married men were marked with tensions, and married women could be suspicious and jealous.

The friendships of these single women were, therefore, mainly with other single women. They also tended to socialize with people (and particularly single women) within their own ethnic grouping, and lesbians tended to socialize with other (particularly single) lesbians. The single women reinforced the validity of each other's life—styles in a family—centred society. They had time, they were available, they had shared interests, and they share a sense of being *different*, even deviant. Single women were able to shift from *outside* to *inside* in friendships with other single women.

> We [single women] are with square ends with one another, we have all sorts of hobbies, we travel, and do all sorts of things together. (Helena, Finland)

> [Other single women] become important because we're similar. You know, you sort of seek refuge with people who are like yourself. (Lorna, Britain)

> If you're single you seek out single friends. Or you seek others kinds of misfits, I guess. — I guess I see myself as a misfit —

because the culture is so heavily into, you know, monogamous relationships. (Sue, Cal, USA)

Networks of friends were supportive and protective; they were assigned some of the activities and emotions normally associated with families. The women tried to achieve, with varying degrees of success, some of the intimacy normally associated with familial relations. Achieving this intimacy was not necessarily easy, precisely because of that association, and also because of the tensions between connectedness and separateness. Independence tended have a price tag even though, in their friendships, the women often strived for independence without isolation.

I do not suggest that women who are married find it easy to cope with the dependent status marriage as an institution assigns them, but I do suggest that it is easier for them to take the pattern of their lives for granted. Their life—styles are reinforced in *familist* societies, whereas the life—styles of single women are subject to more conscious construction, though under the shadow cast by the institution of marriage (Chandler 1991). It is important to add, nevertheless, that single women above the age of 35 years have already done a lot of that construction work, and many are relatively comfortable with their single status.

Single mothers

The position of single mothers is both similar and different to that of single women with no children. Single mothers experience hardships and difficulties not experienced by others. There are great variations in societal patterns though. In the United States and Great Britain lone mothers are less likely to do paid work, and the social and welfare services available to them do not encourage or enable them to do so (see Chandler 1991; Hobson in this volume); some differences between the United States and Great Britain exist (Maclean 1991). In the Nordic countries single mothers are encouraged to engage in paid work, and services are constructed in such a way that this possibility is facilitated (Arber and Lahelma 1992). Hence Finnish single mothers are less likely to be impoverished than their British and (especially) American counterparts. But nowhere have the hardships connected with single parenting been removed; as long as familism is prevalent, legislation for the provision of services alone could not remove such hardships. Familism is also integral in assumptions about the best environment for children; there is a strong sense that single mother families are incomplete and problematic. They are compared with the yardstick of normality with the nuclear family as an ideal.

Single motherhood in the context of familism contains difficulties and hardships, but also joys and pleasures. The diversification of family formations indicates social and ideological changes. Familism is prevalent, but not all encompassing. Particularly in metropolitan areas single parenthood has increased and become more commonplace and more accepted. The women in this study who wanted children and went ahead and had them (having not planned their pregnancies) had not experienced a great deal of external pressure. A large proportion of people in attitude surveys have indicated that single parenthood is acceptable. Making a decision to embark on single parenthood, however, is not easy. Most people themselves would want to have children in the context of marriage and a family (see Thornton 1989). But because of the increase in single motherhood and because of the liberalisation of attitudes vis—a—vis other people's family formations, women who do become single parents in large cities have not been faced with a great deal of *personal* criticism.

In my study, 22 women had not wanted children. Women who wanted children but did not have any had decided that they did not want children alone. A partner was considered important for financial reasons. Although women had learned to manage with the financial resources available and most women were not poorly paid, economic considerations were important when making decisions about children. Second, partners would be a source of practical support. Dealing with children alone was considered too hard, often because of observations of single friends. Third, partners would provide emotional support someone to discuss and share the joys and pains of parenthood with. Fourth, there were social reasons. Many women thought it was important for a child to have a father. They often referred to their own relationships with their fathers. Those who had not been brought up with a father or whose fathers were relatively distant had experienced a sense of loss which they would not want their children to experience.

For some women not having children was very painful. But still the decision to have a child outside the nuclear family was difficult. Nave—Herz in this volume found this to be true in Germany too. Though single motherhood brings many positive experiences, only six women in this study (out of the 23 who had children) first had them as solo mothers; three of these pregnancies were unplanned. Having a child alone is still a major decision.

Conclusion

As Hobson argues, solo mothers are a litmus test group of gendered social rights. Similarly, Sarvasy (1992) suggests that, for women to achieve full citizenship, the needs of most vulnerable women must be met. For example, if single women with children are faced with hardships, those are problems for households headed by single mothers. But it also means that married women with children tend to be cautious about leaving difficult relationships because they fear future uncertainty.

Most of the single women in this study were voluntary; some of them, though reasonably satisfied with their present lives, were eager to marry or establish partnerships in the future, but others wanted to remain single. Nevertheless they had had to struggle to establish their independence while struggling to define the content of that independence not as autonomous separation but as connectedness to others. How women achieve such interdependence and challenge otherness in social relations is still one of the broader dilemmas confronting all women. Solving that dilemma facilitates the construction of multiple patterns of of lives, *public* and *private* intertwined.

Notes

1   I would like to thank Sinikka Aapola, Elina Lahelma and Kaisa Kauppinen for their comments on this article.

2   Thirteen of the Finnish interviews were conducted by Sinikka Aapola, my research assistant; the rest of the interviews were conducted by me.

3   Sourcs: England and Wales — percentages calculated from *Marriage and Divorce Statistics*, series FM2, No. 2, London, HMSO; Finland — percentages calculated from data in *Structure and Population and Vital Statistics 1988*, Central Statistical Office in Finland; United States — percentages calculated from data from the *United States census, Population Characteristics, Current Population Reports*, series, no. 433 p. 20. The percentages remained similar in 1990.

4   Yampolskaya, S. (1993), *Single women in Russia*, an unpublished paper.

5   Very poorly paid women were not represented in this study.

11 Single motherhood: An alternative form of life?

Rosemarie Nave-Herz

Problem outline

In the past single mothers had a very low status in all European countries. In certain times and states they had to endure public punishment (house of correction, flogging, etc.) (Peiper 1966 p. 234). The severity of the sanctions varied according to different eras but also according to differences between regions and individual social classes. In the poorer classes single mothers were more readily accepted (Elliot 1986; Trost 1989).

As the bourgeois ideal of family became prevalent from the 17th century on, single motherhood, especially in the upper class, became more and more unthinkable. For this reason, women had to marry in the earliest possible stages of pregnancy. If not, the mother could expect a hopelessly cruel fate, as described in Goethe's Faust, as well as in many other plays and novels.

René König has pointed out that there was *an antipathy towards illegitimate births in nearly every known society because they made it difficult to 'place' the child within the existing system of relatives* (1969). For this reason the public and the family would insist on legitimization by means of marriage to the father of the child or to another man. Negative social sanctions therefore were not aimed at those who became unmarried mothers, but rather at those who remained so. König neglected, however, to limit his comments to patriarchally structured societies (and in particular to bourgeois families), where the family membership and thereby the origin of the children can more easily lead to problems.

Under the auspices of the new women's movement, the removal of all prejudices against the single mother and her child has been demanded. Moreover, single motherhood has also been proclaimed to be an alternative form of life to the traditional parental family.

The legal framework has changed so that the *state of not being married* has assumed a totally different meaning to the one it had 20 or 30 years ago. At that time it *revealed* a sexual relationship not publicly tolerated and, due to the existing legal position, it had to be accepted as *fate*. Moreover, medical research has also increased the ability to plan having children. Finally the availability of contraceptives and their greater degree of reliability in birth control made the possibility of making a decision as to whether to have children or not more conscious.

Socioeconomic surveys in different countries show, however, that even today single and, especially, unmarried mothers still belong to the socially underprivileged: poverty is highest among single mothers. All in all, they have at their disposal the lowest per capita household income. Furthermore, single mothers in particular are stricken with problems of poor health, suffer from a lack of social contacts and helpful relationships, and often have housing problems (Popey, Rimmer and Rossiter 1983 p. 85; Mulroy 1988; OECD 1990; Berger—Schmitt, Glatzer et al. 1991 p. 13; Goldberg et al. 1992).

This deficient social situation is more marked among unmarried mothers in comparison with other women rearing their children alone. Unmarried mothers are financially worse off. They seem to withdraw into their shells; they have a higher rate of unemployment (Neubauer 1988, p. 122; see also Napp—Peters 1985, p. 62).

The results of mass statistical analyses of data do not rule out that there might exist, nevertheless, a group of single women, small in quantity and therefore, not of statistical significance, whose social situation can be described as being in contrast to that of the majority.

Mother families,[1] due to consciously chosen unmarried motherhood, could constitute a new form within the present—day plurality of forms of living.

For the industrial nations the plurality of family forms of life and the possibility of choosing between various forms of existence are given as characteristics of their modernization. The increase in the number of illegitimate births in the last few years in several Western countries could be interpreted as a conscious decision for the choice of the life—form *single parents without a marriage contract* and as a conscious turning—away from the traditional form of the family. For example, the number of children born out of wedlock increased in Germany and also in the United States by roughly 50 percent (Paul 1992), and in England by about 13 percent (Elliot 1986). Even if many of the children born outside wedlock are legitimized when the parents subsequently marry, the trend continues to rise (Espenshade 1985; Teachman et al. 1987; Schwarz 1989). Lüscher and Engstler have also established an increase in the number of unmarried mothers for Switzerland.

A statistical increase, however, does not necessarily imply increased tolerance, and an equal standing of this form of life with the parent family presupposes a greater degree of choice according to the theorem of modernization. One could also propose the antithesis and claim that the choice of the form of life *single parents* (without a marriage contract) is not made nearly as rationally as is assumed in the concept of modernization. Those concerned could, under certain circumstances, continue to adhere to the model of the *complete family* or to the model of the family based on legal marriage. Therefore this form of life could perhaps be regarded more as an interim phase lasting up until the marriage with the father of the child or with another partner, rather than as a consciously chosen alternative family form lasting up to the post—parental phase. Furthermore, as has been shown by Trost (1980), the increase in the number of children born to unmarried mothers does not mean that these mothers are single in the sense that the newborn comes to a non—existent family. In fact many of these women/mothers are cohabiting under marriage—like conditions with the father of the child, especially in Nordic countries.

Despite many investigations concerning single parenthood, little is known about unmarried mothers, especially about their decision to *live alone with the child*.[2]

I shall examine the reasons why unmarried mothers live in single—parent families (and the conditions under which there was a conscious decision in choosing this form of life.

To answer my questions I refer to two studies. One was carried out in the United States, after which my co—workers and I tried to test the results with regard to the situation in Germany. Our study comprised a total of 26 interviews with single mothers and 177 evaluated questionnaires.

The decision to have a child without being married

In her empirical study about single mothers in the United States Eiduson (1980) found a group of women, who she calls *nest—builders*. They:

> ... had consciously planned their pregnancy and had sought out a particular man to be the father of the child. They lived alone and differed from the other women in the random sample in that they were well—educated and ambitious in their careers. They showed a high degree of satisfaction in their life situations with regard to economic, social and psychic aspects.

Because this small group of single mothers was composed of those belonging to a particular cultural milieu, they could be ascribed a model or a *trendsetter function* in certain circumstances. I have asked whether this type of *nest builder* exists also in Germany.

According to Eiduson the *nest—builders consciously planned their pregnancy and sought out a particular man to be the father of the child.* Therefore they can appear in theoretical terms as rationally acting decision makers.

In recent history, changes with regard to birth control have taken place to such an extent that the *pill* has not only made possible the planning or prevention of pregnancy, but has also left the decision of whether or not to have children more or less entirely to women. About 30 years ago, birth control measures were the responsibility of the man.

However, among the women in our random sample, there had been no rational decision taken to deliberately become pregnant. They all had unplanned pregnancies, regardless of their level of education, career position or age. In this respect our data corresponded with the

189

findings of other surveys which show that, in spite of current medical possibilities, pregnancies occur frequently as a result of rational calculation (see Wahl et al. 1980; Notz 1991).

In the literature many reasons are given for unintentional conception, for example the increasing refusal of women to take contraceptives; the overstrain of at least 30 years of disciplined behaviour; a *secret desire to have children*. From the qualitative interviews, it was possible to interpret specifically a lack of planning and some psychological reasons, the main one being the *secret desire to have children*.

After unintentional conception, the lack of planning in relation to pregnancy resulted in a dilemma followed by the decision to accept the unexpected child. This situation was positively substantiated.

The vast majority of the women who were interviewed had already known their partner for a long time before the child was born. Therefore the pregnancy was seldom the result of a casual acquaintance. Eighty—two percent said that the relationship had been going on for longer than six months; 28 percent were living together with the child's father in a non—marital community of life. The qualitative interviews also showed that none of the women interviewed wanted the child's father merely to be the *procreator of their child*, as expressed in the *nest—builder* thesis. It must be emphasized that many fathers took no part in the rational decision to have a child.

What became evident from the qualitative interviews was the procedure that the decision process frequently followed. Some of the women were faced with the situation in which they were forced to decide between the three goals of partner, child or abortion. All these unmarried mothers came to the same decision in their order of preference between the alternative goals, and life with the child was given the top priority. There was *unequivocality of benefit* as defined by the theory of decision making — in some cases, however, only after overcoming psychological ambivalences.

Examples:

> For me there was somehow no question about it. It's going to born and that's it. And I just decided to have the child and then

Single motherhood: An alternative form of life?

he said: *Go and have an abortion.* There was no way I was going
to do that; it doesn't matter if he wants it or not; it's none of his
business, if that's the way then he should decide; but the child
has a father, even if he doesn't care about it; but it still has a
father.

The decision was not always an easy one.

I had the feeling . . . of looking like a fool, having to decide
between the child and the relationship, and the feeling of being
left totally alone and lonely, really, so that sometimes I couldn't
sleep, that I was really very depressed. And that was, was
terrible. And it was also a terrible burden; well, I wasn't like
that the whole time, now and again I was furious as well . . . In
the meantime he didn't want to recognize the child because he
said it had been my decision, not his.

The quantitative survey confirmed that the decision by the mothers
in our sample who remained unmarried to have the child was taken
by them alone. Often, this decision was taken against the will of the
father. In only one—third of the cases did the father take part in the
decision to have the child.

Table 11.1
Decision to have the child

Decision makers	Percentage
Woman alone	55
Independent of the wishes of the father	35
Against the will of the father	21
Both partners together	33
Don't know	11
(N)	(177)

In contrast to the findings of Eiduson, in our sample, it was not only
the better educated women who made a decision to have their child in
opposition to or independently of the point of view of their partner.

Elementary school pupils represented 58 percent, 67 percent had an intermediate high school certificate, 47 percent were technical college graduates, and 51 percent had a high school diploma.

The high percentage of unmarried mothers who decided to have their child against or independently of the wishes of the child's father (table 11.1) indicates that a new form of living seems to be emerging. This finding differs from **that of** others as regards the circumstances of its formation: the conscious and positive decision to start a family as a mother—child unit without the subsystem of marriage.

The decision to have a child but not to marry

The thesis of the *nest—builders* is also based on the assumption that marriage no longer holds any attraction for certain women.

In our survey several women (17 percent) stated that, at the time their child was born, they were opposed generally to a formal contract of marriage. The correlation between rejection and completion of education was high (approximately —0.30). In the interview, however, a shift from the original rejection of marriage to an acceptance of it could be ascertained. Retrospectively, some distanced themselves from their rejection of a formal marriage and described their previous position more as an *attitude of protest* or as pressure to conform within a certain cultural milieu.

> And in the meantime I certainly no longer have those ideological reasons against marriage in the same form as I had before. Basically I never wanted to get married, never found it worthwhile to let yourself get so tied up. I always found it so stupid so why should I do it? I can decide for myself and for that reason, especially when I was pregnant, it wasn't particularly urgent because it's the usual thing to get married when you're pregnant . . . That was a kind of a small personal protest, not to do it. Especially since T's parents (the partner's) asked us on their bended knees to get married.

The majority (83 percent), however, did not reject marriage in general during their pregnancy. In answer to the question as to why a marriage was not contracted with the child's father, 31 percent emphasized that they were not sure *whether it was a 'lasting' partnership*. They were only skeptical of that particular relationship and did not speak out against either the institution *marriage* or in favour of marrying *at any price*, but stated that marriage should be of a certain quality and durability.

For many of the unmarried women interviewed in our sample, their partner relationships had ceased to exist by the time the child was born. In many cases an unplanned pregnancy (often not accepted on the part of the partner) seems to bring about a turning point in a relationship between an unmarried mother and her partner. The partnership had either broken up during the pregnancy (42 percent) or, in many cases, after the child was born or shortly afterwards. At the time of the interview, 91 percent of the mothers had remained unmarried and the partnership with the child's father had ceased to exist.

Therefore, even a decision taken jointly to have a child and living together is not necessarily a strong guarantee of the stability of the informal partner relationship. In general, the thesis can be put forward the thesis that an unwanted and unplanned pregnancy exerts pressure in certain situations so that the partner system undergoes changes because of it. The relationship is either dissolved as shown in our survey of mothers who remained unmarried or, as established by other studies from different European countries and the United States (with the exception of Sweden and Denmark), it is *transported* into a formal marital relationship (Dyer and Berlins 1982; Davis 1983; Nave—Herz 1984; Carlson 1985; Lüscher and Engstler 1990).

In contrast to the past, for the vast majority who remain unmarried, it is not a question of their child having been deserted by the father. On the contrary, many of the mothers (53 percent) had made their own decision regarding the separation from their partners. Differences with reference to level of education or career position could not be ascertained. Thirty—four percent of those questioned stated that they had made this decision jointly with their partner. Only 14 percent of the women questioned were saved the trouble of making this decision — the child's father had already left them.

Given that the relationships with partners were dissolved in nearly all cases by the women themselves or together with their partners, it seems that, during the psychologically and physically very strenuous period of early infancy, the informal motherhood, a partnership may not offer any relief to the young mother, but actually increases her burden. Some interview passages with the unmarried mothers indicate this:

> Probably there was always a subconscious fear if he is just a little bit irritated by K at the moment . . . or basically just by both of us, then he'll go away. And if I make it nice and pleasant for him, and maybe he won't notice that the child is annoying him, and then everything will be okay. And I think in a way it all just blew back in my face.

> Well, I'm neglecting my studies, I spend my time looking after A. and do nothing just for myself. And I know that I can't go on for long like this, because I will become so dissatisfied, that I . . . will take it out on M and A.

In these quotations we are reminded of the fact that many women feel they are under too much strain with regard to new problems in their relationships. Some do not know how long they will be able to cope with the constant burden of child rearing and *stress in their relationships*. Life for three women and its low degree of institutionalization called for a renegotiation of the partnership. This renegation occurred regardless of whether or not the household was shared with the child's father. Such a situation places an unusually heavy burden on the mothers. They tend to choose separation as a result.

Summary

In our random sample there were no *nest—builders* as defined by Eiduson, because unmarried motherhood was not defined as a goal of their actions.

In the case of those interviewed, unwanted pregnancy resulted in pressure to make decisions in certain situations. For all, there was a clear order of preference between the alternative goals. They decided to accept the unplanned child and knew well that, because of this decision, the partner relationship would no longer be durable. This turned out to be true. The child was valued above the relationship.

If the mothers interviewed had positively decided in favour of their form of life (i.e., starting a family without the subsystem of marriage or partnership), then the vast majority of them were still not *opponents of marriage*. Their conscious decision to opt for this form of life cannot be interpreted as merely a decision against formal marriages and families or cohabitation, with the exception of a small minority. This finding signifies, however, that the mother family and the mother—child unit can well represent a new subjectively accepted and planned family form in the course of the increasing process of individualization, but not in the sense of a conscious rejection of the two—parent family. Moreover, in this decision, we can see the priority of the family over marriage or cohabitation.

Notes

1 In the following I differentiate between parent families and single—parent families which are divided further into mother families and father families.
2 Even in the *Handbook of Marriage and the Family*, edited by M.B. Sussman and S.K. Steinmetz (1987), there is no description of this family form but all other family forms are reported in detail.

12 Light and heavy culture in American and Japanese advice books for women

Arlie Russell-Hochschild/Kazuko Tanaka

> Nowadays husbands and wives, parents and children don't say *hello* to each other in the morning. Sometimes not only does the wife not prepare breakfast, she doesn't even get out of bed. If you think this is sex equality and that the man is a *tender husband* you're mistaken.
>
> Soshitsu Sen, *What a Beautiful Woman*, 1980 pp. 22—23. Best selling advice book in Japan.

Is this a *lazy* wife, a depressed woman or a tired working mother? Is her husband *tender* or is he duped? If it is a working mother, is her job outside the home a loss or a gain? Building on Elina Haavio—Mannila's research on working mothers, we focus in this chapter on the cultural meaning of being a working mother. Using best—selling advice books for women published between 1970 and 1990 in Japan and the United States, we compare how the different cultures of these two capitalist giants conceived the working woman and her unresolved dilemmas. In particular, we probe the taken for granted premises that underlie each culture's ideas about her. In each culture these premises, we argue, form part of larger cultural bargains between men and women.

In some ways, Japanese and American women face the same story of the working mother's double day. For the last 50 years, half of the women in Japan have worked outside the home, a rapidly growing number of them in large companies and a relatively smaller but growing number of them, also as mothers of small children. Two—

thirds of all American women work, as do half the mothers of children six years old and under.[1] Thus, a higher proportion of American mothers work, but as Soshitsu Sen's statement at the beginning suggested, for those who are working mothers, the complaints are the same. But the contexts are different. Both Japan and the United States have an expanding industrial economy, a declining kin system, and cultures adapting to both shifts. Japan is a homogeneous society, barreling from the 19th century hierarchical feudalism to co—leadership of the 21st century industrial world. Japanese women have emerged from the bottom of the feudal hierarchy to the lower quadrant of modern economy. Women make up about a fifth of college and university students, and about 90 percent of junior college students. Japanese language, customs and rites have much more sharply divided men from women in Japan than men from women in the United States In the Japanese language, the character for *wife* symbolizes *inside house*. An advice book by Minoru Hamao, the former tutor of the Emperor and two princes, recommends separate school textbooks for Japanese boys and girls (1972).

American women have inherited a society less divided by sex and more open to the call of freedom and equality. A younger, larger (252 million) society, the United States is a more pluralistic society of settlers and newcomers. There, in the last 200 years, women have gone from being husband helpers on small farms to factory hands and domestic workers, and then to clerical and service workers. In contrast to Japan, however, American women are now branching into *male* trades, professions and management. Women make up about half of the students in the two and four year colleges and universities. The historic ideals of diversity and equality helped absorb many immigrant groups into America, and it seemed a short step in the 1900s and again in the 1960s for American feminists to say *us too*.

Women's advice books and cultural judgements

To understand the cultural lens through which people look at working mothers, advice books are a good place to begin. Best—selling advice books represent a cultural vote. Just as a study of politics includes a look at election returns, so the study of gender culture should include

the most widely read books in a society. From larger lists of best—
selling non—fiction books in Japan and the United States, we selected
17 Japanese and 28 American books that by title, cover, or table of
contents were directly addressed to women or addressed to social
issues of direct concern to women. We also read a few other books,
nonbest—sellers for women, some best—sellers for men, or for both
sexes. We excluded books focused on weight loss, smoking,
alcoholism, personal grooming, financial planning, sexual technique,
spiritualism, or moral uplift.[2]

Through what they say, authors propose a way of seeing things that
is based on a set of cultural premises. In actively selecting which
traditions to drop and which to keep in a *way of seeing things*, we
argue, authors play the role of cultural judges. They do not passively
transmit culture. They actively, selectively interpret and reconstruct it
so as to resolve problems readers face. In their enthusiasm for a book,
readers are saying that an author's *way of seeing* is relevant to their
lives. If it is relevant, it is living culture, culture people use. It is
culture people have in their heads when they think about or become a
working mother. We explored these contents, the authors' style of
giving advice, the tone of the advice, in search of the cultural
principles they reflect. In turn, we see these principles as themselves a
contested terrain, in which contending parties try out collective cultural
bargains over gender.

The weight of tradition

In comparing Japanese and American advice books, we found some
differences we expected and some we did not. To begin with, most
writers of advice books in Japan are men, while most in the United
States are women. Eight out of the 12 authors (of the 17 Japanese
advice books; one author wrote three) are men. Of the 28 American
books, 19 were by sole authors, and, of the 19, 14 authors were female,
and only five were male.

In addition, Japanese advice books are predominantly books of
morality and manners. They focus on the proper thing to do and the
inner virtues which proper behavior reflects. Authors tend to be
reserved, seldom personal, almost never confessional. In contrast,

most American advice books of the 1970s and 1980s were books of popular psychotherapy. Instead of morality and manners, they focused on healthy feelings. In such books, authors often tell about their own fear, dependency, or marital troubles before going on to describe their triumph over these. Only a few best—selling American advice books in this period were morality and manners books.

Japanese advice books focus relatively more on outer comportment, less on inner feelings, though sometimes they argue that outer behavior expresses the inner self. In the 1982 book *How To Be Considerate of Others*, Kenju Suzuki, a male author, instructs women in the intricate art of bowing. In another nonbest—seller, *Tenderness Makes Women Beautiful*, Suzuki tells women to speak softly, to remember to nod during conversations, to avoid wide strides, crossed legs and sudden loud laughs which reveal the upper gums *like a horse* (showing the lower gums is okay). In contrast, American advice books focus on inner feelings which may, but need not, reflect in one's face or behavior. For example, two American male authors, Connell Cowan and Melvyn Kinder in their 1985 *Smart Women, Foolish Choices* advise women how to recognize hidden dependency needs and how to end an *addiction to love*.

Compared with their American counterparts, Japanese advice books devote more space to collective life. For example, the 1970—1971 best—selling three—volume *Introduction to Rites of Passage* by Kazuko Shiotsuki, a female writer, appreciatively details the rites, festivals and celebrations which she sadly fears are in decline. She describes how the families of oldest sons should greet the families of younger sons or daughters to celebrate New Year's Day. She describes how to display dolls — the prince, the princess, three ladies—in—waiting, five male musicians — to celebrate Girl's Day and how to display warrior dolls with weapons to celebrate Boy's Day. (Boy's Day was renamed *Children's Day* and made into a Japanese national holiday. Girl's Day remains a more minor holiday.) Shiotsuki is not among the most traditional of advice—book writers; she proposes modifications in ceremonies — such as the traditional wedding — that leave the ceremonies seeming proper but modified to modern, urban needs. When she wrote this trilogy of ritual life in the early 1970s, half of Japanese women were in the labor force. But in affirming value only in the ritual life, Shiotsuki tacitly resists a major cause of its decline: women's march into paid work.

Among American advice books, no equivalent to *Introduction to Rites of Passage* exists. The Japanese texts suggest a different organizing principle than does the American writings. Japanese authors discuss the past as if it holds great weight. The past is there, people agree on what it is, and they disagree only on whether it is worth preserving. American authors write about the past as if it were light, thin, easy to remember wrongly, malleable. Not only do Japanese and American traditions differ in content, tradition itself feels different. The Japanese books seem to fall naturally along a continuum of total affirmation of the past, partial incorporation and total rejection of it. The basic question is how an author faces the past, the particular point of reference being the model of the upper middle—class woman of the 19th century Meijei Era. Kenji Suzuki's *The Story of Womanliness*, and Shoshitsu Sen's *How Beautiful She Is* affirm the past while *Introduction to Rites of Passage*, already mentioned, adapts tradition to modern circumstance. Such books as *Women's Capacity Depends on Language* by Kumiko Hirose, a female author, rejects tradition, especially linguistic practice.

A different organizing principle arises for the American books. The orienting question is not *Do you or don't you accept the past?* but *How light or heavy does the past feel?* The nearest equivalent to *Introduction to Rites of Passage* is Judith Martin's *Miss Manners' Guide to Rearing Perfect Children*, which is less serious in tone and more cavalier about tradition. Another book on proper dress, *The Woman's Dress for Success* book is by an author, John Molley, who describes himself as a *wardrobe engineer* (1977). He bases his advice, not on wise traditions, but on a scientific study of male executives' responses to various colors, cuts, and textures of female workers' clothes. Even the most traditional American advice book of the 1970s and 1980s, Marabel Morgan's 1973 *The Total Woman, a Fundamentalist Christian Guide to Housewives*, feels curiously modern by contrast with its Japanese counterparts. Morgan makes a case for tradition, not by saying tradition is *true* or *right* but by saying it is useful. If women learn to be deferential and sexually alluring, she suggests, their husbands will not abandon them as many husbands are doing to wives today. Morgan also suggests wearing Hollywood—type costumes to seduce one's husband each evening —

dress and manner that are utterly alien to 19th century notions of a decent, modest lady. She invents tradition, then nimbly buttresses her message by drawing on many sources — the Bible, business, psychotherapy — all at once, as if any one source of legitimacy lacks sufficient authority. Although her message is that women should defer to their husbands, a traditional message, she says it in a post—modern way. Thus the deeper difference between Japanese and American culture lies in how tradition feels.

The traditional Japanese woman: Beautiful, deferential, motherly

In addition to the different *feel* of tradition in the two cultures, the content of Japanese advice books is more patriarchal. The books advance virtues of beauty, motherliness and deference, virtues that would make an exhausted working mother feel guilty. Of the 17 best—selling Japanese advice books, nine are traditional. By traditional, we mean opposing women's equality with men. Four are modern, in the sense of advocating women's equality with men, and two are mixtures of both. In contrast, of the 28 best—selling American advice books, 15 are modern, 9 are traditional, and 4 are mixtures of both.

Taken as a whole, the largest group of Japanese advice books deals with cultural practices and the moral virtues of women that shine through whatever she is doing. A smaller number deal with heterosexual love, parent—child relations, or old age. The largest group of American advice books (about half) deal with male—female love and marriage, often with a focus on appraising men and one's emotional response to them. Far fewer deal with *virtues* or the proper role of women — and those that do focus on aspects of character from a psychological, not a moral, viewpoint. As in Japan, about a fifth of the books focus on parent—child relations. None of the American books focus on old age. Some traditional books such as Soshitsu Sen's *What A Beautiful Woman* (1980) extol the virtue of the woman who cares about how she looks. Sen describes a novelist's memory of his mother:

She had six children, so in the morning she was so busy. But none of these children ever saw her in a sloppy nightgown or dirty clothes. This is because she woke up earlier than the children. She opened the small window and under the window she began dissolving her face powder in water, and in one moment she applied the powder, combed her hair, and put on her kimono very neatly. So in my mind, my mother is always beautiful.

In addition to beauty, traditional Japanese advice books stress modesty and deference. In *How to Discipline Girls* (1972) Minoru Hamao says:

Mothers should defer to their husbands anytime in front of daughters. My wife often tells my daughters, *since father is coming back soon, let's wait to eat*. If he is late, his wife lets the kids eat early and waits to eat later with him. Not only in matters of eating, but in any important matter, my wife gives me the final decision. If my daughter wants money, her mother tells her . . . *if Daddy says okay, I'll give it to you*.

Most important, the Japanese wife should be motherly — both to her child *and* to her husband. In *A Story of Womanliness* (1983) Kenji Suzuki proudly tells how his wife picks out his underwear, socks, shirt, jacket and handkerchief each day. Again, Suzuki tells about falling down and scraping his knee when he was a small boy, and coming upon a small girl, who:

. . . took out a handkerchief from the sleeve of her kimono, while asking me, *Kenchan, are you all right*? and bandaged my wound. This was my first experience of the tenderness of girls. I wish my wound still hurt so Sacchan could come to my house. That was when girls were tender.

Modern Japanese woman: Independent and motherly in the workplace

Modern Japanese advice books focus on women's independence and on what stands in the way of it: Japanese culture. Unlike American modern books, which see few cultural obstacles in the way of *having it all*, modern advice books in Japan focus on sake custom. Perhaps the best example of this is *Women's Capacity Depends on Language* (1985) by Kumiko Hirose, a well—known radio announcer at the Japanese Broadcasting Corporation. In her book, she describes her struggle to be heard when paired with a male announcer: *I could ask no questions and guests on the program looked only at the male co—anchor. I became like a 'tsuma', a decoration at the side of the sashimi on the dinner plate.* Her struggle led her to call for a change in the way men and women speak the Japanese language. Japanese men and women are taught to speak with different intonations, pitch and vocabulary, so that women speak a deferential dialect of Japanese. The polite gender—neutral *I* (Watashi) differs from the more aggressive *I* (Ore) which is used by men. Hirose calls for a unisex Japanese language so that women may assume equal authority in public life — though she herself feels she can't use male language at work. Given what seems *natural* to a woman in Japan and given her desire to bond with her listeners, Hirose feels she can not simply make the private choice to speak in the male language. She feels a change in culture has to come first.

Hirose's struggle against Japanese culture, and her personal success, seems to her perfectly compatible with close, motherly and daughterly bonds with family and friends. Hirose talks to her radio listeners as to friends and family, creating in this way a mock kin system. When she falls ill, fans write in. When they fall sick, she writes or sends gifts. She struggles against being a decorative *tsuma* in the male world of Japanese radio. But she does not do this *on her own*, cowgirl style, as so many American advice books recommend. She tells us how she took courage from her female listeners when she was on the verge of quitting her Saturday afternoon program:

> The most important reason I didn't quit was that I received a card from a middle aged woman who said, when I was in the hospital I was deeply comforted to listen to you on the radio.

For me, who had almost become neurotic [over her struggle with male co—workers at the radio station], her words were like rays of sun.

Again, she says of her listeners, *Your warmth helped heal me from my isolation and loneliness, so I will never let you feel lonely and isolated.* In addition, she describes how she tried to gain the support for her struggle at work from her skeptical mother—in—law. Seeing how hard she works, her mother encourages Hirose to invite her mother—in—law to see her life on the set, and so appreciate her work. (She doesn't mention if it works.) Hirose does not write about her family and friends as if they were inherently incompatible with her fierce battle to win equality at work. She writes about how to make them compatible.

A few modern Japanese advice books focus on how to fit work with raising small children. Kingsley Ward in *Letters of a Business Man to his Daughter* (1989), the best—selling Japanese translation of a Canadian author describes how his wife (not he) took a leave from a high—powered executive job, when the children were small, to become a free—lance writer. He also tells how she later became famous as a screenwriter for children's television programs. She adapted to her children's needs *and* she was a success.

Other modern books focus on a more active role for fathers. Kingsley Ward calls on young fathers to change diapers, drive children to the doctor, wash dishes and shop in good spirit (1989). Again, in Yuzo Kayama's 1981 *This Love Forever: A Young Captain's Diary of Childrearing* (1981), the author, a famous actor who plays a daring adventurer, describes changing diapers at 3:00 a.m., throwing a ball, or playing train with his four tots. Though his wife, a homemaker, does more at home than he, his model is an advance over the stereotype of the Japanese salary man who, as the saying goes, comes home, sits down and utters three words, *dinner, bath, sleep.* Kayama's book is similar to Bill Cosby's, 1987 American best—seller, *Fatherhood.* Both are biographies of male media stars married to homemakers, and both celebrate active fathering from the safe distance of the primary breadwinner role.

There is the good news and bad in all this for the working mother in Japan. On one hand, tradition runs stronger in Japan. In the eyes of most conservative Japanese advice book writers, the mother who goes out to work, even if she must, is feared to be a *loss* to womanliness, motherliness, even basic manners. On the other hand, Hirose proudly gives and receives help. She honors and cultivates relationships of social support.

Traditional American woman: A joke

In contrast to traditional advice books in Japan, most American books seem to look at tradition as if glancing back over one's shoulder at a bygone age. Dr. James Dobson's *Parenting Isn't For Cowards* (1987) calls for traditional parenting while humorously commenting on modern times. Quoting a poem, *Where Have All the Grandmas Gone* (Dobson 1987), he says,

> In the dim and distant past,
> When life's tempo wasn't fast
> Grandma used to rock and knit,
> Crochet, chat and baby—sit . . .
> But today she's in the gym
> exercising to keep slim,
> She's off touring with the bunch,
> Or taking clients out to lunch . . .

Even more than the content of traditional advice books, the spirit is different. In contrast to best—selling Japanese traditionalists, who strike a serious, nostalgic or scolding tone, many best—selling American traditionalists are humorists. Erma Bombeck's three best—selling books, *Motherhood, the Second Oldest Profession, Aunt Erma's Cope Book*, or *The Grass is Always Greener Over the Septic Tank* are books — not about the perfect, beautiful, motherly housewife, but about her comic opposite. Bombeck makes fun of being unbeautiful, noting that every time she sees her neck in a mirror, she's reminded that she hasn't made chicken soup in a while. She makes fun of being deferential to her husband. When her husband asks her if she married him because she loved him or because he could repair broken household appliances, she stares back. Finally he says, *okay, I'll fix the broken sink.*

205

She even makes fun of motherliness. At one point she writes in her diary, *I'm terribly concerned about what's his name* (1972). At another point she complains that ... *the high point of my day is taking knots out of shoestrings — with my teeth — that a kid has wet on all day long* (1972). When, after moving to the suburbs to raise their family, her husband questions why she needs a second car, she makes fun of the isolation of the housewife in the suburbs. Explaining why she wants a car, she says:

> I'll be able to go to the store, join a bowling league, have lunch downtown with the girls, volunteer ... I want to see the big, outside world ... I want to rotate my tires with the rest of the girls. Don't you understand? I want to honk if I love Jesus! (1972)

Bombeck embraces the role of suburban homemaker not through serious nostalgia — as in the Japanese analog — but by making fun of the role she embraces. Again, in *Love and Marriage* (1990) Bill Cosby, the African American comedian, notes that he is the man of the house but that his wife, Camille, has the *keys to the house*. Among Japanese books, humor is more often located at the modern end of the continuum, as in Shusaku Endo's *Lazy Man's Guide to Love* (1973), not at the more anxious, traditional end.

Related to humor is the theme of fun. Traditional American advice books, like those by Marabel Morgan, Erma Bombeck and Bill Cosby, make the case that traditionalism is good, not — as in Japan — because it is *right*, but because it is *fun*. Thus the deepest rationale for tradition is not what it stands for in some objective sense but how it feels. Behind this subjectivism is a taste of American pragmatism. For, if a social pattern feels right in the modern Tilt—a—Whirl age where traditions need continual testing, it is a sign that aspects of traditional culture work.

Modern American woman: Autonomous and asocial

Best—selling modern American advice books welcome the working mother. They prepare an emotional path for her. If the traditional

American books assume an air of exchanging funny stories in the livingroom after dinner, the modern books put the reader on the psychoanalyst's couch for a serious review of her *issues*. Often focused on troubles with men, books such as C. Cowan's and M. Kinders' *Smart Woman, Foolish Choices* or Robin Norwood's *Women Who Love Too Much*, devote their serious tone not to reverence for past, but to a *healing* of the modern heart.

American modern advice books also give less honor, if not less attention, to the social support of family, friends and co—workers. There is no analog among the progressive American advice books to Kumiko Hirose's invitation to her mother—in—law to come and watch her in the studio. There is much less grateful mention of depending on the encouragement of a mother or good friend. From time to time, American advice books mention the support of a friend or a relative, but these are offered in passing without appreciative mention for their helpfulness.

Most extreme in its spirit of *going it alone* is Colette Dowling's *The Cinderella Complex* (1981), translated into Japanese but never a best—seller there. Dowling tells the tale of Simone de Beauvoir's internal struggle *to exorcise her urge to be dependent* on Jean Paul Sartre. One way she expressed this urge was to face challenges and test her endurance by hiking up steep mountains:

> Alone I walked the mists that hung over the summit of Sainte—Victoire, and trod along the ridge of the Silon de Roi, bracing myself against a violent wind which sent my beret spinning down into the valley below. Alone again, I got lost in a mountain ravine on the Luberon range. Such moments, with all their warmth, tenderness, and fury, belong to me and to no one else.

While Hirose, the Japanese newscaster, focuses on a moment during which she takes courage from an older female fan, in the American text, the spotlight is on the woman *on her own*. Both Hirose and Dowling's De Beauvoir struggle to express themselves. Both do express themselves. Both have social bonds to others. We imagine that both need the support of others. But the books seem to us to place different cultural values on this need. In Japanese advice books, social bonds are more likely to be credited with enabling a woman to achieve her goals. American advice books are more likely to view such bonds as neutral or even as an impediment to achievement.

In addition to the value placed on attachment, there is a difference in the object of attachment. Of all American advice books, none is devoted exclusively to the topic of the elderly, and in the others it is mentioned very little. When old age is mentioned — as it is, for example, in Helen Gurley Brown's *Having It All* — it is mentioned not as an occasion to help others but as an aspect of self to disguise. In the Japanese best—seller *How To Grow Old Together* (1978) Hajime Mizuno addresses the conflict between women's paid work outside the home and care of the elderly. It suggests that the elderly, themselves, should develop interests on their own. In addition, as they retire, men will have to learn to be more considerate of their wives. As Mizuno notes:

> It is said if you don't use your brain when you're old, the brain ages faster. If you stay at home without doing anything and ask your wife, oiy oiy, give me tobacco. Give me a light. Give me my newspapers. — if you act like this — your brain will age very fast and the final destination will be senility.

A Japanese popular saying about retired salary men is, *you stick to your wife like wet fallen leaves to feet*. The modern advice books say, *get your own tobacco, and help around the house*. Ironically, in America as in Japan, it is mainly women who care for the elderly. By avoiding the topic of old age, American advice books also avoid a basic problem for working mothers.

On the whole, the American advice books suggest two sides of American individualism. The *good side* of American individualism allows American women to benefit from the opportunities of advanced capitalism. But the *bad side* leads Americans to avoid the link between individualism and contest. It leads to a focus on the *right* personality — assertive, confident — and not on the right national day—care program, the best flexible schedule at work, or a helpful set of friends and family.

Comparing cultural stretch: Content and tone

The Japanese advice books reflect a far wider range of standpoints on the role of women than do their American counterparts. At the conservative extreme is *How to Discipline Girls* (1972) by Minoru Hamao, a former tutor of the Emperor and two princes. Hamao advises that *mothers should show respect for their husband's higher authority under all circumstances.* At the other extreme is Kumiko Hirose, the radio announcer. Among the American books, the extremes are closer together. That is, the Emperor's former tutor is farther away from the radio announcer, than, say Marabel Morgan, American author of *The Total Woman* is from Colette Dowling, author of *The Cinderella Complex.* One reason for this difference may be the more rapid pace of change in Japan than in the United States.

The range in tones of authority is also far wider among the Japanese than among the American advice books. Some authors write with a tone of stern command, as if to say, *I have the unquestioned right to tell you what to do.* The advice of the Emperor's former tutor, for example, takes the form of a hundred commands (*You should . . ., You should not . . .*) The rules are absolute; they do not depend on a context. And the author poses himself as the sole arbiter of the rules. In a preface to *How To Discipline Girls* (1972), Minoru Hamao notes:

> This is for parents who raise girls and for young women about to marry and for women students. I want these people to read my book, and I also want critiques from teachers or other educators . . .

He invites no critiques from the girls themselves.

Other Japanese authors write in a spirit of an older sister: *Why don't you try this; it might work.* This range of tone is probably due to the greater difference, in Japan, between the way *female* and *male* authors — at least conservative older males — grip authority. Between the early 1970s and the late 1980s, the gender gap in the style of giving advice closed somewhat, leaving three types of voice — the old male authoritarian voice, the new male more democratic voice, and the new female democratic voice. In the American books, the old male authoritarian voice is missing.

Although most of the traditional Japanese books were written by men, it is not traditionalism which predicts the authoritarian tone. It is being male. The traditional female author, Yaeko Shiotsuki, grand master of the Japanese tea ceremony and author of the best—selling, three volume *Introduction to Rites of Passage* (1970), begins modestly:

> When the editor encouraged me to write this book, I worried about my limited ability to write, but I decided to accept this opportunity and consulting other professionals in the field, I finally finished it.

Feminist female Japanese authors — Fumi Saimon and Kumiko Hirose, adopt a more assertive, but also more self—revealing, equalizing, and sisterly tone that makes them more like American female — and even American male — authors. For example, Fumi Saimon, a female humorist ends her 1990 *The Art of Loving* with this:

> Why could I write of love? ... If a person is born a genius and can solve difficult equations at a glance and he writes about his experience passing an entrance exam for Tokyo University, then what use is it for most people? It's the same with love. If a woman just by walking down the street is approached by men who want to ask her to go to bed, or gets proposals from the very rich, or is sent words of love by artists, and writes about her experiences of love, this is useless to most girls (though it's very interesting just as a story). The regular person should be satisfied with falling in love once or twice in a life ... I myself have fallen in love from the bottom of my heart once or twice. And these are the treasures of my life. If you can experience true love, once or twice in life, this is a big success for the average person ...

American women authors do not differ in tone from male authors, mainly because the male authors wield authority gently. Instead of commanding *You should, or you should not* ... in *Smart Women, Foolish Choices* (1985), American male authors, Dr. Connell Cowan and Dr. Melvyn Kinder say:

Perhaps you are wondering who we are, and why we think we have something to say to smart women about their relationships with men. We are clinical psychologists who maintain individual practices of psychotherapy . . .

As men, we believe we **understand** how other men think, feel and react. We're going to **tell** you about strategies that work with men and . . . we will **reveal** insights and strategies that we hope will convince you that what now may appear to be a stand off between the sexes can instead be your opportunity to claim delightful, fulfilling experiences with men.

In making something so personal as their sex relevant to the credibility of their advice, Cowan and Kinder resemble such female writers as Robin Norwood (*Women Who Love Too Much*) or Susan Forward and Joan Torres (*Men Who Hate Women and the Women Who Love Them*).

The greater stretch between cultural extremes in both content and voice suggests more rapid changes in the 1970s and 1980s in Japan than in the United States. It suggests a deeper change in the relation between gender and authority. For giving advice is telling people what to do. However nicely, and personally in doing so, the advice—giver assumes authority. American female writers seem far more comfortable with their authority than their Japanese counterparts. In this respect, the medium is part of the message.

Conclusion

To summarize, the best—selling Japanese advice books that appeared between 1970 and 1990 incline toward morality and manners, American books toward personality. Japanese books focus relatively more on collective life — rites, rituals — American books, on the individuals person. Although Japan is the more culturally homogeneous society of the two, its range of views on women is wider. Ironically, in diverse America, the books ae more homogeneous. Japanese books praise women for their attention to beauty, deference and motherliness, not brilliance, creativity, public speaking or drive. But the few feminist Japanese books seem to synthesize a drive for independence with a value on ties to friends and family. In all these ways, the traditional and modern Japanese books are more similar to each other than they are to American books.

The books differ in a deeper way too. American traditional books hold tradition lightly, pointing to what is humorous or fun about it. Even the serious American traditionalists use lighter appeals — focusing on how *useful* a view is, not how *right*. American modern books focus far more closely on how to find, keep or drop a man, and have relatively little to say about children or the elderly. Underlying each set of advice, seems to be different ideas about social ties. The emotional model underlying the Japanese books seems to be a social web with the young, middle—aged and old. The emotional model underlying the American books seems to be a closed circle surrounding a 30ish woman, man and their children.

A model of culture

But in both cultures, beliefs and practice are the stuff of cultural collective bargaining. Cultural customs such as the Watashi *I* and the Ore *I*, in Japanese, the restrictions on how women laugh or walk, are not simply laid out like objects in a museum. Advice books for women in Japan and the United States we propose, describe the cultural practices and beliefs that are bargained about. They tell us what modernizing women and their allies and traditional men and their allies each bring to the imaginary cultural bargaining table. In this view, some customs are a tool in the hands of those who uphold patriarchy. Other customs are a tool in the hands of those pressing for equality. Some are useful to both or neither. Customs held lightly, with humor, are worth less in trade—offs than customs which are sacred. The affirmation or challenge of culture in books such as these is part of a quiet struggle about the legitimacy of *good terms* for the working mother.

In both countries, the current male position is similar; only in Japan it is held more strongly: We'll let you work as long as you don't withdraw your motherly services at home and show the same devotion to work as men at work. In Japan, women have been wedged in between these two provisos and are beginning to challenge the first. In the United States, relatively more women have challenged the

212

first proviso, but given in to the second. In the end, for Japanese women, the problem is to promote the gender revolution. To accomlish this goal, they will have to challenge the gender divisions that run so deep, including the gender division built into everyday language. Japan's more communal ethos, we argue, is also partly a problem for Japanese working mothers, since it is mainly women who do the work of maintaining this *ethos*. On the other hand, this communal ethos, this *systems approach,* is a way of seeing things that can help protect Japanese women from falling into the trap of a stalled revolution in which women are individually *emancipated* in a society that leaves each woman to cope on her own. It helps them value social support.

For American women, the problem is getting out of a stall in the revolution and finishing the job of equality. For them, the way advice books talk gets in the way. In America, a woman can rise *on her own* but she can also fall *on her own.* Whether she rises or falls depends less on her private initiative than on state or community efforts to set up the day care, the flexible workplace, and the services that can make work and family go together well. The do—it—yourself ideology of American advice books blind women to this fact.

We will have to struggle differently with our cultures to resolve our different dilemmas by forging different cultural bargains based on the cultural resources at hand. But in each case, the aim should be to press for full equality, while valuing ties to family and friends, and for larger social supports for the working mother. With such a bargain as a basis, a working mother can wake up rested, help her husband get breakfast, and sit down to a relaxed meal with the children before going off to work.

Notes

1   The Japanese have historically honored the male family line and strongly stressed maternal sacrifice and children's dependence, and, according to Masahiro Yamada, a sociologist at the University of Tokyo, have built capitalism on the basis of it

213

— adult men transfer their dependence to the company and, like their mothers, sacrifice themselves to it in the process of building capitalism. Today, while the tradition of maternal sacrifice remains, other aspects of the Japanese family is changing. Parents less often arrange their children's marriages, children more often make their own *love* match. Marriage is less *compulsory*; fewer marry; those who do marry more often live independently of their parents and, compared with the previous generation, have fewer children. Although very low to begin, the divorce rate has risen since the 1960s to a high of one out of four today. Outside certain ethnic enclaves, marriages in the United States were never arranged. But people marry later, marry less, and when they marry have fewer children. They are also more prone to divorce.

2   We chose best sellers in hard cover or paperback, in the trade and mass market for the years 1970 through 1990. For ratings for the American books, we relied on Ben Bowker's *Eighty Years of Best Sellers* and ratings published by *Publisher's Weekly*. The criteria used by *Publisher's Weekly* to determine a best—seller changed through the years, and we have followed their changes. The American system for determining a best seller was the number of books publishers shipped to bookstores.The Japanese system was to poll the owners of major bookstores.

3   Until the 1900s, most advice books in America were also authored by men.

4   Just as in labor struggles, there are labor—management *collective bargains*, so collective bargains emerge between women and men. Both are bargains between groups, not simply between given individuals who may dissent against a wider agreement. Both are attempts to reconcile contending demands, and both change from time to time. The difference is that, in economic life, collective bargaining is about money and work benefits. In cultural life, collective bargaining is about visibility, honor, authority. In economic life, it concerns the issues are conscious, in cultural life, issues which are often unconscious.

13 The unresolved and unsolvable affective dilemmas of career women

Constantina Safilios-Rothschild

In the 1980s and 1990s in some developed countries such as the United States and the Scandinavian countries, career women have begun to have the comforting illusion that it is possible to combine love and a career. Some of them may even be able to accomplish it for a short time. Soon either the demands of the lover or the demands of an absorbing career catch up with them, and they are sitting on the eternal dilemma of bright and dedicated women: how to manage to enjoy a career and a love fully without *losing themselves*. An almost impossible affective dilemma of dedicated, passionate women was clearly described in 1923 by Alexandra Kollontai, the intellectual feminist of the Russian Revolution, by analyzing the *new image of women* appearing in the post—revolutionary European literature. As we shall see in the following discussion, these images of *les femmes nouvelles* or *les femmes celibataires* of that far away era still describe rather accurately some of the conflicts, problems and ambivalences of modern liberated women on all continents.

I do not discuss the relatively lesser dilemmas of combining marriage with work, the predominant problem of the 1960s. While this combination still presents many difficulties, the difficulties are mostly managerial problems of time and energy allocation. Many women and men can find often tiring, if not exhausting, solutions that may entail a number of compromises for one or both partners in their work or affective lives. They are not easy compromises, but they are usually feasible, especially when the passionate, all—absorbing element in both the work and the affective life of one or of both of them is less intense. In general, the solutions represent accommodations to practical problems such as the needs of the children, the needs of family life and the need to earn a sufficient income to sustain the family. As a part of such accommodations, some women have even managed to leave husbands behind and pursue their careers away from them for more or less lengthy periods. When these separations are not too long, they have often been without serious disruptions in their relationship. Longer separations, however, more often lead to attachments with other partners and to divorce. But leaving a lover for quite a while? Lovers are much more demanding than husbands in terms of presence, reciprocity and physical loving not on the basis of legal rights but on the basis of their feelings of love.

The distinction needs to be made between marriage and love, a love that remains intense, absorbing and demanding and does not get domesticated and changed into a tender habit. Furthermore, the difference between work and career is crucial since the essence of the latter is the degree of identification with the work and the degree of dedication of one's energy, heart and soul.[1] A career is demanding and absorbs one's thoughts, preoccupations and actions. It is under these conditions that a woman is torn between the two passions.

Before the women's movement, even professional women spent a lot of energy presenting an image of themselves to the world that indicated that their work was not so important to them; it could, therefore, be relegated to a secondary position to their family life. In this way, the type of dilemma discussed in this paper was not allowed to be fully developed. In reality, of course, occasionally their careers became important, and it was no longer possible to put on the non—serious facade. And then the marriage was in trouble because men were not comfortable with a wife deeply involved in a career that distracted her attention away from the tender care due to them. The essence of the problem in these cases was in fact a power struggle: men could not maintain the feeling of superiority and control vis—à—vis their wives when the wives' careers changed and became publicly recognized as important, sometimes more important than their own. The competing strong element was the traditional expectation that women had to be devoted mothers and wives and emotionally available to their families. Of course, in many cases, the dilemma posed may have been somewhat different than the one discussed since it may not have involved two passionate pursuits because the affective relationship between the women and their husbands may not have been intense and demanding. In these cases, more *liberated* husbands with such less intense and demanding affective needs were able to even encourage their wives in these pursuits.

In the 1990s, after many social and psychological changes have taken place in men's and women's lives, women feel freer to opt for absorbing, fulfilling careers with less guilt and discomfort. This newly acquired freedom, however, has also more clearly defined their affective dilemmas than before. These affective dilemmas, already discussed by Kollontai in the 1920s, are those experienced by women who cannot accept being defined through the men they love, even when they love them passionately. When love is felt passionately, it becomes threatening to their way of life and the threat is coped with by limiting its duration so as to relegate it to a short phase that passes while work is the stable life orientation.

Many women solve their dilemma by deciding to prefer their careers, which can often give them more stability than their love for a special man. In many African countries, the *single women* are generally urban, well—educated and ambitious, and they opt to not marry but may have children sometimes with successful men with whom they have relations of varying length and intensity. In addition, for the last ten years or so, the popular psychology books in the United States that give advice to women for successful love relationships have in different ways dealt with these affective dilemmas of women seriously involved in their careers, as well as in their own psychological growth and development. Most of these books utilize different techniques to empower women by giving them the necessary insights and skills to allow them to enter love relationships *without submerging their personalities* in the men and in the relationship.

The dilemma is even more difficult when the woman's career requires considerable traveling and sojourns in far away places. Of course, a lover can feel left behind even when the woman is in the same house but absorbed in her career and not emotionally available to fulfill his affective and sexual needs. But the physical separation accentuates her lack of availability, underlines her power position by the fact that she determines when and for how long it is possible to be together and is further threatening since it involves an increased possibility of encounters with other potentially attractive men.

217

What is new in the 1990s is that men have begun to experience the same affective dilemmas since the social, structural and psychological changes that have taken place increasingly offer women careers and emotional or sexual options similar to those of men. In addition, men in love are also expected to display very different roles and to provide emotional support to the women they love, including support for their careers. It is, therefore, becoming more difficult and less acceptable for men to behave in the same selfish and possessive manner as in the past in regard to their lover's career involvement. And the tougher question is: *Can a man and woman who are both dedicated to their careers ever manage to live a passionate love?*

The affective dilemmas of career men and women have become even more complicated. Proof of the experienced stresses and strains is the appearance of a new pattern of intimate relationships that seems to be structurally better adapted: middle—aged women entering into love relationships, in the form of marriage (usually second marriages for the women) or living together with younger men. During the 1980s, this pattern became more common in the United States (and is slower making its appearance in Western Europe) where women in all types of careers, from executives and scientists to factory workers and sales ladies, opt for this type of more compatible type of intimate relationship.

Maybe no one, a man or a woman, can have two passions. When a career is a state of mind going beyond the particular job or tasks that one has and when it involves one's heart and soul, it ceases being an intellectual pursuit. It becomes a strong emotional involvement that is difficult to reconcile successfully with another passion. Men in the past were able to have a career and a lover only when she was willing to efface herself and live for him and through him and his career. She had very limited expectations from him and accepted his physical and emotional absence when he was absorbed in his career. She was satisfied with the fact that an important, dedicated man loved her once in a while.

It is not a coincidence that, when one meets women (in the world) who are dedicated to changing the development scenario for women or women with remarkable careers in science or business, they are either living alone or they are in traditional marriages (often in arranged marriages as in many Asian countries) in which their hearts

218

and souls are not heavily invested. Some go in and out of marriages driven by loneliness and the desire to have *normal* lives. Others make a clear choice in favour of their careers and resign themselves to having brief love encounters or only friendships.

The women's movement and all kinds of far reaching policies have possible helped solve to some extent, some practical problems involved in combining a family with work, but they have not even touched the affective dilemmas of women torn between two crucial passions. And now increasingly men face similar problems. Is the fact that men share this problem the beginning of the solution? Or is this dilemma a truly structural problem that is impossible to solve? Maybe we are asking too much: to love intensely, to have a fulfilling career that realizes us and to have both passions last. Probably the solution lies in a flexible, multiphase pattern throughout women's (and men's) lives. The recent trends in many developed countries have clearly shown that even the most successful men and women in the highest positions cannot count on career stability. So many conditions change outside and inside ourselves that, for each stage, a different pattern of work involvement and intimate relationships may be the most satisfying. In some stages, one may prefer close friendship relationships with men and women over love relationships, while in others, one may opt for the traditional form of marriage. It may be therefore, that women and maybe also men may have to be content with short—lived passionate love and go on steadily with one's absorbing career as long as it lasts, but they must be prepared to be flexible and creative even in this area.

Notes

1   The term career does not refer only to professional or managerial women. In fact, it may not apply to all professional or managerial women, and it may apply to women in different types of work such as the military jobs, foremen and skilled workers, or even office workers. For it is not the nature of work that determines whether or not it constitutes a career, but rather what the woman invests in it and what it represents to her.

Bibliography

Abel, E.K. and Nelson, M.K. (1990), *Circles of Care: Work and Identity in Women's Lives*, State University of New York Press, Albany.

Abramovitz, M. (1988), *Regulating the Lives of Women. Social Welfare Policy from Colonial Times to the Present*, South End Press, Boston.

Acker, J. (1991), 'Thinking About Wages; The Gendered Wage Gap in Swedish Banks', *Gender and Society*, Vol. 5, pp. 390—407.

Alanen, R. (1981), 'Päivähoidon yhteyksistä naisten asemaan ja perheeseen', (in Finnish). *Sosiaalipolitiikan pro gradu —tutkielma*, Helsingin yliopisto, Helsinki.

Alestalo, M. (1991), Julkisen sektorin laajentuminen. *Sosiaalipolitiikan vuosikirja*, Vol. 16, pp. 7—36.

Allen, K. (1989), *Single Women/Family Ties; Life Histories of Older Women*, Sage, London.

Amott, T. (1990), 'Black Women and AFDC: Making Entitlement out of Necessity', in Gordon, L. (ed.), *Women, The State and Welfare*. University of Wisconsin, Madison.

Anttonen, A. (1990), 'The Feminization of the Scandinavian Welfare State', in Simonen, L. (ed.), *Finnish Debates on Women's Studies*, Tampereen yliopisto, Naistutkimusyksikkö, Työraportteja No. 2, pp. 3—25.

Arber, S. and Lahelma, E. (1993) 'Women, Paid Employment and Ill-health in Britain and Finland', *Acta Sociologica*, Vol. 36, No.2, pp. 121-138.

220

Baalsrud, E.S. and Fougner, B.A. (1992), 'Chain of Women', in Baalsrud E.S. (ed.), *Free and Equal? Female Voices from Central and Eastern Europe*, Norwegian Equal Status Council, No. 2.

Baker, T.L. and Sween, J.A. (1982), 'Synchronizing Post—Graduate Career, Marriage, and Fertility', *Western Sociological Review*, No. 13 (1), pp. 69—86.

Baldwin, P. (1990), *The Politics of Social Solidarity*, Cambridge University Press, Cambridge.

Baldwin, P. (1992), *Citizenship and Welfare: The View from Beveridge*, a paper presented at the conference on Comparative Studies of Welfare State Development, Quantitative and Qualitative Dimensions, University of Bremen, Germany.

Barrett, M. and McIntosh, M. (1982), *The anti—social Family*, Verso, London.

Baruch, G.K. and Barnett, R.C. (1983), *Lifeprints: New Patterns of Love and Work for Today's Women*, McGraw—Hill, New York.

Beck—Gernsheim, E. (1988), 'Von der Pille zum Retortenbaby: Neue Handlungsmöglichkeiten, neue Handlungszwänge im Bereich des generativen Verhaltens', in Lüscher, K. et. al (eds.). *Familiale Lebensformen und Familienpolitik — Übergang zur Postmoderne*, Konstanz, pp. 201—215.

Becker, G.S. (1981), *A Treatise on the Family*, Harvard University Press, Cambridge, Mass.

Bell, R.R. (1984), *Sexuality and cross gender friendships*, paper presented at the National Council on Family Relations Annual Meetings, San Francisco, CA.

Berger—Schmitt, R., Glatzer, W. et. al. (1991), 'Die Lebenssituation alleinstehender Frauen', *Schriftenreihe des Bundesministers für Frauen und Jugend*, Bd. 2. Stuttgart.

Bernard, J. (1972), *The Future of Marriage*, World Publishing Co, New York.

Bimbi, F. (1990), *Parenthood in Italy: Asymmetrical Relationships and Family Affection*, paper for the working—meeting on 'European Parents in the 1990s', Suzdal.

Bombeck, E. (1976), *The Grass Is Always Greener Over the Septic Tank*, McGraw Hill, New York.

Bombeck, E. (1983), *Motherhood, The Second Oldest Profession*, Dell Publishers, New York.

Borchost, A. (1994), 'Scandinavian Welfare States —patriarchal, gender neutral, or women friendly?', *International Journal of contemporary Sociology*, Vol. 1, No. 3.

Bowen, D.E. and Cummings, T.G. (1990), 'Suppose We Took Service Seriously?', in Bowen D.E., Chase R.B., Cummings T.G. and Associates, (eds.), *Service Management Effectiveness*, Jossey—Bass Inc., San Francisco, pp. 1—14.

Bowker, B. (1977), *Eighty Years of Best Sellers*, R.R. Bowker, New York.

Brief, A.P. and Nord, W.R. (1990), *Meaning of occupational work*, A collection of essays, Lexington Books, Lexington, MA.

Brown, H.G. (1982), *Having It All*, Pocket Books, New York.

Carlson, E. (1985), 'Couples Without Children: Premarital Cohabitation in France', in Davis, K. (ed.), *Contemporary Marriage*, Russell Sage Foundation, New York, pp. 111—132.

Chandler, J. (1991), *Women Without Husbands: An Exploration of The Margins of Marriage*, Macmillan, London.

Chodorow, N. (1978), *The Reproduction of Mothering: Psychoanalysis and the Sociology of Gender*, University of California Press, Berkeley.

Christensen, A. and Heavey, C.L. (1990), 'Gender and Social Structure in the Demand/Withdraw Pattern of Marital Conflict', *Journal of Personality and Social Psychology*, No. 59, pp. 73—81.

Cosby, B. (1987), *Fatherhood*, Berkley Press, New York.

Cosby, B. (1989), *Love and Marriage*, Bantam Books, New York.

Coser, R.L. (1991), *In Defense of Modernity*, Stanford University Press, Stanford.

Cowan, C. and Kinder, M. (1985), *Smart Women, Foolish Choices*, Signet Books, New York.

Crary, M. (1987), 'Managing attraction and intimacy at work', *Organizational Dynamics*, No. 15(4), pp. 27—40.

Crosby, F.J. (ed.) (1987), *Spouse, Parent, Worker: On Gender and Multiple Roles*, Yale University Press, New Haven.

Davis, K. (1983), 'The Future of Marriage', *Bulletin of the American Academy of Arts and Sciences*, pp. 15—43.

Davis, K. (1985), *Contemporary Marriage*, Russell Sage Foundation, New York.

Deaux, K. (1992), 'Personalizing Identity and Socializing Self', in Breakwell, G. (ed.), *Social Psychology of the Self—Concept*, Academic Press Ltd., London.

De Gruyter, A. and Erickson, R.J. (1991), *When Emotion is the Product: Self, Society, and (In) Authenticity in a Postmodern World*, unpublished Doctoral Dissertation, Washington State University, Pullman, WA.

DeVault, M.L. (1991), *Feeding the Family: The Social Organization of Caring as Gendered Work*, University of Chicago Press, Chicago.

Dobson, J.C. (1987), *Parenting Isn't For Cowards*, Word Publishing, Dallas.

Dowling, C. (1981), *The Cinderella Complex*, Pocket Books, New York.

Duggan, J. (1993), *The Effect of Family Policy on the Household Division of Labor: A Comparison of East and West Germany*, paper presented to the German Socio—Economic Panel User Conference, Berlin.

Dyer, C. and Berlins, M. (1982), *Living together*, The Hamlyn Publishing Group Ltd., Feltham/Middlesex, England.

Eckelaar, J. and MacLean, M. (1986) *Maintenance After Divorce*, Claredon Press, Oxford.

Eiduson, B.T. (1980), 'Contemporary Single Mothers', in Katz, L.G. (ed.), *Current Topics in Early Childhood Education*, Norwood, N.J., pp. 65—76.

Elliot, F.R. (1986), *The Family: Change or Continuity*, MacMillau Education Ltd., London.

Endo, S. (1973), *Lazy Man's Guide to Love*, Kodanska, Tokyo.

England, P. (1992), *Comparable Worth: Theories and Evidence*, Hawthorne, NY.

Epstein, C.F. (1970), *Woman's Place*, University of California Press, Berkeley.

Epstein, C.F. (1973), 'Positive Effects of the Multiple Negative: Explaining the Success of Black Professional Women', *American Journal of Sociology*, No. 78, January, pp. 912—935.

Epstein, C.F. (1981), *Women In Law*, Basic Books, N.Y., Second Edition (1993), University of Illinois Press, Chicago.

Epstein, C.F. (1987), 'Multiple Demands and Multiple Roles: The Conditions of Successful Management', in Crosby, F.J. (ed.), *Spouse, Parent, Worker: On Gender and Multiple Roles*, Yale University Press, New Haven, pp. 23—35 .

Epstein, C.F. (1988), *Deceptive Distinctions: Sex, Gender and the Social Order*, Yale University Press, New Haven.

Epstein, C.F. (1992), 'Tinkerbells and Pinups: The Construction and Reconstruction of Gender Boundaries at Work', in Lamont, M. and

Fournier, M. (eds.), *Cultivating Differences: Symbolic Boundaries and the Making of Inequality*, University of Chicago Press, Chicago, pp. 232—256.

Espenshade, T.J. (1985), 'The Recent Decline of American Marriage', in Davis, K., (ed.), *Contemporary Marriage*, Russell Sage Foundation, New York, pp. 53—90.

Esping—Andersen, G. and Korpi, W. (1987), 'From Poor Relief to Institutional Welfare States: The Development of Scandinavian Social Policy', in Esping—Andersen, G. and Korpi, W. (eds.), *The Scandinavian Model: Welfare States and Welfare*, State Research, Sharpe M.E.

Feree, M.M. (1995), 'Patriarchies and Feminisms: The Two Women's Movements of East European Transitions', *Social Politics: International Studies of Gender, State, and Society*, Vol. 2.

Finch, J. and Groves, D. (eds.), (1983), *A Labour of Love: Women, Work and Caring*, Routledge & Kegan Paul, London.

Flood, L. and Klevmarken, A. (1990), 'Tidsanvändning i Sverige 1984', in Jonung, C. and Persson, I., (eds.) *Kvinnors roll i ekonomin*, (in Swedish), Allmänna Förlaget, Lånatidsutredningen, Bilaga 23, Stockholm.

Forward, S and Torres, J. (1986), *Men Who Hate Women and the Women Who Love Them*, Bantam Books, New York.

Fraser, N. (1994), 'After the Family Wage: Gender Equity and the Welfare State', *Political Theory*, Vol. 22., November.

Fraser, N. (1990), 'Women, Welfare and the Politics of Need Interpretation', *Unruly Practices*, University of Minnesota Press, Minneapolis.

Fraser, N. and Gordon, L. (1994), 'Dependency: Inscriptions of Power in a Keyword of the Welfare State', *Social Politics: International Studies of Gender, State, and Society*, Vol. 1, Spring.

Fraser, N. (1989), *Unruly Practices. Power, Discourse and Gender in Contemporary Social Theory*, University of Minnesota Press, Minneapolis.

Friedland, R. and Alford, R.A. (1991), 'Bringing Society Back, Symbols, Practices, and Institutional Contradictions', in Powell, W.W. and DiMaggio, P.J. (eds.), *The New Institutionalism in Organizational Analysis*, University of Chicago Press, Chicago, pp. 232—265.

Garnaghan, E. and Bahry, D. (1990), 'Political Attitudes and the Gender Gap in the USSR', *Comparative Politics*, pp. 379—399.

Gerstenberger, H. (1985), 'The Poor and Respectable Worker: On the Introduction of Social Insurance in Germany', *Labour History, A Journal of Labour and Social History*, No. 48, May, pp. 69—85.

Giele, J.Z. (1991), *Life Patterns of Mature Women in the National Longitudinal Surveys, 1967—82*, final Report to the Research Support Program of the Murray Research Center, Radcliffe College, Waltham, Mass., Heller School, Brandeis University.

Giele, J.Z. (1993), 'Women's Role Change and Adaptation, 1920—1990', in Hulbert, K. and Schuster, D. (eds.), *Educated American Women of the Twentieth Century*, Jossey—Bass, San Francisco.

Giele, J.Z. (1995), *Two Paths to Women's Equality: Temperance, Suffrage, and the Course of American Feminism*, Twayne Publishers, Macmillan, New York.

Giele, J.Z. and Gilfus, M. (1990), 'Race and College Differences in Life Patterns of Educated Women', in Antler, J. and Biklen, S. (eds.), *Women and Educational Change*, N.Y., SUNY Press, Albany.

Gilligan, C. (1982), *In a Different Voice: Psychological Development and Women's Development*, Harvard University press, Cambridge.

Gittins, D. (1985), *The Family in Question: Changing Household Ideologies and Familiar Ideologies*, Macmillan, London.

Glass, J., Tienda, M. and Smith, S.A. (1988), 'The Impact of Changing Employment Opportunity on Gender and Ethnic Earnings Inequality', *Social Science Research*, No. 17, pp. 252—276.

Gleason, P. (1983), 'Identifying Identity: A Semantic History', *The Journal of American History*, No. 69, pp. 910—931.

Glenn, E.N. (1992), 'From Servitude to Service Work: Historical Continuities in the Racial Division of Paid Reproductive Labor', *Signs*, No. 18, pp. 1—43.

Goldberg, W.A., Greenberger, E. and Hamill, S. (1992), 'Role Demands in the Lives of Employed Single Mothers With Preschoolers', *Journal of Family Issues*, pp. 312—333.

Gongla, P.A. and Thompson, Jr.E.H. (1987), 'Single—Parent Families', in Sussman, M.B. and Steinmetz, S.K., *Handbook of Marriage and the Family*, Plenum Press, New York/London, pp. 397—418.

Goode, W.J. (1960), 'A Theory of Role Strain', *American Sociological Review*, No. 25, pp. 483—496.

Gordon, L. (1990), 'The New Feminist Scholarship on the Welfare State', in Gordon L. (ed.), *Women, the State, and Welfare*, University of Wisconsin Press, pp. 9—35.

Gordon, L. (1991), 'The New Feminist Scholarship on the Welfare State', in Gordon, L., (ed.), *Women. The State and Welfare*, University of Wisconsin, Madison.

Gordon, L. (1994), *Pitied But Not Entitled: Single Mothers and the Historv of Welfare*, Free Press, NewYork.

Gordon, T. (1994), *Single Women: On the Margins?*, Macmillan, London and New York University press, New York.

Gorelick, S. (1991), 'Contradictions of Feminist Methodology', *Gender & Society*, Vol.5, No 4, pp.459—477.

Grabher, G. (ed.), (1993), *The Embedded Firm: On the Socioeconomics of Industrial Networks*, London/New York.

Groonos, C. (1990), *Service Management and Marketing*, D.C. Heath, Lexington, MA.

Gustafsson, S. (1990), 'The Labor Force Participation and Earnings of Lone Parents: A Review of Swedish Policies and Institutions with Some Comparisons to West Germany', OECD Outlook: Lone—Parent Families, *Social Policy Studies*.

Gustafsson, S. and Bruyn—Hundt, M. (1992), 'Incentives for Women to Work: A Comparison between the Netherlands, Sweden, and West Germany', *Journal of Economic Studies*, Vol. 18.

Gutek, B.A., Cohen, A.G. and Konrad, A.M. (1990), 'Predicting social—sexual behavior at work', A contact hypothesis, *Academy of Management Journal*, No. 33, pp. 560—577.

Haas, L. (1992) *Equal Parenthood and Social Policy: A Study of Parental Leave in Sweden*, State University of New York Press, Albany, New York.

Haavio—Mannila, E. (1983), 'Cross—Gender Relationships at Work and Home over the Family Life Cycle', in Steinmetz, S.K., (ed.), *Family and Support Systems across the Life Span*, Plenum Press, New York, pp. 197—212.

Haavio—Mannila, E. (1983), 'Economic and family roles of men and women in Northem Europe', in Lupri, E., (ed.) *The Changing Role of Women in Family and Society*, Helsinki.

Haavio—Mannila, E. (1989), *Life Patterns of Women in Cross—Class Families*, paper presented at Gender and Class: Intemational

Developments in Theory and Research Conference, September 18—20, Antwerp.

Haavio—Mannila, E. (1981), 'Finland: Economic, Political and Cultural Leadership', in Epstein, C.F. and Laub Coser, R. (eds.), *Access To Power: Cross—National Studies of Women and Elites*, Allen & Unwin, London, pp. 53—75.

Haavio—Mannila, E. (1986), 'Inequalities in Health and Gender', *Social Science of Medicine*, No. 22, 2, pp. 141—149.

Haavio—Mannila, E. (1989), 'Influence of Work Place Sex Segregation on Family Life', *Marriage and Family Review*, No. 14, pp. 107—126.

Haavio—Mannila, E. (1994), 'Erotic relations at work', in Alestalo, M., Allardt, E., Rychard, A. and Wesolowski, W. (eds.), *The transformation of Europe: Social conditions and consequences*, IFIS Publishers, Warsaw.

Haavio—Mannila, E. (1991), 'Emotional Relations at Work', *Finnish Work Research Bulletin*, No. 2b, pp. 12—15.

Haavio—Mannila, E. and Kauppinen, K. (1992), 'Women and the Welfare State in the Nordic Countries', in Kahn, H. and Giele, J. (eds.) *Women's Work and Women's Lives — The Continuing Struggle Worldwide*, Westview Press, Boulder.

Haavio—Mannila, E. and Kauppinen, K. (1995), 'Changes in the Status of Women in Russia and Estonia', in Piirainen, T. (ed.) *Change and Continuity in Eastern Europe*, Dartmouth, Aldershot, pp. 173—203.

Haavio—Mannila, E., Jallinoja, R. and Strandell, H. (1984), *Perhe, työ ja tunteet — ristiriitaisuuksia ja ratkaisuja*, (Family, Work, and Feelings — Contradictions and Solutions). (In Finnish), WSOY, Juva.

Haavio—Mannila, E., Kauppinen—Toropainen, K. and Kandolin, I. (1986), 'The Effect of Sex Composition of the Workplace on Friendship, Romance, and Sex at Work', in Gutek, B.A., Stromberg, A.H. and Larwood, L. (eds.), *Women and Work: An Annual Review*, No. 3., Sage, Beverly Hills, pp. 123—137.

Haavio—Mannila, E. and Rannik, E. (1985) *Vertaileva tutkimus Eestin ja Suomen perheestä, työstä ja vapaa—ajasta*, (Comparative Study on Family, Work and Leisure in Estonia and Finland). (In Finnish), NL TTYK, Helsinki.

Haavio—Mannila, E. and Snicker, R. (1980), 'Traditional Sex Norms and the Innovative Function of Afternoon Dancing', *Research in the Interweave of Social Roles: Women and Men*, No. 1, pp. 221—245.

Hamao, M. (1972), *How To Discipline Girls*, Kobunsha, Tokyo.

Hartmann, H. and Spalter—Roth, R. (1994), 'AFDC Recipients as Caregivers and Workers: A Feminist Approach to Income Security Policy for American Women', *Social Politics: International Studies in Gender, State, & Society*, Vol . 1, pp. 211—223.

Hayes, C.D., Palmer, J.L. and Zaslow, M.J. (eds.), (1990), *Who Cares for America's Children: Child Care Policy for the 1990s*, National Academy Press, Washington, D.C.

Helson, R. and Picano, S. (1990), 'Is the Traditional Role Bad for Women?' *Journal of Personality and Social Psychology*, No. 59, pp. 311—320.

Hernes, H.M. (1987), *Welfare states and woman power: essays in state feminism*, Norwegian University Press, Oslo.

Hirdman, Y, (1990a), 'Genussystemet', *Demokrati och makt i Sverige*, (in Swedish), SOU 44, Maktutredningens huvudrapport, Stockholm, pp. 73—116.

Hirdman, Y. (1990b), *Att lägga livet tillrätta — Studier i svensk folkhemspolitik*, (in Swedish),Carlsson Bokförlag, Stockholm.

Hirose, K. (1985), *Woman's Capacity Depends on Language*, Lyonsha, Tokyo.

Hirschman, A.O. (1970), *Exit, Voice, and Loyalty: Responses to Decline in Firms, Organizationss and States*, Harvard University Press, Cambridge, Mass.

Hobson, B. (1993), 'Gendered Discourses and Feminist Strategies in Welfare States: The Debate Over Married Women's Right to Work in Sweden and the United States', in Koven, S. and Michel, S., (eds.) *Mothers of the New World: Gender and Oriqins of Welfare States in Westem Europe and North America*, Routledge, Kegan and Paul, New York.

Hobson, B. (1990), 'No Exit, No Voice: Women's Economic Dependency and the Welfare State', *Acta Sociologica*, No. 33, pp. 235—250.

Hobson, B. (1994), 'Solo Mothers, Policy Regimes, and Welfare States', in Sainsbury, D. (ed.) *Engenderinq Welfare States: Combining Insights of Feminism and Mainstream Research*, Sage Publications, London.

Hobson, B. (1991a), *No Exit, No Voice. A Comparative Analysis of Women's Economic Dependency and the Welfare State*, Center of Women's Studies, Stockholm University.

Hobson, B. (1991b), *The Debate over Women's Right to Work in Sweden and the United States During the 1930s: A Comparative Perspective on Gendered Discourses and Strategies in Welfare States*, paper Presented at the Annual Meeting of the Social Science History Association, New Orleans.

Hochschild, A. (1983), *The Managed Heart*, University of California Press, Berkeley.

Hochschild, A.R. (1986), 'The Economy of Gratitude', in Franks, D. (ed.), *The Sociology of Emotions: Original Essays and Research Papers*, Jai Press, Greenwich, Conn., pp. 95—111.

Hochschild, A. & Machung A. (1989), *The Second Shift - Working Parents and the Revolution at Home*, Viking Penguin Books Ltd., Harmondsworth.

Holter, H. (ed.), (1984), *Patriarchy in a Welfare Society*, Universitetsforlaget, Oslo.

Home Help 1986, 1988, 1990 (1992), National Agency for Welfare and Health, *Social security*, No. 2, Helsinki.

Hormuth, S.E. (1990), *The Ecology of the Self: Relocation and Self—Concept Change*, Cambridge University Press, Cambridge.

House, J.S., Umberson, D. and Landis, K.R. (1988), 'Structures and processes of social support', *Annual Review of Sociology*, No. 14, pp. 293—318.

Jallinoja, R. (1983), *Suomalaisen naisasialiikkeen taistelukaudet*, (in Finnish), WSOY, Helsinki.

James, W. ([1890] 1983), *The Principles of Psychology*, Harvard University Press, Cambridge. Ma.

Jameson, F. (1984), 'Postmodernism, or the Cultural Logic of Late Capitalism', *New Left Review*, No. 146, pp. 53—92.

Jones, K. (1990), 'Citizenship in a woman—friendly polity', *Signs*, Vol. 15 (1).

Joshi, H. (1990), 'Obstacles and opportunities for Lone Parents as Breadwinners in Great Britain', OECD Outlook, One—Parent Families, *Social Policy Studies*, No. 6.

Julkunen, R. (1990), 'Women in the Welfare State', *The Lady with the Bow. Feminist Essays from Finland*, Otava, Helsinki, pp. 140—166.

Julkunen, R. (1993), 'Suomalainen sukupuolimalli — 60—luku käänteenä', in Anttonen, A. et al. (eds.) *Hyvinvointivaltio, naiset ja Suomen malli*, (in Finnish), Vastapaino, Tampere.

Kahn, R.L. and Katz, D. (1960) 'Leadership practices in relation to productivity and morale', in Cartwright, D. and Zander, A. (eds.), *Group dynamics: Research and Theory*, Row, Peterson, Evanston, IL, 2nd ed., pp. 554—570.

Kahne, H. and Giele, J.Z. (eds.) (1992), *Women's Work and Women's Lives: The Continuing Struggle Worldwide*, Westview Press, Boulder, Colo.

Kalns—Timans, A. (1992) 'Latvian Women: the Way Forward?', in Trapenciere, I. and Kalnina, S. (eds.) *Fragments of Reality: Insights on Women in a Changing Society*, VAGA Publ., Riga, pp. 32—44.

Kamerman, S.B. and Kahn, A.J. (1988), 'What Europe does for single—parent families', *The public interest*, pp. 70—86.

Kammerman, S., and Kahn, A. (1986), 'Women, Children, and Poverty: Public Policies and Female—Headed Families in Industrialized Countries', in Gelpi, B. et al. (eds.), *Women and Poverty*, Chicago University Press, Chicago.

Kammerman, S., and Kahn, A. (1991), *Child Care, Parental Leave. and the Under 3's: Policy Innovation in Europe*, Auburn House, New York.

Kammerman, S. and Kahn, A.: (1986), 'Women, Children, and Poverty: Public Policies and Female—Headed Families in Industrialized Countries', in Gelpi, B. et. al. (eds.), *Women and Poverty*, Chicago University Press, Chicaco.

Kammerman, S. and Kahn, A., (1991), *Child Care, Parental Leave, and the Under 3's: Policy Innovation in Europe*, Auburn House, New York.

Kanter, R.M. (1977), *Work and Family in the United States*, Russell Sage Foundation, New York.

Kauppinen, K., Haavio—Mannila, E. and Kandolin, I. (1989), 'Who benefits from working in non—traditional workroles: Interaction patterns and quality of worklife', *Acta Sociologica*.

Kauppinen—Toropainen, K. and Kandolin, I. (1991), 'Työn ja kodin vaatimusten yhdistäminen', (Combining of Work/Family—Demands). (In Finnish), *Työ ja ihminen*, No. 5:3, pp.295—312.

Kauppinen—Toropainen, K., Kandolin, I. and Haavio—Mannila, E. (1988), 'Sex Segregation of Work in Finland and the Quality of Women's Work', *Journal of Organizational Behavior*, No. 9, pp. 15—27.

Kayama, Y. (1981), 'This Love Forever: Yakadaisho's Diary of Childrearing', Kobunsha, Tokyo.

Kelly, R.F. and Voydanoff, P. (1985), 'Work/Family Role Strain Among Employed Parents', *Family Relations*, No. 34, pp. 367—374.

Kirner, E. and Schulz, E. (1992), 'Das `Drei—Phasen—Modell' der Erwerbsbeteiligung von Frauen—Begruendung, Norm und empirische Relevanz', in Ott, N. and Wagner, G. (eds.), *Familie und Erwerbstaetigkeit im Umbruch*, Deutsches Institut für Wirtschafts—forschung, Berlin, Sonderheft, p. 148.

Knijn, T. (1991), *Citizenship, Care, and Gender in the Dutch Welfare State*, paper presented at the Conference on 'Gender, Citizenship and Social Policy', Social Science History Association, New Orleans.

Knijn, T. (1994), 'Fish Without Bikes: Revision of the Dutch Welfare State and its Consequences for the (In)dependence of Single Mothers', *Social Politics*, Vol.1, No. 1.

Kohn, M.L. and Schooler, C. (1973), 'Occupational Experience and Psychological Functioning: An Assessment of Reciprocal Effects', *American Sociological Review*, No. 38, February, pp. 97—118.

Konecko, C. (1982), 'One Undergraduate Looks at 'Life'; Coding the Children and Work Questionnaire', *Bryn Mawr Alumnae Bulletin*, Winter, pp. 24—26.

König, R. (1969), 'Soziologie der Familie', in König, R. (ed.), *Handbuch der empirischen Sozialforschung*, Enke, Stuttgart, pp. 172—305.

Kulawik, T. and Reidmuller, B. (1991), 'Institutionelle Arrangements und die Lebenssitution der Alleinstehenden Frauen', in Ruidmuller, et. al. (eds.), *Die Lebenssituation der alleinstehenden Frauen in der Bundesrepublik Deutschland*, Schriftenreihe des Bundesministerium für Frauen und Jugend, Stuttgart.

Kurikka, M. (1992), *Päivähoidon politiikan naispolitiikka'*, *pro gradu — tutkielma*, (in Finnish). Tampereen yliopisto, Politiikan tutkimuksen laitos, Tampere.

Kuronen, M. (1989), 'Onnellinen ja ongelmallinen äitiys. Tutkimus lasten hoidon ja kasvatuksen asiantuntijoiden äitiyttä koskevista käsityksistä' (in Finnish), *Tutkimuksia*, Tampereen yliopisto, Sosiaalipolitiikan laitos, Sarja B, No. 2, Tampere.

Kuusipalo, J. (1990), 'Finnish Women in Top—Level Politics', in Keränen, M. (ed.), *Finnish 'Undemocracy': Essays on Gender and Politics*, The Finnish Political Science Association, Helsinki, pp. 13—36.

Kvande, E. and Rasmussen, B. (1989), *Women in Men's Organizations — A Structural Model of Analysis*, paper presented in the 15th Nordic Sociological Congress, Aalborg.

Lambert, S. (1990), 'Processes Linking Work and Family: A Critical Review and Research Agenda', *Human Relations*, No. 3, pp. 239—257.

Land, H. (1983), 'Poverty and Gender: The Distribution of Resources within the Family', in Brown, M. (ed.), *The Structure of Disadvantage*, Heineman, London.

Land, H. (1994), 'The Demise of the Male Breadwinner in Practice but not in Theory: A Challenge for Social Security Systems', in Baldwin, S., Falkingham, J., (eds.), *Social Security and Social Change: New Challenaes to the Beveridge Model*, Harvester Wheatsheaf, London.

Langan, M. and Ostner, I. (1991), 'Gender and Welfare: Towards a Comparative Framework', in Room, G. (ed.) *Towards a European Welfare State?*, SAUS, Bristol, pp. 127—150.

Lapidus, G.W. (1978), *Women in Soviet Society. Equality, Development, and Social Change*, University of CA Press, Berkeley, Los Angeles, London.

Lapidus, G.W. (1992), 'The Interaction of Women's Work and Family Roles in the Former USSR', in Kahne, H. and Giele, J.Z. (eds.) *Women's Work and Women's Lives. The Continuing Struggle Worldwide*, Boulder, San Francisco, Westview Press, Oxford, pp. 140—164.

Leidner, R. (1993), *Fast Food, Fast Talk: Service Work and the Routinization of Everyday Life*, University of California Press, Berkeley.

Leira, A. (1992), *Welfare States and Working Mothers*, Cambridge University Press, Cambridge.

Lewis, J. and Ostner, I., (1994), 'Gender and the Evolution of Social Policies', *Zes—Arbeitspapier*, No 4/94. Centre for Social Policy Research.

Lewis, J. (1991), 'Models of Equality for Women: The case of State Support for Children in Twentieth—Century Britain', in Bock and Thane (eds.), *Maternity & Gender Policies: Women and the Rise of European Welfare States, 1880's—1950's*, Routledge, London, pp. 73—93.

Lifton, R.J. (1986), *The Nazi Doctors: Medical Killing and the Psychology of Genocide*, Basic Books, New York.

Lifton, R.J. (1993), *The Protean Self*, Basic Books, New York.

Likert, R. (1967), *The human organization: Its management and value*, McGraw—Hill, New York.

Lister, R. (1993), 'Tracing the contours of women's citizenship', *Policy and Politics*, Vol 21 (1).

Lister, R. (1994), 'The Child Support Act: Shifting Family Financial Obligations in the United Kingdom', *Social Politics: International Studies of Gender, State. and Society*, No. 1.

Lobel, S.A., Dutton, J.E. and O'Neill, R. (1992), *Nurturing: Elaborating our understanding of important roles, skills, and contexts in organizations*, paper presented at the 8th Annual Conference of Women and Work, Arlington, Texas.

Lobel, S.A., Quinn, R.E. and Warfield, A. (1990), *Toward a gendered vision of the workplace: Images of relationships*, paper presented at the Academy of Management Meetings, San Francisco.

Lobel, S.A. (1993), 'Sexuality at work: Where do we go from here?', *Journal of Vocational Behavior*, No. 42, pp. 136—152.

Lorence, J. (1992), 'Service Sector Growth and Metropolitan Occupational Sex Segregation', *Work and Occupations*, No. 19, pp. 128—156.

Lüscher, K. and Engstler, H. (1990), 'Pluralität in Grenzen—Eine sozio—demographische Typologie aktueller Formen der Familien—gründung in der Schweiz', *Zeitschrift für Bevölkerungswissenschaft*, No. 16, pp. 407—413.

Lyson, T. (1986), 'Industrial Transformation and Occupational Sex Differentiation: Evidence From New Zealand and the United States', *International Journal of Comparative Sociology*, No. 27. pp. 53—68.

MacLean, M. (1991), *Surviving Divorce: Women's Resources After Separation*, Macmillan, London.

MacLennan, E. (1992), 'Politics, Progress, and Compromise: Women's Work and Lives in Great Britain', in Kahne, H. and Giele, J.Z. (eds.), *Women's Work and Women's Lives: The Continuing Struggle Worldwide*, Westview Press, Boulder, Colo.

Mainiero, L.A. (1986), 'A review and analysis of power dynamics in organizational romances', *Academy of Management Review*, No. 11, pp. 750—762.

Marchenko, T. and Shlapentokh, V. (1992), 'Family Values in the Rise While Women Fall in Russia', *Feminist Issues*, No. 12(2), pp. 43—47.

Marcia, J.E. (1980), 'Identity in Adolescence', in Adelson, J. (ed.) *Handbook of Adolescent Psychology*, John Wiley, New York.

Markus, H. and Nurius, P. (1986), 'Possible Selves', *American Psychologist*, No. 41, pp. 954—969.

Marshall, T.H. (1963), *Class, Citizenship, and Social Development*, Doubleday, Garden City, N.Y.

Martin, J. (1984), *Miss Manners' Guide to Rearing Perfect Children*, Athenium Publishers, New York.

Mayo, E. (1933), *The human problems of an industrial civilization*, MacMillan, New York.

McAuley, A. (1981), *Women's Work and Wages in the Soviet Union*, Allen and Unwin, Boston.

McLanahan, S., Sorensen, A., and Watson, R. (1990), 'Sex Differences in Poverty', 1950—, 1980, *Signs*, No. 15.

McLanahan, S. and Booth, K. (1989), 'Mother—Only Families: Problems, Prospects, and Politics', *Journal of Marriage and the Family*, No. 51, August, pp. 558—80.

Mead, G.H. ([1934] 1962), (ed.), *Mind, Self & Society: From the Standpoint of a Social Behaviorist*, University of Chicago Press, Chicago.

Merton, R.K. ([1948] 1968), *Social Theory and Social Structure*, The Free Press, Glencoe, IL.

Miki, T. (1973), *The Art of Childrearing*, Kodansha, Tokyo.

Miki, T. (1974), *Woman's Expression*, Shodensha, Tokyo.

Milkman, R. and Pullman, C. (1991), 'Technological Change in an Auto Assembly Plant', *Work and Occupations*, No. 18, 2, pp. 123—147.

Millar, J. (1993), *Poverty and the Lone Parent Family: The Challenge to Social Policy*, Avebury, Gower.

Miller, J.B. (1986), *Towards a New Psychology of Women*, 2nd ed., Beacon, Boston.

Mizuno, H. (1978), *How To Grow Old Together*, Volumes 1 and 2.

Molley, J. (1977), *The Woman's Dress For Success Book New York*, Warner Books.

Morgan, M. (1973), *The Total Woman*, G.K. Hall, Boston.

Mozny, I., 'Ot komplementarnosti k universalizatsii: O sotsialnyh roliah muzhtsiny', (In Russian). (From complementarity to universality: About the social roles of men and women). *Sotsiologitsheskiie Issledovaniia*, No. 4, pp. 88—91.

Mulroy, E.A. (1988), *Women as Single Parents*, Auburn House Publishing Company, Dover, Mass.

Mänttäri, S. (1991), 'Nainen kolmen maailman asukkaana', (Woman as Inhabitant of Three Worlds). (In Finnish). *TA Julkaisuja*, Sarja D, 1, Helsinki.

Napp—Peters, A. (1985), *Ein—Eltern—Familien. Soziale Rand—gruppe und neues familiales Selbstverständnis?*, Juventa Verlag, Weinheim u. München.

Narusk, A. (1988), *Pered, kus kasvavad teismelised*, (Families with teenagers). (In Estonian), Valgus, Tallinn.

Narusk, A. (1989), *Podrostok iz horosei semji*, (Adolescents from a good Family). (In Russian), Perioodika, Tallinn.

Narusk, A. (1992), 'Parenthood, Parentship, and Family in Estonia', in Björnberg, U. (ed.), *European Parents in the 1990s. Contradictions and comparisons*, Transaction Publ., New Brunswick, London, pp. 155—171.

Narusk, A. (ed.) (1995a), *Every—day life and Radical Social Changes in Estonia*, ETAK, Tallinn.

Narusk, A. (1995b), 'The Estonian Family in Transition', *Nationalities Papers*, Vol. 23, No 1.

Nave—Herz, R. (1989), 'Gegenstandsbereich und historische Entwicklung der Familienforschung', in Nave—Herz, R. and Markefka, M. (eds.), *Handbuch der Familien— und Jugendforschung*, Neuwied, Luchterhand, pp. 1—18.

Nave—Herz, R. (1984), *Familiäre Veränderungen seit 1950 — Eine empirische Studie*, Abschlußbericht/Teil I., Universität Oldenburg, Institut f. Soziologie, Oldenburg.

Nelson, B.J. (1990), 'The Origins of the Two—Channel Welfare State: Workmen's Compensation and Mothers' Aid', in Gordon, L. (ed.), *Women, the State, and Welfare*, The University of Wisconsin Press, pp. 123—151.

Neubauer, E. (1988), 'Alleinerziehende Mütter und Väter — Eine Analyse der Gesamtsituation', *Schriftenreihe des Bundesministeriums für Jugend, Familie, Frauen und Gesundheit*, Kohlhammer, Stuttgart.

Norwood, R. (1985), *Women Who Love Too Much*, Pocket Books, New York.

Notz, G. (1991), *Du bist als Frau um einiges mehr gebunden als der Mann*, Dietz, Bonn.

Nurminen, E., Roos, J.P. (1990), *Models of Parenting between Generations and Classes*, paper for Vienna—project 'European Parents in the 1990s', Jan. 21—25, Suzdal.

Nyberg, A. (1989), *Tekniken: Kvinnornas befriare*, Linköping.

O'Connor, J. (1990), *Gender, Class, and Citizenship in Comparative Analysis: Theoretical and Methodological Issues*, paper presented at the Meeting of the International Sociological Association, Madrid.

OECD, Social Policy Studies (1990), *Lone—Parent Families — The Economic Challenge*, No. 8 , Paris.

Okin, S. M. (1989), *Gender. Justice and the Family*, Basic Books, New York.

Ollila, A. (1994), 'Naisliike, nationalismi ja kansanvalistus: Miksi Martta—yhdistys halusi riveihinsä 'kaikkien kansanluokkien naiset'?, in Anttonen, A. et al. (eds.), *Naisten hyvinvointivaltio*, (in Finnish), Vastapaino, Tampere.

Orloff, A. (1993), 'Gender and the Social Rights of Citizenship: The Comparative Analysis of Gender Relations in the Welfare States', *American Socioloqical Review*, Vol. 58 (June).

Orloff, A.S. (1993), 'Gender and the Social Rights of Citizenship', *American Sociological Review*, No. 58, June, pp. 303—328.

Osheverova, L. (1992), 'If the State Doesn't Take Care of the Family, There Will Be No one To Take Care of the State', *Izvestia*, p. 2.

Ostner, I. (1993), 'Women in Slow Motion: Women, Work, and the Family in Germany', in Lewis, J., (ed.) *Women. Work, and Welfare*, Edward Elgar, Cheltenham.

Ott, N. (1992), *Intrafamily Bargaining and Household Decisions*, Springer—Verlag, Berlin.

Pahl, J. (1988) 'Earning, Sharing, Spending: Married Couples and Their Money', in Walker, R. and Parker, G., (eds.) *Money Matters: Income. Wealth, and Financial Welfare*, Sage, Beverly Hills, Calif.

Palme, J. (1992), *Nations of Welfare: Comparing Income Inequalities Among the Pre—Retirement Elderly*, paper presented at the Department of Sociology, Stockholm University, November 24.

Parsons, T. (1942), 'Age and Sex in the Social Structure of the United States', in Parsons, T. (ed.), *Essays in Sociological Theory*, Free Press, 1954, New York, pp. 89—103.

Parsons, T. and Bales, R.F. (1955), *Family, Socialization, and Interaction Process*, Free Press, New York.

Pateman, C. (1989), *The Disorder of Women: Democracy, Feminism, and Political Theory*, Stanford University Press, Stanford.

Pateman, C. (1988a), 'The Patriarchal Welfare State', in Gutmann A. (ed.) *Democracy and the Welfare State*, Princeton University Press, Princeton, pp. 231—260.

Pateman, C. (1988), *The Sexual Contract*, Stanford University Press, Stanford, Calif.

Pateman, C. (1989), *The Disorder of Women*, Stanford University Press, Stanford.

Paul, C. (1992), 'Eheschließungen, Ehescheidungen, Geburten— und Sterbefälle von Ausländern', *Wirtschaft und Statistik*, pp. 767—773.

Paules, G.F. (1991), *Dishing it Out: Power and Resistance Among Waitresses in a New Jersey Restaurant*, Temple University Press, Philadelphia.

Pearlin, L.I., (1989), 'The Sociological Study of Stress', *Journal of Health and Social Behaviour*, Vol. 30, pp. 241—256.

Peattie, L., and Rein, M. (1983), *Women's Claims: A Study in Political Economy*, Oxford University Press, New York.

Pedersen, S. (1993), *Family and Dependence and the Origins of the Welfare State: Britain and France 1914—1945*, Cambridge University Press, Cambridge/England.

Peiper, A. (1966), *Chronik der Kinderheilkunde*, 4. Aufl., Thieme, Leipzig.

Persson, I. (1991), 'The Third Dimension—Equal Status Between Swedish Women and Men', in Persson, I. (ed.), *Generating Equality in the Welfare State: The Swedish Experience*, Norwegian University Press, Oslo.

Phillips, A. (1991), *Engendering Democracy*, Basic Blackwell, Cambridge, England.

Pleck, J.H. (1992), 'Work—Family Policies in the United States', in Kahne H. and J.Z. Giele (eds.), *Women's Work and Women's Lives: The Continuing Struggle Worldwide*, Westview Press, Boulder, Colo.

Popay, J., Rimmer, L. and Rossiter, C. (1983), 'One Parent Families', *Parents, Children and Public Policy*, Study Commission on the Family, London.

Popenoe, D. (1987), 'Beyond the Nuclear Family — A Statistical Portrait of the Changing Family in Sweden', *Journal of Marriage and the Family*, pp. 173—183.

Porokhniuk, E. and Shepeleva, M. (1975), 'How Working Women Combine Work and Household Duties', in Novikova, E. (ed.), *Women's Work and the Family*, Profizdat,. Moscow, pp. 267—180.

Porter, L.W., Steers, R.M., Mowday, R.T. and Boulian, P.V. (1974), 'Organizational commitment, job satisfaction, and turnover among psychiatric technicians', *Journal of Applied Psychology*, No. 59(5), pp. 603—609.

Posadskaya, A. (1993), 'The Role and Task of National Machinery for the Advancement of Women in the Period of Social and Economic Reform in the Countries of Eastern Europe and the USSR', in Rantalaiho, L. (ed.), *Social Changes and the Status of Women: The Experience of Finland and the USSR*, University of Tampere, Tampere, pp. 49—56.

Quinn, R.E. (1977), 'Coping with Cupid: The formation, impact and management of romantic relationships in organizations', *Administrative Science Quarterly*, No. 22(1), pp. 30—45.

Rantalaiho, L. (1993), *The Finnish Gender Model — Surfaces and Deep Structures*, seminar presentation at the Wissenschaftszentrum, February 9, Berlin.

Rein, M. (1982), *Women in the Social Welfare Labor Market*, WZB Working Papers, Berlin.

Rimachevskaya, N. (1993), 'Socio—economic Changes and Position of Women in the Union of Soviet Socialist Republics', in Rantalaiho, L. (ed.), *Social Changes and the Status of Women: The Experience of Finland and the USSR*, University of Tampere, Tampere, pp. 35—47.

Rosenberg, S. (1988), 'Self and Others: Studies in Social Personality and Autobiography', in Berkowitz, L. (ed.), *Advances in Experimental Social Psychology*, Academic Press, New York, pp. 57—95.

Ross, C.E. and Mirowsky, J. (1992), 'Households, Employment, and the Sense of Control', *Social Psychology Quarterly*, No. 55, pp. 217—235.

Rudolph, H. (1992), 'Women's Labor Market Experience in the Two Germanies', in Kahne, H. and Giele, J.Z. (eds.), *Women's Work and Women's Lives: The Continuing Struggle Worldwide*, Westview Press, Boulder, Colo.

Saarinen, A. (1992), 'Feminist Research — An Intellectual Adventure', *Publ. Series*, No. 4, the University of Tampere, Research Institute of Social Sciences, Tampere, Centre for Women's Studies and Gender Relations .

Saimon, F. (1990), *The Art of Loving*, P.H.P, Kenkyujo, Tokyo.

Sainsbury, D. (1989), 'Dual Welfare and Sex Segregation of Access to Social Benefits: Income Maintenance Policies in the UK, the U.S, the Netherlands, and Sweden', *Journal of Social Policy*, Vol. 22, No. 1, pp. 69—88.

Sapadin, L. (1988), *Gender and friendships: Hers and his, same—sex and cross—sex*, paper presented at the 96th annual convention of the American Psychological Association, Atlanta, GA.

Saraceno, C. (1994), 'The Ambivalent Famialism of the Italian Welfare State', in *Social Politics: International Studies of Gender. State and Society*, Vol. 1, pp. 60—83.

Saraceno, C. (1984), 'Shifts in Public and Private Boundaries: Women as Mothers and Service Workers in Italian Daycare', *Feminist Studies*, No. 10, pp. 7—29.

Sarvasy, W. (1992), 'Beyond Difference Versus Equality Policy Debate: Posatsuffrage Feminism, Citizenship, and the Quest for a Feminist Welfare State', *Signs*, Vol. 17, No. 2, pp. 329—362.

Schwarz, K. (1989), 'In welchen Familien wachsen unsere Kinder auf', *Zeitschrift für Familienforschung*, No. 2, pp. 27—48.

Sen, S. (1981), *What A Beautiful Woman*, Shufutoseikatsush, Tokyo.

Shiotsuki, Y. (1970, 1971), *Introduction to Rites of Passage*, Volumes I—III, Kobunsha, Tokyo.

Shlapentokh, V. (1984), *Love, Marriage, and Friendship in the Soviet Union: Ideals and Practices*, Praeger, Publisher, New York.

Shweder, R.A. (1993), 'Why Do Men Barbecue? and Other Postmodern Ironies of Growing Up in the Decade of Ethnicity', in *America's Childhood, Journal of the American Academy of Arts and Sciences*, Vol. 122, No. 1, pp. 279—308.

Siim, B. (1993), 'Gender, Citizenship, and Political Participation for Women in Scandinavian', *Social Politics; International Studies of Gender, State, and Society*, Vol. 1.

Siim B. (1987), 'The Scandinavian Welfare States — Towards Sexual Equality or a New Kind of Male Domination?', *Acta Sociologica*, Vol. 30, No. 3—4, pp. 255—270.

Siim B. (1988), 'Towards a Feminist Rethinking of the Welfare State', in Jones, K—B. and Jonasdottir, A.G. (eds.), *The Political Interests of Gender*, Sage Publications, London, pp. 160—186.

Siltanen, J. and Stanworth, M. (1984), 'The politics of private woman and public man', in Siltanen, J. and Stanworth, M. (ed.), *Women and the Public Sphere*, Hutchinson, London.

Simon, B.L. (1987), *Never Married Women*, Temple University Press, Philadelphia.

Simonen, L. (1990), 'Contradictions of the Welfare State, Women and Caring. Municipal Homemaking in Finland', *Acta Universitatis Tamperensis*, Ser A, Vol. 295, University of Tampere.

Skocpol, T. (1992), *Protecting Soldiers and Mothers: The Political Origins of Social Policy in the United States*, Harvard University Press, Cambridge, Mass.

Smith, J. (1984), 'The Paradox of Women's Poverty: Wage—Earning Women and Economic Transformation', *Signs*, No. 10, pp. 291—310.

Sono, A. (1970, 1971), *For Whose Sake Do You Love*, Bungeishuju, Tokyo.

Sorensen, A. and McLanahan, S. (1987) 'Married Women's Economic Dependency, 1940—, 1980', *American Journal of Sociology*, Vol. 93.

Staples, R. (1981) 'Black Singles in American', in Stein, P. (ed.), *Single Life: Unmarried Adults in Social Context*, St. Martin's Press, New York.

Stein, P. (ed.) (1981), *Single Life: Unmarried Adults in Social Context*, St. Martin's Press, New York.

Stryker, S. (1987), 'Identity Theory: Developments and Extensions', in Yardley, K. and Honess, T. (eds), *Self and Identity: Psychosocial Perspectives*, Chichester, New York, pp. 83—103.

Sulkunen, I. (1987), 'Naisten järjestäytyminen ja kaksijakoinen kansalaisuus' in Alapuro R. (ed.) *Kansa liikkeessä*, (in Finnish), Kirjayhtymä, Helsinki, pp. 157—172.

Sulkunen I. (1991), *Retki naishistoriaan*, (in Finnish). Hanki ja Jää, Helsinki.

Sussman M.B.; Steinmetz, S.K. (1987), *Handbook of Marriage and the Family*, Plenum Press, New York/London.

Sutherland, M.B. (1990), Report at the seminar 'Women's Studies and the Social Position of Women in Eastern and Western Europe, Hague, the Netherlands, *Publications of European Network for Women's Studies*, pp. 22—27.

Suzuki, K. (1982), *How To Be Considerate Of Others*, Kodansha, Tokyo.

Suzuki, K. (1983), *How To Be Considerate of Others II*, Kodansha, Tokyo.

Suzuki, K. (1983), *A Story of Womanliness*, Shogakukan, Tokyo.

Teachman, J.D.; Polonko, K.A. and Scanzoni, J. (1987), 'Demography of the Family', in: Sussman, M.B. and Steinmetz, S.K. *Handbook of Marriage and the Family*, Plenum Press, New York/London, pp. 3—36.

Thoits, P.A. (1986) 'Multiple Identities and Psychological Well—being: A Reformulation and Test of the Social Isolation Hypothesis', *American Sociological Review*, No. 48, pp. 174—187.

Thomas, D.L. and Wilcox, J.E. (1987), 'The Rise of Family Theory: A Historical and Critical Analysis', *Handbook of Marriage and the Family*, Sussman, M.B. and Steinmetz, S.K. (eds.), New York: Plenum Press, pp. 81—100.

Thornton, A. (1989), 'Changing Attitudes toward Family Issues in the United States', *Journal of Marriage and the Family*, No. 52, pp. 993—1014.

Tidmarsh, K. (1993), 'Russia's Work Ethic', *Foreign Affairs*, No. 93, pp. 67—77.

Tronto, J.C. (1987), 'Beyond Gender Difference to a Theory of Care', *Signs*, Vol. 12, No. 4, pp. 644—663.

Trost, J. (1975), 'Married and Unmarried Cohabitation: The Case in Sweden with some comparisons', *Journal of Marriage and the Family*, pp. 677—682.

Trost, J. (1980), *The Family in Change*, International Library, Västerås/Sweden.

Trost, J. (1989), 'Nicheheliche Lebensgemeinschaften', in Nave—Herz, R. and Markefka, M. (eds.), *Handbuch der Familien— und Jugendforschung*, Familienforschung, Neuwied, Luchterhand, pp. 363—374.

Tsui, A.S. (1984), 'A role set analysis of managerial reputation', *Organizational Behavior and Human Performance*, No. 34(1), pp. 64—96.

Ungerson, C. (1990), *Gender and Caring, Work and Welfare in Britain and Scandinavia*, Hemel Hempstead.

Ungerson, C. (1987), *Policy is Personal: Sex, Gender, and Informal Care*, Tavistock Publications, London.

Ungerson, C. (ed.) (1990), *Gender and Caring. Work and Welfare in Britain and Scandinavia*, Harvester Wheatsheaf, New York, pp. 8—33.

241

Urdze, A. and Rerrich, M. (1981), *Frauenalltag und Kinderwunsch — Motive von Müttern für oder gegen ein zweites Kind*, Campus, Frankfurt.

Urquhart, M. (1984), 'The Employment Shift to Services: Where Did it Come From?', *Monthly Labor Review*, April, pp. 15—22.

Voydanoff, P. (1987), 'Work and Family Life', Sage, Newbury Park, CA.

Wager, M. (1988), 'Naiseutta etsimässä. Tutkielma naisen identiteetistä', (Searching for Femininity. Research on Woman's Identity.). (In Finnish), TA *Julkaisuja*, Sarja D, No. 2, Helsinki.

Wahl, K., Tüllmann, G., Honig, M.A. and Gravenhorst, L. (1980), *Familien sind anders. Wie sie sich selbst sehen, Anstöße für eine neue Familienpolitik*, Reinbek b. Hamburg, Rowohlt.

Ward, K. (1983), *How To Be Considerate of Others II*, Kodansha, Tokyo.

Ward, K. (1983), *A Story of Womanliness*, Shogakukan, Tokyo.

Ward, K. (1989), *Letters of a Businessman To His Daughter*, Tokyo, Shinchosha, Tokyo.

Ward, K.B. and Pampel, F.C. (1985), 'Structural Determinants of Female Labor Force Participation in Developed Nations, 1955—75', *Social Science Quarterly*, No. 66, pp. 654—667.

Warfield, A. (1987) 'Co—worker romances: Impact on the work group and on career—oriented women', *Personnel*, No. 64(5), pp. 22—35.

Wærness, K. (1978), 'The Invisible Welfare State: Women's Work at home', *Acta Sociologica*, Special Congress Issue: The Nordic Welfare States, Supplement Vol 21, pp. 193—225.

Wharton, A.S. (1993), 'The Affective Consequences of Service Work: Managing Emotions on the Job', *Work and Occupations*, No. 20, pp. 205—232.

Wharton, A.S. and Erickson, R.J. (1993), 'Managing Emotions on the Job and at Home: Understanding the Consequences of Multiple Emotional Roles', *Academy of Management Review*, No. 18, pp. 1—30.

Wharton, A.S. and Erickson, R.J. (1993), 'Managing emotions on the job and at home', *Academy of Management Review*, No. 18(3), pp. 457—486.

Wilson, E. (1977), *Women and The Welfare State*, Tavistock Publications, London.

Wippler, R. (1986), 'Oligarchic Tendencies in Democratic Organisation', *The Nederlands' Journal of Sociology*, Vol. 22, No 1, Apr., pp. 1—18.

Wippler, R. (1990), 'Cultural Resources and Participation in High Culture', in Hechter, M., Opp, K.D. and Wippler R. (eds.), *Social Institutions, Their Emergence, Maintenance and Effects*, Aldine de Gruyter, New York, pp. 187—205.

Wolfe, A. (1989), *Whose keeper? Social Science and Moral Obligation*, University of California Press, Berkeley.

Wood, D.A. and Erskine, J.A. (1976), 'Strategies in canonical correlation with application to behavioral data', *Educational and Psychological Measurement*, No. 36(4), pp. 861—878.

Wright, P.H. (1985), 'The acquaintance description form', in Duck, S. and Perlman, D. (eds.), *Understanding personal relationships*, Sage, Beverly Hills, pp. 38—62.

Yakovleva, G. (1972), 'K voprosu o polozhenii rebenka odinokoi materi', *Productive Activity of Women and the Family*, (in Russian), Belorussian State University BGU, Minsk, pp. 206—217.

Young, I. M. (1990), *Justice and the Politics of Difference*, Princeton University Press, Princeton.